Everything for Everyone

The Radical Tradition That Is Shaping the Next Economy

Nathan Schneider

NATION
BOOKS
New York

Nation Books
116 East 16th Street, 8th Floor
New York, NY 10003
www.nationbooks.org
@NationBooks

Printed in the United States of America

First Edition: September 2018

Published by Nation Books, an imprint of Perseus Books, LLC, a subsidiary of Hachette Book Group, Inc.

Nation Books is a co-publishing venture of the Nation Institute and Perseus Books.

The Hachette Speakers Bureau provides a wide range of authors for speaking events. To find out more, go to www.hachettespeakersbureau.com or call (866) 376-6591.

The publisher is not responsible for websites (or their content) that are not owned by the publisher.

Print book interior design by Six Red Marbles Inc.

Library of Congress Cataloging-in-Publication Data
Names: Schneider, Nathan, 1984– author.
Title: Everything for everyone: the radical tradition that is shaping the next economy / Nathan Schneider.
Description: First Edition. | New York: Nation Books, [2018] | Includes bibliographical references and index.
Identifiers: LCCN 2018007566| ISBN 9781568589596 (hardcover) | ISBN 9781568589602 (ebook)
Subjects: LCSH: Cooperative societies—History—21st century. | Capitalism—Social aspects. | Political participation.
Classification: LCC HD2956 .S465 2018 | DDC 334—dc23
LC record available at https://lccn.loc.gov/2018007566

ISBNs: 978-1-56858-959-6 (hardcover); 978-1-56858-960-2 (ebook)

LSC-C

10 9 8 7 6 5 4 3 2 1

I bow to the economic miracle, but what I want to show you are the neighborhood celebrations.

—Chris Marker, *Sans Soleil*

Contents

Introduction

Equitable Pioneers

My maternal grandfather came into the world just north of Johnstown, Colorado, in 1916. It's a place of high, dry plains under the Rocky Mountains, which stretch far off along the western horizon. On cassette tapes recorded a few years before his death, he and my grandmother bicker about those days. She'd come from Lincoln, Nebraska, and, like my grandfather, was the child of German-speaking migrants whose ancestors had lived for centuries in Russia's Ukrainian conquests. She complains that his parents were hard and cruel for not keeping him in school longer than it took to learn reading and some math. He fires back, not kindly—saying you can't apply "modern standards" to the way it was then and there, when he slept with his brothers year-round in an open lean-to on the sugar-beet farm where the family tenanted, no heat or light at night except what scarce wood could provide. My grandparents were about the same age, and of the same peculiar ethnicity, but town and country then were two entirely distinct worlds.[1]

Modern standards eventually came to the farms around Johnstown, but not inevitably. Although cities like Lincoln had electric lights by the time my grandmother was born there, electric

1

companies had no interest in stringing power lines to dispersed farmhouses. Electricity arrived only in the 1940s with the expansion of the Poudre Valley Rural Electric Association—a company organized and owned by its customers, set up with financing through the Rural Electrification Act, which President Franklin Roosevelt steered through Congress in 1936. Poudre Valley REA is still running, still a cooperative, and is an aggressive adopter of solar farms. It's part of a resident-owned grid that delivers power to about 75 percent of the territory of the United States.

As a teenager, my grandfather moved in with his older brother in Greeley, where he started working at an auto-parts store. He made extra money connecting power lines to German-speakers' farms and selling them their first washing machines. After a wartime spell in the army, he began a career as a roving hardware-store manager, then as an executive, and finally, as the director of Liberty Distributors, which became one of the larger hardware firms in the country during his tenure.

Liberty's members, and my grandfather's bosses, were regional hardware wholesale companies; together, they bought saws and sandpaper and other goods that would be sold in local stores and lumberyards. Each member company held one share and one vote, and members split any surpluses. It was a co-op. Since the onslaught of big-box chains, it's mostly thanks to co-ops like this that the small hardware stores my grandfather loved can persist at all. Perhaps the co-op model helps solve a family mystery, too—how Grandpa managed to build a national company without becoming especially rich.

Liberty did about $2 billion in business annually in today's dollars during the early 1980s, serving three thousand or so stores. The company's mission, according to the company handbook, was to fulfill its members' "continued desire through a cooperative effort to meet with the economic pressures facing each business."[2] It also allowed a more flexible arrangement than the conformity expected by other co-ops such as Ace Hardware. But, like them, its job was survival.

Liberty is not the only co-op I've encountered in my family's past. When I take a ride in a nearly automated tractor with one of

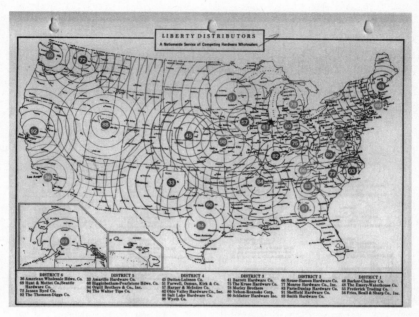

*A map of Liberty Distributors' member wholesalers, from the 1980
company directory.*

my grandfather's nephews, who still farms near Greeley, he tells me
about how he brings his sugar beets to Fort Morgan for processing.
He is a member of the Western Sugar Cooperative, a descendant of
the same Great Western Sugar Company that brought our ancestors
to Colorado after they arrived at Ellis Island in 1907.[3] Thanks to the
co-op, he keeps up the old family crop.

Nobody told me when I was growing up that this particular
way of doing business had so much to do with our family history.
Why should they? Why would the kind of company matter?

More than a century later, here I am. I was raised back east,
lived on both coasts, and then wound up moving—returning—
from New York City to Colorado with my wife and our unborn
son, who would enter the world an hour's drive from the name-
less spot where my grandfather did. Compared to what it was in
his time, Colorado is another kind of place, a land of ski resorts
and hydraulic fracturing and tech startups. Cooperative business
shores up the area's burgeoning affluence—the mortgage-lending

credit unions, the babysitting time-banks, the consumer-owned
REI stores for skiwear and climbing gear. High-country electric
co-ops helped plan out some of the famous resort towns. But
Colorado is still a place where people have to create an economy
of their own to get by. When I take a ride with an East African
driver-owner of Green Taxi or meet a child-care co-op member
who speaks only Spanish, I remember my grandfather's immigrant
parents a century earlier.

It wasn't investigating my family history that put me on the
lookout for cooperatives. I started looking because of stirrings I noticed as a reporter among veterans of the protests that began in
2011, such as Occupy Wall Street and Spain's 15M movement.
Once their uprisings simmered, the protesters had to figure out how
to make a living in the economy they hadn't yet transformed, and
they started creating co-ops. Some were doing it with software—
cooperative social media, cloud data, music streaming, digital currencies, gig markets, and more. But this generation was not all lost
to the digital; others used cooperation to live by dirt and soil.

The young radicals turned to the same kind of business that
my buttoned-up, old-world, conservative grandfather did. Following them, I began following in my grandfather's footsteps before I
even knew it.

Both he and the protesters professed principles derived from
a small group of neighbors in mid-nineteenth-century Britain—
the Rochdale Society of Equitable Pioneers. These Equitable Pioneers were mostly weavers working too hard for too little in textile
mills, and they set up a store where they could buy flour and can-
dles on their own terms. Equitable co-ownership and co-governance
were practical tools for accomplishing this task. Through their
democracy, they cut costs, ensured quality, and spun the threads
that would help stitch together a global movement. But any movement can fray with time. Each generation has needed its own
equitable pioneers. And these pioneers, I've learned, can leave
marks far beyond their neighborhood stores.

Co-ops tend to take hold when the order of things is in flux,
when people have to figure out how to do what no one will do
for them. Farmers had to get their own electricity when investors

wouldn't bring it; small hardware stores organized co-ops to compete with big boxes before buying local was in fashion. Before employers and governments offered insurance, people set it up for themselves. Co-ops have served as test runs for the social contracts that may later be taken for granted, and they're doing so again.

This book is a sojourn among the frontiers of cooperation, past and present—*cooperation* not in the general sense of playing nice, but in the particular sense of businesses truly accountable to those they claim to serve. It's about the long history and present revival of an economy in which people can own and govern the businesses where they work, shop, bank, or meet, sharing the risk and the rewards. These represent a parallel and neglected tradition that runs alongside the usual stories we tell ourselves about how the world as we know it came to be and what is possible there. New cooperators are rearranging this tradition into inventive, networked guises, as if the future depends on it.

Cooperative enterprise can be as old as you want it to be, and a lot of the basic ideas go back as long and far as human economies in general. I'll offer a partial history in the coming chapters, told through the eyes of those reliving pieces of it now. This history carries evidence, from one century to another, that people can govern their own lives, if we give ourselves the chance. Cooperation is tradition and innovation, homegrown yet foreign to the ways of the world around it. It's part of my family's story, and it's a new generation of equitable pioneers. It's like the French peasant-prophet Peter Maurin used to say about things of this sort: "A philosophy so old that it looks like new."[4] It's a philosophy whose discreet return I've had the chance to witness and document, a philosophy of utopian trouble and dull practicality, a philosophy carried out over and over, yet one that we habitually forget or outright deny we are capable of fulfilling. Well, we are.

———

It's really not so surprising that I didn't grow up knowing of my grandfather as a cooperator. After World War II, in a United States still reeling from the labor struggles of the 1930s and fearful of communist revolutions abroad, an implicit deal was struck: democracy would be for the voting booth alone, not the boardroom. Law and culture concurred. Most large co-ops that persisted—Liberty Distributors among them—did their best to blend into the corporate order. Vulnerable as they were to Red-baiting, democratic businesses cast themselves as good-old American capitalism.[5]

This strategy, however, meant forgetting part of why those co-ops were created in the first place. The social reformers at work during my grandparents' youth had a habit of invoking the vision of a "cooperative commonwealth," an economy made up of interlocking but self-governing enterprises, which put control over production and consumption in the hands of the people most involved in them. Those people would choose what to produce, how to do it, and what to do with the profits. The commonwealth, and the gradual, evolutionary process of getting there, offered an antidote to the authoritarian tendencies then ascending on the right and the left; for six-time Socialist Party presidential candidate Norman Thomas, writing in 1934, "the only effective answer to the totalitarian state of fascism is the cooperative commonwealth." Farmers had been setting up purchasing and marketing co-ops for decades to counteract the power of urban industrialists. W. E. B. Du Bois, meanwhile, was documenting and celebrating the commonwealth among the "communal souls" in African American cooperative businesses.[6]

All this rested on a faith that ordinary people could choose their destinies. One of the most memorable slogans from the labor struggles in those days was a saying of child-laborer-turned-organizer Rose Schneiderman: "The worker must have bread, but she must have roses, too." If "bread" was the buying power of wages, "roses" was the right to the free time that came from reasonable working hours—time for enjoyment and self-management. Schneiderman said those words in a 1912 speech to a room of a few hundred wealthy women in Cleveland. Women's suffrage was the immediate subject and crusade of Schneiderman's speech, but to her, the ballot meant more than voting for politicians every few years. It was the key to a commonwealth.

Her organization during that period, the Women's Trade Union League, regarded "self-government in the workshop" as an overriding demand; the momentary struggles over hours and wages and suffrage were a means to that end. The International Ladies' Garment Workers' Union, for which she had also worked, pursued the commonwealth by organizing co-owned apartments for its members.[7]

Serious businesspeople nowadays tend to regard any alternative to the investor-owned corporation as aberrant or impossible. But the alternatives actually preceded the models that prevail today. In Britain, the first legislation for co-ops passed four years before joint-stock companies got their own law in 1856. Legal scholar Henry Hansmann has suggested that we regard investor-owned companies as a distorted kind of cooperative, bent in service of investor interests over anyone else's.[8] The kind of business that now seems normal was once strange; someday it might seem strange again. Perhaps the strangeness is creeping back.

Surveys suggest that something like 85 percent of workers worldwide don't feel engaged in their jobs. As a stopgap, consultants teach corporate managers to instill the fictional "sense of ownership" that so many people want to experience in their economic lives—for employees, and consumers as well. The internal website for Walmart "associates" is MyWalmart.com; "It's *your* store," Albertsons supermarkets used to tell their customers. Harvard Business School's Francesca Gino, among others, has documented productivity benefits when employees experience "psychological ownership." A pair of former Navy SEALs turned executive coaches preach "extreme ownership." But keeping up this facade is hard work, especially when it has no relationship to reality. It could be more efficient to set up at least a partial ESOP, or employee stock-ownership plan. Partial employee ownership, as at Southwest Airlines or W. L. Gore, is a long-standing tradition in US business, but even that rarely comes up in the management lit.[9] Strange indeed. Why does it seem so hard to take the desire for genuine participation seriously?

As I began encountering the new cooperative frontiers, I learned to notice remnants of past and partial commonwealths still at work around me. When I travel now, I see them fly by everywhere, points of interest missing their commemorative plaques. In the most drab of parking lots, I look around and there they are, dotting the strip malls. These traces of commonwealth have begun to seem like a secret society, an inverted reality lurking inside what claims to be reality, economies that reject the rules by which the economy supposedly plays. In these traces, even tucked within competitive markets, cooperative advantage holds its ground.

Each example pokes a hole in the usual story about how the world came to be as it is, challenging tall tales about progress made from competition and the pursuit of profit. No, there have been other principles at work.

Pass a Best Western hotel or a Dairy Queen or a Carpet One on the highway—can you see the purchasing co-ops built into their franchise models? How about in an antique store that doubles as a sales office for State Farm, still a cooperative-like mutual owned by its car-insurance policyholders? In a Whole Foods Market, and even its adopted parent, Amazon, perhaps there are still ghosts of the organic food co-ops that helped create the demand Whole Foods feeds on, and that it then swallowed. Are there traces left in Burley bike trailers, passing by on the shoulder, of the days when that company was worker owned? As I've driven by the King Arthur Flour factory in Vermont, or Publix grocery stores in Florida, or the New Belgium brewery in northern Colorado, I see some of the more than fourteen million US workers who benefit from an ESOP.[10] Pass a cluster of solar panels in farm country, and chances are it delivers power to members of the area's cooperative electric utility, financed by a hundred-billion-dollar cooperative bank in a city many miles away. Pick up a local newspaper in a diner, and half its heft is wire stories from the Associated Press, a co-op since its founding before the Civil War. The rusty grain silo in a farming town, the laundry service for my region's hospitals, a brutalist credit union building I pass every day—co-op, co-op, co-op.

The International Cooperative Alliance calculates that the largest cooperatives globally generate about $2.2 trillion in turnover and employ about 12 percent of the employed population in G20 countries. As much as 10 percent of the world's total employment happens through co-ops. According to the United Nations, the world's 2.6 million co-ops count over 1 billion members and clients among them, plus $20 trillion in assets, with revenue that adds up to 4.3 percent of the global GDP. The country with the largest total number of co-op memberships—though many members don't know themselves as such—is the United States, home to more than forty thousand cooperative businesses.[11] A national survey found that nearly 80 percent of consumers would choose co-ops over other options if they knew they had a choice.[12] I'm still learning where and how to notice them.

Portions of the commonwealth have trouble noticing each other, too. The worker-owners of an urban house-cleaning co-op might not recognize the cowboy cooperation of ranchers buying feed together, or the hackers sharing cooperative servers while pounding away at their code. A fair-trade spice distributor and a worker-owned mental-health center have offices next door to each other in my town, but they've never talked with each other about being co-ops. With practice, the commonwealth appears. Some of the big, older co-ops have even started displaying their cooperative identity again, as something to be claimed rather than hidden. Whether they admit it or not, they've each turned to democracy out of need.

Economist Brent Hueth finds that cooperatives arise most often when there are "missing markets," when the reigning businesses fail to serve an unmet demand or utilize latent supply.[13] While coffee companies ran a race to the bottom in environmental and labor practices, co-ops engineered a fair-trade movement that went the other way, from the worker-owned roaster Equal Exchange to consumer-owned grocery stores and countless grower co-ops around the world. When competing banks needed to collaborate with each other more reliably, they formed Visa and the SWIFT network as cooperatives. Democracy can be creative and flexible where top-down models fear to tread.

Still, cooperation remains a minority logic in the global economy, and the kinds of hopes that today's equitable pioneers stumble toward are anything but inevitable. Authoritarian, neo-feudal tendencies have found fresh appeal in many quarters; surveys suggest that, worldwide, the desire for democratic politics is on the decline. Young people in the United States increasingly consider democracy—as they know it, at least—a poor way to run a country.[14] Cooperatives themselves have fallen victim to this. Many large credit unions, electric co-ops, mutual insurance giants, and the like have lost the kind of member involvement that they had at their founding, and managers find it just as well not to remind their members that they are, in fact, co-owners. The result is stagnation, usually, or sometimes outright graft. If the world is forgetting its capacity for democracy, the co-ops are, too.

When politicians talk about spreading democracy, they typically have in mind an expansion to more and more countries, forcibly or otherwise, of representative governments and accompanying political rights.[15] But democracy might spread in forms other than ballot boxes. It can spread like Schneiderman's roses into ever more hours of our days, into our workplaces and markets and neighborhoods, and into what becomes of the wealth we generate. It can start to take root in levels of the social order where it was previously absent. Otherwise, democracy becomes a spectator sport—as real, and yet as out of reach, as reality TV.

When tech people talk about "democratizing" something, like driving directions or online banking, what they really mean is *access*. Access is fine, but it's just access. It's a drive-through window, not a door. Access is only part of what democracy has always entailed—alongside real ownership, governance, and accountability. Democracy is a process, not a product.

Apple's Orwell-themed 1984 Super Bowl commercial presented the personal computer as a hammer in the face of Big Brother; later that year, after Election Day, the company printed an ad in *Newsweek* that proposed "the principle of democracy as it applies to technology": "One person, one computer." The best-selling futurist handbook of the same period, John Naisbitt's *Megatrends*, likewise promised that "the computer will smash the pyramid," and with its networks "we can restructure our institutions horizontally."[16] What we've gotten instead are apps from online monopolies accountable to their almighty stock tickers. The companies we allow to manage our relationships expect that we pay with our personal data. The internet's so-called sharing economy requires its permanently part-time delivery drivers and content moderators to relinquish rights that used to be part of the social contracts workers could expect. Yet a real sharing economy has been at work all along.

———

During the 2016 International Summit of Cooperatives in Quebec, I attended a dinner at the Château Frontenac, a palatial hotel that casts its glow across the old city. Quebec City has an especially well-developed commonwealth; many residents can recount a typical day with a litany of one co-op after another— child care, grocery stores, workplaces, and so on. We heard from Monique Leroux, then president of the International Cooperative Alliance, the sector's global umbrella organization. A selection of Canada's legislators, government ministers, and foreign emissaries rose in turn as the emcee announced their names and titles. Among them were cooperative managers from every corner of the world, dressed the way the establishment was supposed to dress before the rise of startup bros and hedge funders, enjoying a meal worthy of the lavish benefit dinners I used to attend as a freeloading guest in New York City. Their credit unions and farm co-ops and wholesalers represented a non-negligible chunk of the global economic order. And though these cooperative titans personally claimed spoils lower than those of their peers in investor-owned conglomerates—maybe a few hundred thousand dollars a year rather than many millions—the ironies of any establishmentarian gathering were present there, too.

Keith Taylor, a co-op researcher at the University of California–Davis, texted me from the United States: "i imagine youre seeing a lot of lip service for members and communities... w/no representation." Pretty much.

Ironies and all, the fact of that elegant dinner bore a revelation. Most of the younger cooperators I'd been among the past few years, working in isolation and starting from scratch, didn't know a gathering like this was possible. The scene in Quebec was a reminder that the cooperative movement—even its most bureaucratic participants refer to it as a "movement"—is no theoretical or utopian phenomenon. I met directors of co-ops from around the world owned by their workers, their farmers, their depositors, their residents, and their policyholders. They brought many languages and many sorts of formal dress. As a group, they had little in common except a set of agreements held and honed over time about how to make cooperation work in an acquisitive world.

The International Cooperative Alliance first met in 1895 in London. The principles it would adopt to define and guide the international movement derived from the rules that the Rochdale Pioneers set out for themselves in 1844. These principles have evolved over the years. The most recent list, approved in 1995 by the ICA and framed on the wall in the boardrooms and kitchens of co-ops the world over, are these:

1. Voluntary and open membership
2. Democratic member control
3. Member economic participation
4. Autonomy and independence
5. Education, training, and information
6. Cooperation among cooperatives
7. Concern for community

Alongside the principles, in its materials on "cooperative identity," the ICA promulgates a list of values that inform the principles' meaning: self-help, self-responsibility, democracy, equality, equity, and solidarity.[17] Much resides in these principles and values; their meanings will unfurl in the pages to come. I'll refer to them again. They're a monument as much as they're a method. They're violated as systematically as they're followed across the ever-partial global commonwealth. And yet they're a moving, beating heart.

The arteries and veins of the cooperative idea are participation and control. Those who use an enterprise should be those who own and govern it. It's not just a vessel for absentee speculators. When participants are owners, the firm becomes worth more than what an owner can extract from it. A co-op's members might be individuals, or businesses, or other co-ops, but in any case the model invites them to come as their whole selves. They have the freedom to seek more than profit.

Co-ops of any substantial size hire staff to manage the day-to-day, but for big decisions or board elections, the rule is one member, one vote. Investor-owned companies give greater control to those who own more shares, but a cooperative counts its members according to their solidarity, not their investment. As co-owners, they're all on the hook for how they govern. The enterprise stands or falls by how they direct it. Thus the fifth principle—the part about education.

This kind of responsibility calls for a lifetime of learning about the particulars of the business at hand, toward the wisdom that self-management requires. Co-ops are supposed to constantly equip their members with the knowledge and skills they need to be good stewards; they are also expected to broadcast their mission and model to the public beyond. In this and much else, co-ops can team up. The sixth principle enjoins them to align their efforts through federation and collaboration, turning their cooperation into an advantage in competitive markets. Finally, because a co-op's owners are the people who live where it operates, they have every reason to care how it affects their communities. The community is not an externality, it's part of the business.

These principles are a series of feedback loops. Each is meant to reinforce the others to produce viable businesses that serve their members and the common good. But they're not a guarantee of anything.

The commonwealth has stalled in areas and industries where it once thrived. A gulf separates the generations that built much of its past and the newcomers trying to reinvent a commonwealth for themselves. The newcomers conjure up experiments with Bitcoin but don't bother voting in their local credit union's election. And the credit union's management may actually prefer it that way; when I asked my own credit union's CEO if he would like to see more than the handful of members who come to the annual meeting, he said credit unions aren't like that anymore. To vote in my mutual car-insurance company's annual meeting, I still have to send in a request by physical, mailed letter to an address tucked away in fine print.

For people to use their power, they have to remember, or be reminded, that they have it or could have it in the first place. As much as co-ops arise out of economics, they depend on a supportive, nourishing culture from below and enabling policy from on high. They depend on a democracy that is dexterous, not fixed and frozen in time. Their lifeblood is participation and commitment. Yet the values and principles amount to nothing if there isn't a solid basis in business.

———

Does cooperation count as capitalism, or something else? Some co-op directors have insisted to me it is. If capitalism means freely associating in the economy, or ingenuity and innovation, or the rough-and-tumble of setting up a business, or price-based reasoning—then, yes, cooperation overlaps with it. But if capitalism means a system in which the pursuit of profit for investors is the overriding concern, cooperation is an intrusion. Participation is what co-ops are accountable to, not just wealth. It's an inversion of that capitalist order, but one that can nevertheless persist in that order's midst.

Sure, many people invest in the stock of companies with which they shop, work, bank, or insure. But that kind of ownership isn't the same as co-op membership. The rules surrounding stock markets presume that owners want only financial gain. For instance, after the 2017 Grenfell Tower fire killed seventy-one people in London, the shareholders of a complicit supplier sued their company—not for the loss of life or the moral negligence, but for shareholder losses; ExxonMobil employees similarly sued the company over its climate-change deceptions—in pursuit of lost value in their stock options.[18] Nothing else would hold up in court. This kind of system contorts the actual people involved.

It sees only a tiny sliver of their humanity. These capital markets have created a machine, a kind of profit-sniffing artificial intelligence, in whose service its subjects work, buy, invent, and even rest. If we're to take on existential market externalities such as poverty and climate change, we need companies capable of seeing the world in the way people do.

———

Just as cooperatives co-created the industrial world, they are at work on what comes next. They're vying among other candidate regimes, from the easy money of venture capitalists to the corporate darlings of authoritarian governments. And the prospects for a cooperative commonwealth may never have been better. When the Wharton School business guru Jeremy Rifkin spoke to the International Summit of Cooperatives in Quebec, he assured his listeners that their tradition was the way of the future. "Co-ops will be the ideal venue to scale this new digital revolution," he said. "Even if you didn't exist, you're the model we'd have to create."

Social movements are betting on the model, too. Some beleaguered labor unions in the United States and Europe are devising a new vocation and a new strategy through unionized co-ops—recovering a union-cooperative symbiosis that was more prevalent a century ago. Defenders of the environment, from indigenous tribes to Pope Francis, have turned to cooperation in pursuit of what has come to be called climate justice. So it appears also in struggles for racial justice; the Movement for Black Lives, for instance, uses cognates of *cooperative* forty-two times in the Economic Justice portion of its official platform, which insists on "collective ownership" of the economy, "not merely access." Upstart politicians, such as Jeremy Corbyn of the United Kingdom's Labour Party and Bernie Sanders in the United States, have put co-ops in their platforms as well.[19]

This isn't new. The Scandinavian social democracies grew from the root of widespread co-ops and folk schools. The US civil rights struggle of the 1960s mobilized the self-sufficiency black farmers had already built through their co-ops. Although best known for his obstructive resistance against British rule of India, Mohandas K. Gandhi viewed the "constructive program" of spinning wheels and village communes as the real center of his strategy.[20] Cooperation, however, cannot be claimed as the purview of any one political outlook or party—neither in my grandfather's time nor today. Electric co-ops and credit unions may have found their early advocates in Washington, DC, among progressives, but they now find more affinity with right-wing lawmakers willing to roll back cumbersome regulations. The 2016 party platforms of both Democrats and Republicans encouraged employee ownership. Among younger cooperators, one frequently encounters devotees of the right-libertarian Ron Paul.

Yet the commonwealth is anything but inevitable; I would give more credit to capitalism than Rifkin did. As much as digital networks empower peer producers, they are furnishing unprecedented global monopolies and previously unimaginable feats of surveillance. There's no guarantee that the equitable pioneers will win out. But taking cues from the shreds of past cooperation they encounter, they're devising futures that challenge both the co-op configurations of my grandfather's era and the imperatives that capital imposes now. The stories I'll be telling are not about cooperation-the-venerable-achievement but cooperation-the-work-in-progress.

These newer co-ops aspire to reach further and encompass more than their predecessors. Cooperators want to confront the intersectional dividing lines of identity that too easily determine the economy's winners and losers, including in co-ops. They exhibit a tendency that has come to be called open cooperativism, an extra emphasis on the first cooperative principle's openness for a network-enabled age. They venture to the radical edges of transparency. They adopt complex, multi-stakeholder ownership structures to account for these complex challenges; I know of at least one co-op that reserves a board seat for the Earth itself.[21] Rather than merely serving their members and their members' surroundings, these cooperators want to do good in the world beyond. They secure B Corp certifications, based on metrics of social impact, to prove it. They share common property in ways that seek to dispense with property altogether.

If this is where the cutting edge points, it's toward a kind of paradox: employing the method of cooperative ownership so as to wither ownership away. The new equitable pioneers have bold ideas, as their predecessors did, but they also run the risk of capriciousness, of neglecting sturdy institutional forms on behalf of a specious liberation.

Among the enigmatic utterances of the philosopher Jacques Derrida was a habit of referring to "democracy to come."[22] Democracy can never be a static or stable condition, he believed, because its most basic commitments are forever in tension with one another—equality and diversity, freedom and accountability. We never quite possess democracy in any full sense, except to the degree that we strive toward it, attempting to reconcile its tensions by kneading them over and over into our lives. These are the tensions, for instance, between the dignitaries' dinner in Quebec and the wry text messages of my friend Keith, or between data-sharing over cloud servers and old-fashioned property. Without continual striving, what once seemed like democracy becomes ossified and unresponsive. What we discover from this striving today will shape the social contracts to come.

One can't know when or where the breakthroughs might occur. A commonwealth arises from the persistent hope that more and fuller democracy is possible, and through the persistent risk that human beings might trust themselves and each other with their destinies. In this book I've attempted to compose a portrait of that risk, and of that hope.

1

All Things in Common
Prehistory

Gregorian chant and free jazz are two kinds of music that sound nothing alike. One came from the monasteries of medieval Europe, where nuns and monks intoned scriptural verses in unison. The other was an invention of African Americans who were in but not of the white monoculture of the 1950s and early 1960s, discarding fixed melodies and rhythms for cacophonous liberty. It is hard to imagine forms more different. Both, however, are the sounds of self-governance.

The band plays in the dark. People onstage and off go about their business. The percussionist pounds out one beat for a while, then changes to another. The upright bassist thumps along to that same beat, until venturing elsewhere, then reconverging some minutes later. Same with the piano, the sax, and whatever else is in that session. A lot of the time they're each in their own tempo and key, if any, working something out for themselves. And then they come together—when they feel like it—and it's a relief to a listener used to more dictatorial orchestration. Harmony becomes precious when it's not a given, and soon the discord obtains a beauty of its own. That's the sound of freedom and free association, of living by choice and not coercion.

Sun Ra, an Afrofuturist composer with free-jazz influences, proposes playing a song, in his 1974 film *Space Is the Place*, so as to "teleportate the whole planet": "Then we'd have a multiplicity of other types of destinies. That's the only way."[1] These sounds are accompaniments to surviving by improvised economies, to living in a world whose rules aren't for you.

The monks sing to the dark. It's before dawn between the cold stone walls of the chapel. Every morning of their lives, they utter first the same words: "Lord, open my lips, and my mouth will proclaim your praise." Their voices are one, as much as is possible for fallen, sinful beings with only the aid of grace. This is work; they call it the Divine Office. Soon the sun will rise. After more prayers, the monks go out into the fields and barns that surround the cloister and begin the manual work that helps maintain the monastery, with the same lockstep as that of their prayers in the chapel.

In the chapel many of them are tired, but they stay awake for each other like fellow soldiers on a battlefield. A short monastic poem, found in a twelfth-century French manuscript, reports the responses of God, the devil, and the abbot to a young monk who falls asleep during prayers. The devil is optimistic about winning the monk's soul for himself. The abbot asks for help from God, who declines to intervene in such a minor incident. No one takes the matter as seriously as the monk himself, who expresses his regret in gruesome form: "Sooner would I have my head cut off than fall asleep again."[2]

This is the music of mutual accountability—whether in the stinging shame of sleep or in the slow finding of a common beat. This is *ora et labora*, the ancient mixture of prayer and work that goes back to the apostle Paul making tent pegs to support his preaching. This is *kujichagulia* and *ujamaa*, the Swahili notions of autonomy and cooperation, adopted by descendants of slaves. The music is part of these. And it's part of a usable history for those turning to cooperativism again.

———

There's a temptation, in the course of a book such as this, to abuse our ignorance of the prehistoric past by claiming it as a time in which we all cooperated. One could begin even before there was a human *we*—enter tales of evolutionary history that stress the survival value of symbiosis and sociality among organisms instead of ruthless, solitary competition.[3] Picture the blobs in primordial goo feeding each other useful enzymes, or bonobos licking filth off their young. In the long, grand story of the universe, cooperation has been a fact of nature. But resist the easy way out: it is not the only fact. The friendly and the cutthroat have each contributed to our mysterious origins, and it's at least partly true to emphasize either one.

I will not dwell much, either, on the early human side of what museums consider natural history—our mythologies of tribal, "primitive" societies, which rest on an assumption that general facts hold consistent for a tremendous range of groupings of human beings across ages and biomes, societies either too remote or too extinct to talk back. Even Margaret Mead, an anthropologist not shy of drawing strong conclusions, could conclude little more from her editorship of a volume titled *Cooperation and Competition Among Primitive Peoples* than that "competitive and cooperative behavior on the part of individual members of a society is fundamentally conditioned by the total emphasis of that society"— that is, *it depends*. But suffice it to say that in societies without stockbrokers, where survival is a daily activity carried out among a smallish number of interdependent people, economy ends up being a more egalitarian affair than the rest of us are probably used to. It's no accident that some newfound cooperators today have taken to calling their transnational affinity groupings "neo-tribes."[4]

The Nobel-laureate political economist Elinor Ostrom spent decades studying how various communities the world over manage what she termed "common-pool resources"—the stuff they share and use together. These systems might govern fisheries or forests or waterways or bodies of knowledge through strategies formed over centuries. Ostrom found that such systems exhibit certain features. As if echoing the cooperative principles listed earlier, she identified seven main "design principles":

1. Clearly defined boundaries
2. Local rules adapted to local conditions and needs

3. Mechanisms for those affected by the rules to change them
4. Monitoring of participant behavior
5. Appropriate consequences for rule violators
6. Processes for conflict resolution
7. Free and flexible self-organization[5]

To these Ostrom added an eighth principle, for larger systems: a pattern of nesting, so that smaller decisions happen in smaller groupings, which in turn defer to larger institutions for larger challenges—the principle of federation. This, like Ostrom's other principles, overlaps plentifully with modern cooperation. Her findings point toward a vast prehistory for this subject matter.

Cooperative precedents appear around the world, from lending circles referred to in Confucian texts to African merchants' caravans. But the lineage that I will dwell on here is one that happened to achieve particular influence in the global economic order, starting with the civilizations that formed around the Mediterranean Sea. There were the ancient Jewish Essene communes, which in some respects prefigured the farming-village *kibbutzim* that helped build modern Israel. Islam likewise instituted the principle of the *waqf*, a set of shared property held in perpetuity for the common good, and *takaful*, a system of mutual insurance. Such institutions existed throughout the region, from Greek secret cults to Roman burial societies. They could be subversive enough that Julius Caesar tried to ban them.[6]

Traces of a commonwealth appeared with particular vividness in the Christian church's first days. Twice in the Book of Acts, soon after Jesus leaves his followers to their own devices, they begin pooling property. Here is the first time, in Chapter 2:

> Awe came upon everyone, and many wonders and signs were done through the apostles. All who believed were together and had all things in common; they would sell their property and possessions and divide them among all according to each one's need.[7]

The same practice reappears in Chapter 4, where, just after another experience of "signs and wonders," we read that "the community of believers was of one heart and mind, and no one claimed that any of his possessions was his own, but they had everything in common." The next chapter tells the story of Ananias and Sapphira, who die sudden deaths after attempting to withhold from the community part of their earnings from a sale of land. When their story ends, again, "Many signs and wonders were done among the people at the hands of the apostles."[8] Evidently, there is a link between the experience of divine activity in the world and the sharing of property among members of the Christian community; dishonest dealing in this arrangement has dire consequences. The lesson of Ananias and Sapphira casts its warning from St. Peter's Basilica in Rome, where a depiction of it appears on the canvas over the Altar of the Lie.

A chapter later, the apostolic commune experiences more growing pains. The original apostles find the task of resource management beyond their ken; the needs of widows are being neglected. They ask the community to select seven trusted representatives to carry out the distributions.[9] Their cooperation, as in modern cooperatives of any significant scale, required electing a board.

This cooperative imprint in its scriptures keeps coming back to haunt Christendom, despite its most imperial pretensions. Monasteries first appeared in the fourth century, just after the emperor Constantine made Jesus Christ the official god of Rome. Strenuous believers fled to the desert, where they could practice their faith in solitude and simple communities, away from the corruptions of empire. The economic spirit of the apostles reappeared among them. Citing Acts, the North African, early fifth-century Rule of St. Augustine instructs monastics, "Call nothing your own, but let everything be yours in common." About a century later in Italy, Benedict of Nursia went further in his rule, stipulating, "As often as anything important is to be done in the monastery, the abbot shall call the whole community together," discussing the matter with everyone before making a decision.[10] The Rule of

St. Benedict prescribes election of the abbot by the community and expects the community to support itself through shared businesses. Both rules emphasize obedience to the abbot or abbess over democratic deliberation. But they also enjoin an egalitarian spirit and a collaborative economy.

The spirit of Acts returned in force during the thirteenth-century mendicant movement, when barefoot preachers spread across Europe, contrasting their poverty with the lavish lifestyles among church officials and in wealthy monasteries. Clare of Assisi, Francis of Assisi's friend and colleague, enshrined in her rule for Franciscan sisters a particular measure of countercultural self-governance. The draft of the rule that Pope Innocent IV proposed for her order required that the sisters' elected abbess gain the approval of the male friars' minister general, a provision St. Clare struck from the final version. She also added the practice of a weekly meeting—which apparently the pope deemed unnecessary for women—in which the sisters would gather to confess their offenses and discuss "the welfare and good of the monastery." She stressed the inclusion of all community members in this process, noting, "the Lord often reveals what is best to the lesser among us."[11]

As Clare and Francis's movement grew in influence, church leaders sought to manage it. The most contested question was that of whether Franciscan communities would have to hold property or retain radical poverty.[12] Some early Franciscan scholars developed sophisticated legal arguments to insist that the friars could have *use* of goods like food and clothing without actually *owning* them. They cited the economy of the Garden of Eden to this effect, a state of nature in which the first people shared stewardship of the whole world. But this strategy foundered, and church law would require their order to hold its own property. Rome deemed ownership necessary to protect the Franciscans' poverty and communalism from an acquisitive outside world.

If possession for the sake of sharing seems like a contradiction, it wasn't a new one. Gratian's twelfth-century *Decretum*, the compendium of canon law that thereafter steered governance in the church for eight hundred years, held that "all things are common to everyone." By the lights of natural law, at least, private property is an aberration, though under the conditions of fallen human society it's a necessary arrangement. This paradox has come to be called, including in the current Catholic catechism, the universal destination of goods.[13]

What a strange phrase: *the universal destination of goods*. It holds that everything—in the final analysis, even if we can barely act this way here and now—is somehow everyone's. This doesn't pretend to offer a practical business model, yet it asks that any provisional, proprietary business somehow reflect the communal reality beneath. And as impossible an expectation as this seems, it keeps coming back.

———

The cave dwellings in Matera, Italy—the Sassi—are said to have been inhabited for nine thousand years. Staggered terraces of masonry facades line ragged cliffs that fall into canyons. After World War II, the Sassi became the country's most notorious slum, and the government emptied residents into modern apartments on the plateau above. For decades the ancient caves lay empty. Pier Paolo Pasolini and Mel Gibson both filmed movies about Jesus there. In the 1990s, a band of cultured squatters began to move in and renovate, leading the way for a tourist industry in the otherwise sleepy city. UNESCO declared the caves a World Heritage Site; the sides of Matera's police cars now boast "Cittá dei Sassi." Most of Matera's sixty thousand residents, however, live not in that romantic past but in a present where it's not altogether clear what they have to offer in the global economy. Decent work is hard to find, and the city is hemorrhaging its youth.

In early 2014, the ancient caves of Matera became home to an experiment: an unMonastery, the first of its kind. For the dozen or so unMonks who moved there from across Europe and North America, plus the hundreds following their progress online, it carried the quixotic hope of an underemployed generation regaining control of the technology that increasingly commodifies and surveils their lives. Monasteries ushered civilization through the Dark Ages, harboring scholars and inventors and the technology of writing; perhaps unMonasteries, sparing the dogma and self-flagellation, could keep alive the promise of a liberating internet.

The unMonastery's gestation began in 2011. The Council of Europe's ominous-sounding Social Cohesion Research and Early Warning Division sought, in the words of its chief, "to have a better idea of the extent of insecurity in society." The international body sponsored the invention of what came to be called Edgeryders, "an open and distributed think tank" of people working through an online social network and a series of conferences. Anyone could join, but those who did ended up being mostly young, tech-savvy, and entrepreneurial, and mostly from Western Europe. What united them was not a political ideology, but the dead-end conditions of austerity and the hope of figuring out better ways forward. They produced a report about the economic crisis, which they called a "guide to the future." Soon the council's funding ended, but Edgeryders pressed on as an online network with more than two thousand members and an incorporated entity. The group began presenting itself as a company in the business of "open consulting."

At the end of their first meeting in June 2012, a small circle of Edgeryders, with glasses of wine in their hands and under the shadow of a Strasbourg church, dreamed up the unMonastery. The idea was this: find a place with unmet needs and unused space that could lend a building to a group of young hackers. Live together cheaply, building open-source infrastructure with the locals. Repeat until it becomes a network.

The unMonastery vision went viral among the Edgeryders. It fit into a widely felt longing at the time, evident in many parts of Europe and North America where protest had been breaking out, to start figuring out practical alternatives to the failed order. This was the period, too, of National Security Agency whistleblower Edward Snowden's leaks, of persecuted hacker Aaron Swartz's suicide, of blockades against techie commuter buses in San

Francisco. Google became one of the world's leading lobbyists, and Amazon CEO Jeff Bezos bought the *Washington Post*. The internet could no longer claim to be a postpolitical subculture; it had become the empire.

As tech achieved its Constantinian apotheosis, old religious tropes seemed to offer a return to lost purity, a desert in which to flee, the stark opposite of Silicon Valley. A bonneted "Amish Futurist" began appearing at tech conferences, asking the luminaries about ultimate meaning, as if she came from a world without the internet. Ariana Huffington cashed in with her mobile app, GPS for the Soul.

For a year and a half, the unMonastery idea developed and grew. Edgeryders brought their favorite conceptual vocabularies to bear: social innovation, network analysis, open source. They also brought their experience with hackerspaces, makerspaces, and co-working. Alberto Cottica, an Italian open-data advocate and leading Edgeryder, perused the Rule of St. Benedict and discovered its author to be a network-savvy, evidence-based social innovator.

"Each monastery is a sovereign institution, with no hierarchy among them," Cottica explained in the Edgeryders' online discussions. "The Rule acts as a communication protocol across monasteries." He compared Benedict to Jimmy Wales, the founder of Wikipedia, and Linus Torvalds, creator of the open-source operating system Linux. "The rule was—still is—good, solid, open-source software."

In Brussels, Cottica learned about Matera's bid to be declared a European Capital of Culture by the European Union and saw an opportunity for his fellow Edgeryders. The bid proposal centered around the theme of "ancient futures"—"in order," it said, "to give voice to forgotten places, areas often pushed to the outskirts of modernity, yet which remain the bearers of deep values that remain essential." The committee in charge of the bid came to recognize the unMonastery concept, with its supporters throughout the continent, as a useful addition to Matera's portfolio. The city agreed to provide a small cave complex, as well as €35,000 for travel and expenses for four months, which stretched to six.

Dinner outside the unMonastery's caves.

The presiding unAbbot was Ben Vickers, twenty-seven years old, with patches of gray on either side of his well-trimmed hair and a hooded black coat worn over his banded-collar black shirt. While also more or less retaining his post as "curator of digital" for London's Serpentine Galleries, Vickers was the unMonastery's theorist and coordinator; the others generally praised his ability to digest and summarize their various points of view, and to document them on the online platforms they used to communicate. He blasted George Michael songs while setting up breakfast and found a certain glee in the prospect of failure—a turn of mind probably honed during his days in doomed anarchist squats. Documentation, he believed, can trump even failure; others can study the attempt, tweak it, and try again.

Visible from what became the unMonastery's patio, down one cliff and up another, were dark abscesses in the rock, their interiors still bearing remnants of paintings from past use as churches and hermitages. Where the monks and nuns who once lived there had hours of structured prayer each day, the unMonastery had documentation—the basic act of piety in any open-source project. Before an algorithm can be copied, adapted, and redeployed, it must be radically transparent. Monks expose them-selves to God through prayer; unMonks publish their activities on the internet.

Some of the documentation looked outward. Maria Juli-ana Byck, a videographer from the United States, was working on a project to map common resources in town, to help Matera residents—the Materani—connect with each other and collab-orate. There was an "unTransit" app in the works for local time-tables and workshops on the gospel of open data. Also underway on the Materanis' behalf were an open-source solar tracker, an open-source wind turbine, and coding classes in the unMonastery caves for adults and kids.

As in real monasteries, much of the unMonastery's piety went toward scrutinizing the minutiae of daily life. This was of partic-ular concern to a pony-tailed, thirty-one-year-old software devel-oper named elf Pavlik, who had been living for five years without touching money or government IDs. With nearly pure reason, he implored the others to document more and more precisely what came and went, from food to tampons, so they'd learn to budget not by cost but in terms of the resources themselves. Using a soft-ware package called Open Energy Monitor, they kept track of the unMonastery's electricity usage minute by minute, room by room.

Keeping track of the longer view was the job of Bembo Davies, a Canadian-turned-Norwegian widower and grandfather, a vet-eran of the circus and stage who updated his WordPress chronicle in august prose. Accompanying material evidence—skeletal floor plans, a mannequin's headless torso—came from Katalin Hau-sel, an artist who once helped rewrite the official history in her native Hungary. They talked about the unMonastery, even in its first months, as at the beginning of a two-hundred-year history. It didn't seem like so much time to ask for in a place that has been around for millennia.

The unMonastery sat on more precipices than one: it was an emissary of the hubristic tech culture it represented, but also a patient attempt at redemption. While planning ahead for centu-ries, the unMonks practiced the one-step-at-a-time philosophy of

Agile software development; if breakfast wasn't on the table on time, or when they worried about whether they'd done any good for Matera whatsoever, they reminded each other, "Everything's a prototype."

———

The days and nights I spent embedded in those caves were manic with the spectrum of old and new realities that my informant-hosts were trying to stuff into their experience: tech culture, monk culture, nonprofit culture, local culture, art culture, protest culture, entrepreneurial culture, recession culture—all in the space of a few months and a finite budget. They might have called themselves a cooperative were it all not so ephemeral. The want of clarity wasn't so different from what one reads in the sayings of the early Desert Fathers and Mothers, the progenitors of Christian monasticism; none of them knew what they were really up to. Those possibly lunatic ancient hermits kept going around asking each other, in every way they could think of, "What are we doing here?"

Monastic rules, like company bylaws, establish a discipline. They take raw, human material and provide a form into which we can proceed and persist, by which we can tolerate the inevitable coming and going of inspiration. But discipline is no good, either, without the grappling. This is why I don't think we can understand the cooperative past or imagine a cooperative future without these errant, fumbling stories. Like most stories, you don't get to know the end until you get there, if there is an end at all.

———

On a windy day in May, gusts swelled through the unMonastery's first-floor caves, blowing from the walls various colored sticky notes and hand-drawn posters made in meetings heady with excitement and hope. They were schedules, sets of principles, slogans to remember, lists of things to do. A maxim for the Edgeryders' doctrine of do-ocracy, for instance: "Who does the work calls the shots." These relics remained on the floor for hours, apparently provoking insufficient motivation to pick them up.

There had been a kind of monastic routine at the unMonastery in the first weeks. At specified times, the group would sit in circles to share feelings and discuss concerns. A flying drone once captured footage of the theatrical morning exercises that Bembo Davies led. But by May, the circles and the exercises were on indefinite hiatus.

After the seven o'clock wake-up bell rang half an hour late one morning, Davies groaned, on the way to the shower in his underwear, "We're sliding into a prehistoric condition." He lamented on his blog that people had been reverting to talking about the laptops they'd brought as "mine." Benedict's rule has harsh words for private property: "Above all, this evil practice must be uprooted and removed from the monastery."[14]

A few months in, the unMonastery's communications had become a jungle of platforms, many of them proprietary, with few clear lines between inward and outward: the public Edgeryders website, public Trello boards, a closed Google Group, and public folders full of Google Docs. The "ideologically coded"

Software developer elf Pavlik in the unMonastery kitchen.

unMonastery website that elf Pavlik had designed was badly out of date and difficult to use, so a Facebook page had become the main means of sharing information with the world. Before, one unMonk had always refused to use Facebook on principle; it was only after coming to this supposedly open-source hacker commune that he felt compelled to start an account. The unMonastery's vision of an open-source way of life seemed at risk of becoming a wholly owned subsidiary of the status quo.

Back and forth, they debated what the real problem was: The decline of ritual? Attempts to revive the morning exercises kept failing. The lack of ties with people in Matera? They knew there were grumblings among locals about why the city was spending money to support a bunch of foreigners. Too much software, or not enough? Alberto Cottica warned from afar over the Edgeryders platform about fixating on technology rather than on actual social interactions. They disagreed about the rules that governed them, as well as whether there were any in the first place. Losing patience in a tendentious meeting, Rita Orlando, one of the unMonastery's Materan allies, begged, "Let's try to think like a company, even though we are not a company—please!" A company, at least, has to concern itself with doing something of value for someone else.

The last two months of the experiment proved eventful, at least. "Most of the demons have scurried off and work ethic is buzzing away at a good clip," Bembo Davies reported in the last days, with his usual obscurity. Pavlik brought a new cadre of hackers in for a spell, and dozens of local children attended coding classes. A video of a "co-napping" experiment on the streets of Matera went viral online, though it made some Materani cringe. The wind turbine and unTransit projects came closer to having prototypes of their own; they would carry on even though the unMonastery prototype would be closing. A pack of young locals got to work editing their documentary about it. Ben Vickers scrambled to assemble the unMonks' fervent documentation into the "unMonastery BIOS," named after the initialization firmware in a computer—a box full of lessons and design patterns for the iterations to come. He alternated between grandiosity and humility. Vickers wrote, on a thread on the Edgeryders website, that the "unMonastery for me is not a utopian project designed to solve the woes of the world, it operates at the scale of the invention of the fire hydrant."

Rita Orlando lived in Matera before the unMonastery came and remained after it left. She felt frustrated with the aftermath. People in town mostly just saw the project's foreignness and naïveté, not its promise or vision. "We've been too short on time," Orlando said.

Before the end of 2014, at least in part thanks to the visibility the unMonastery lent it, the European Union named Matera one of the 2019 European Capitals of Culture. A few of the un-Monks stayed in town; others tried to open a new unMonastery in Greece. They're still trying to see whether the unMonastery is a protocol that can travel, that can go to other places with unused spaces and unused people who want to do good. A lot of aging religious communities are meanwhile trying to figure out how to put their empty buildings to use these days, while preserving some kernel of their traditions.

The prefix "un" has its uses—for marking a new beginning, for putting aside certain inadequacies of the past—and yet one cannot go on negating and reinventing everything forever. Ancient monks had to learn this, too. First the desert hermits, then the Benedictines, then the Franciscans—each fled the world but then became part of its ongoing reality. A time may come when spiritual-social-technological institutions with features such as those of the prototype in Matera will be content to drop the "un" and call themselves, simply, monasteries.

Metaphors have their usefulness, in the meantime, and the distant Middle Ages offer new cooperators an ample supply of them. While monasteries sought to keep souls apart from the world, another set of institutions served those in the midst of it, where other strategies were needed for imitating the Book of Acts.

———

Some months after my time in Matera, I joined Chris Chavez, Jerone Hsu, and Dan Taeyoung as they splayed themselves out along a suspended I-beam and stray ladder on a roof in the Hell's Kitchen neighborhood of Manhattan. We talked about their new co-working space and the history of the world. The three of them, in their late twenties and early thirties, were overseeing a renovation of the structure beneath them. First built in 1919 as a garage, it was being transformed to include an art studio in the basement, an open-plan office and café at the ground level, and a room for workshops and meditation on the second floor. Chavez greeted construction workers by name as they passed by.

The three began to tell me where they situated their plans, world-historically speaking. "It took a few hundred years to get over the hangover of the Industrial Revolution," Chavez said. He explained that this hangover has lasted well into the digital age, manifesting most recently in the instability wrought by ever-looming waves of automation. It was now time, they believed, to restore a preindustrial template to prominence. They'd decided to reinvent Prime Produce, a small nonprofit that Hsu had founded some years earlier, by modeling it after a medieval guild.

The idea came to them the previous spring, when they organized a retreat for entrepreneurs on the grounds of Bluestone Farm, a community of eco-feminist Episcopal nuns in Brewster, about an hour upstate on the Metro-North Railroad. After some years engaged in varied forms of entrepreneurship, the three were trying to figure out what forms of organization would best suit their peers' shifting work conditions. Neither unions nor chambers of commerce seemed suited to a generation that can't count on having a fixed place of work. The Reverend Leng Lim, a minister and executive coach who lived across the street from the nuns, suggested that Chavez and his compatriots look into guilds.

From roughly the turn of the first millennium to the French Revolution, guilds organized Europe's urban economies. They were associations of independent craftspeople, setting standards for their lines of work and cultivating lively subcultures around their labor. They typically held legal monopolies over crafts in particular jurisdictions; one guild's members might be responsible for all of a town's stone carving, while another would control the market for blacksmithing. Members were also expected to have each other's backs. In *Wage Labor and Guilds in Medieval Europe*, Steven A. Epstein, a historian at the University of Kansas, cites a tenth-century guild that obliged members to rally for mutual defense and vengeance against clients who failed to pay up. "The members also swore an oath of loyalty to each other," Epstein writes, "promising to bring the body of a deceased member to a chosen burial site and supply half the food for the funeral feast."[15] One of Prime Produce's initial members told me that Chavez recruited him with a copy of Epstein's book in hand.

This guild's dozen or so members didn't have plans for funeral insurance just yet, and they weren't defining themselves around a particular trade or industry. They included an architect, an accountant, a food-and-beverage vendor, and a painter. The typical co-working space is run by a company that workers pay for use; by contrast, Prime Produce would make many of its members co-owners of a cooperative, which would manage the proceeds of their dues and pay rent to the sympathetic investors who owned the buildings. Chavez explained that co-ownership can be a way to opt out of the broader economy's pressures—and to reclaim the former meanings of words from before they were conscripted to capitalism.

"The word 'company' doesn't need to exist in a market logic," he said.

Members of medieval guilds typically progressed in rank from apprentice to journeyman to master craftsman—distinctions still used by some trade associations today. Prime Produce would also incorporate three tiers, but based on levels of commitment rather than on experience and proficiency. As a rite of passage, new members would each receive a pair of slippers to wear while inside the space—a "differentiating mechanism," Chavez said, between members and visitors.

Prime Produce wasn't alone in looking to old guilds as the way of the future. Some see a model for organizing freelancers in Hollywood's guild-like set-worker unions, which establish industrywide standards as their members bounce from production to production. Jay Z's Tidal streaming platform sold itself to consumers as a kind of guild for musicians; a group of Silicon Valley business writers has organized itself into the Silicon Guild to help amplify each member's networks; some gig-economy workers have an Indy Workers Guild to distribute portable benefits. In the twentieth century, Charlie Chaplin and his friends formed United Artists to produce their own films, and photographers such as Henri Cartier-Bresson and Robert Capra formed Magnum, a cooperative syndication guild. Less glamorously, the professional organizations for doctors, lawyers, real estate agents, and hairdressers have clung to the guild model, complete with monopoly powers recognized by governments and peers.

As we talked on the rooftop, Prime Produce's founders freely mixed medieval idiom with that of Silicon Alley. Taeyoung cited the computer programming guru Donald Knuth's dictum, "Premature optimization is the root of all evil." That is, if they decided too much ahead of time and in too much detail, they wouldn't be as flexible or as iterative. Hsu described what Prime Produce was doing as "crafted social innovation," a form of "slow entrepreneurship." The guild's appeal wasn't just nostalgic to them but was a means of navigating an often lonely, attention-deficient economy, by cultivating habits of excellence and communizing resources like office space, companionship, and broadband. Adding to the stew of anachronism, Chavez referred to the old guilds as "catalysts" for a better kind of technological progress. "They blocked innovation that dehumanized work," he said. "Guilds were always responsible to people first."

Others might object. Adam Smith referred to the guilds' price-fixing practices as "a conspiracy against the public," and at the start of the French Revolution, they were among the first features of the *ancien régime* dispatched to the institutional guillotine. The usual story since has held that guilds in fact stymied efficiency and technological innovation. Epstein's book sought to correct this narrative, as does the work of the Dutch social historian Maarten Prak. Guilds, Prak told me, "were not opposed to innovation per se; they were opposed to machines taking over." When factory production replaced craft guilds, "work was transformed from rather boring to hopelessly boring." Products became cheaper and more uniform, with fewer workers required to make them. But gone, too, was the fingerprint of the craftsperson. Prak also stresses the importance of what he calls "formal anchoring" for medieval guilds—establishing arrangements with local governments—to sustain themselves "for a longer period than the enthusiasm of the founding members."

Politics meant legitimacy, but it also meant collusion. "It was a sort of deal between small businessmen and the authorities," says Sheilagh Ogilvie, an economic historian at the University of Cambridge who is more critical of the guilds' legacy than Epstein or Prak. Ogilvie believes that guilds enforced an exclusionary economy, barring from their trades whomever they happened not to like, which often meant women, Jews, and immigrants. It was only in the last gasps of the guilds, after they'd lost most of their monopolies and had their most discriminatory habits banned, that Ogilvie thinks their nuisance was minimized.

Thus far, at least, Prime Produce's membership had considerable ethnic, gender, and occupational diversity. And rather than making political deals, the founders seemed content with the synergy of their slippers and their good works. Despite various delays and hitches, no one had yet dropped out. "The ingredient that plays a central role in all this is trust," Qinza Najm, an artist

Qinza Najm, Saks Afridi, and Jerone Hsu on the roof of the Prime Produce building.

who planned to work in the basement studio, told me. After a burglary and a lousy contractor delayed the opening more, they held events about prepackaged culture and participatory design in their construction site.

Before the afternoon on the rooftop was over, another master-member, Marcos Salazar, came to visit. He was taller than the others, his attire less laid-back. Salazar worked as a consultant for cultivating "purpose-driven careers, businesses, and lives." He also organized events for social entrepreneurs in the city and planned to hold some at the Prime Produce space when it became ready.

"I've heard a lot about guilds," he said, as if he'd heard about enough. But when I asked about the slippers, he shrugged and looked at the founders uneasily. They smiled. They hadn't mentioned that part yet.

———

The practical guilds worked alongside the mystics in the monasteries. Each arranged a sort of business meant to put property and commoning into balance. But as the signs and wonders of modern progress began to appear, spreading by printing presses and colonial expeditions, the scales tipped squarely to the side of property. It was a change noticed well enough to merit bloody resistance.

During the torture that preceded his beheading in 1525, the German preacher Thomas Müntzer reportedly confessed to believing that *omnia sunt communia*—all things are common. Perhaps it matters little whether this report from the torturers was truly the position of Müntzer and the popular revolt that he helped lead, or merely a concoction they devised in order to hasten his demise; in either case, they deemed professing this teaching of the apostles and principle of canon law as evidence justifying his execution. The torturers' account went on to say that he believed property "should be distributed to each according to his needs, as the occasion required. Any prince, count, or lord who did not want to do this, after first being warned about it, should be beheaded or hanged."[16]

Müntzer was a contemporary of Martin Luther's who was less adept at siding with the ascendant elites. His movement fell under the swords of princes, as did Müntzer himself. But remnants of the "radical Reformation" of which he was a part persist today in the intentional economies of such Anabaptist sects as the Amish and Mennonites. The Calvinist variant of the Reformation's communal impulses, too, found expression among the Puritans who settled in New England. Although the Puritans' initial experiment in shared farmland and produce was short-lived, their legacy has lived on in New England's town meetings and the congregationalist governance structure that still holds sway in much of US Protestantism. It appears, too, in the medical cost-sharing organizations that offer a faith-based alternative to the corporate health insurance system.[17]

None of these old communards exactly correspond with cooperative enterprise in the modern sense. In certain respects they challenge cooperative principles; expressly religious communes have tended to privilege poverty over ownership and obedience over autonomy. But such precursors do suggest that when modern cooperation did arise, it did not do so as a rude break with the past, but in continuity with customs of commoning and cooperation that people had lived by for ages.

In the Magna Carta and its sister document, the Charter of the Forest, a thirteenth-century English king had to acknowledge the ancient rights of commoners to co-manage and live in the thickest, wildest regions of the realm. One provision protected, for instance, the right of a widow to her "reasonable estovers of the common"—access to supplies that she needed to survive from common land. But during the same centuries in which the Reformation dismantled Rome's spiritual hegemony across Europe, an economy of corporations and capital began to decimate the guilds and the commons. The cataclysm of this process is difficult to appreciate now, centuries later—unless we compare it to the mix of splendor and squalor in the global economic cataclysms now underway. Land that had long been available for shared use became a patchwork of fenced-off enclosures; work that before had been obviously communal started to be regimented into firms.[18]

Among the squeaks in this engine of progress were those who called themselves the Diggers, or the True Levellers—a short-lived and peaceable insurgency in the midst of the English Civil War, led by a drifter named Gerrard Winstanley. Within weeks of occupying a site called St. George's Hill, they declared their intentions in terms that were spiritual, social, and scatological:

> In that we begin to Digge upon *George-Hill*, to eate our Bread together by righteous labour, and sweat of our browes, It was shewed us by Vision in Dreams, and out of Dreams, That that should be the Place we should begin upon; And though that Earth in view of Flesh, be very barren, yet we should trust the Spirit for a blessing. And that not only this Common, or Heath should be taken in and Manured by the People, but all the Commons and waste Ground in *England*, and in the whole World, shall be taken in by the People in righteousness, not owning any Propriety; but taking the Earth to be a Common Treasury, as it was first made for all.[19]

As in the monasteries, the Digger cosmology presumed a God who created everything for everyone; while the Diggers waited for the world to recognize this, they began practicing it in microcosm, through a cooperative community of their own on a pathetic piece of land. Before long they'd be driven from it by goons working for the reigning order, which deemed their views obnoxious and their commoning of land to be trespassing.

Like Müntzer's, the Diggers' position would not carry sway among the contenders groping for control over a shifting world. The feudal commons was up for grabs, and the proposal to replace it with even more commoning, on the model of the first Christians, was inadequately convenient for those who commanded armies. The radical Reformers' ideas have lived on mainly among the partisans of other lost causes who have periodically rediscovered them, from Marxists in interwar Germany to the late 1960s San Francisco counterculture. Müntzer and the Diggers tempt nostalgia, even if what they called for never fully existed. Yet their declarations carry in them, at least, the memory of a world in which habits of commoning were more familiar, in which land was not a commodity, in which work was a shared enterprise. Theirs was a hard world, one that for many reasons we're better off having left behind. But for those now trying to imagine and carry out an economic future more equitably shared among all who inherit and contribute to it, some nostalgia has value. It can remind us of forgotten achievements, of capacities latent among us that may be of use once again.

2

The Lovely Principle

Formation

The Great Depression is not frequently regarded as a time of triumph. But in the 1936 edition of his treatise *Cooperative Democracy*, James Peter Warbasse wrote, "The years since 1929 have seen the greatest advancement in cooperation the country has ever seen." Warbasse, a surgeon, became the first president of the Cooperative League of the United States of America in 1916 and served until 1941.[1] The league was the national umbrella organization for the US cooperative movement, and it lives on today as the National Cooperative Business Association—that is, NCBA CLUSA. It keeps its headquarters in the lobbying district of Washington, DC, and has become a prolific purveyor of international aid. In the early 1920s, the league created the cooperative logo of two pines side by side in a circle, still widely used; in 2000, the NCBA helped secure the creation of the ".coop" top-level domain for co-ops' websites. It has been the US sector's official evangelist.

Warbasse's successor as Cooperative League president, Murray Lincoln, referred to the founder in his memoirs as "a fine, sincere man" and a "crackerjack when it came to expounding theory."[2] Yet Warbasse's enthusiasm in the 1930s was understandable.

The conditions of the Depression had spurred people to form co-operatives across the country. New Deal programs were promoting co-ops, and Congress passed the Credit Union Act in 1934. *Cooperative Democracy* includes a chapter titled "Cooperation Throughout the World" that details a lengthy catalog of cooperative achievements, from French worker-owned factories, Germany's famous consumer-owned banks, and Russia's early Soviet co-ops to parallel achievements as far-flung as China and Japan, with occasional references to the co-ops' run-ins with the ascendant fascist regimes. (The motto of the German movement, whose storefronts became Nazi targets after Kristallnacht: "Cooperation Is Peace.") The book's frontispiece, opposite the title page, is an artist's rendition of twenty-five impressive buildings owned by the British Cooperative Wholesale Society piled on top of each other like a pyramid, a monument to the organized consumer, that

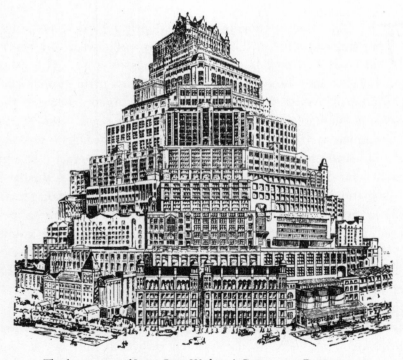

The frontispiece of James Peter Warbasse's Cooperative Democracy.

pharaoh of the cooperative commonwealth on the rise. By this time, the old tradition of shared ownership and enterprise had found a distinctly modern, industrial expression.

As geopolitical as Warbasse's vision gets, it's also a vision of what kinds of people we might become. In the book's final words, he concludes that the point of it all is "the development of superior individuals, appreciative of cultural values, and with a passion for beauty, truth, and justice."[3] He's talking about cooperation as a school, just as the earlier monks regarded their monasteries— not only a better society in which human beings might live, but a means of forming them, forming us, into better human beings. It couldn't be otherwise. The very possibility of such enterprise in the industrial age was not a given but became evident through lessons that had to be learned. This kind of business, with effort and error, had to be formed.

———

By the time of Warbasse's optimism, the cooperative movement was already a century old, more or less. It was a movement of movements, appearing in many countries and languages, including capitalism's Anglophone cradles.

One of the first workers' strikes on record in what would become the United States, among New York City tailors in 1768, birthed a cooperative workshop when the tailors went into business for themselves. Free blacks in New Orleans formed a Perseverance Benevolent and Mutual Aid Association in 1783. As secretary of state under President George Washington, Thomas Jefferson helped craft a tax-relief package for cod fishing that encouraged profit-sharing among workers—a maritime version of his commitment to an economy based on small family farms. A cooperative-like business model undergirded Benjamin Franklin's prototypical public library and fire department in Philadelphia. And the federated democracy of the Iroquois Confederacy, which Franklin and others observed in their dealings with native tribes, likely informed the structure of the Continental Congress through which the colonists organized to shed themselves of British rule.[4] When Alexis de Tocqueville wrote home to France about the young United States, he marveled at its people's talent for association.

The pre–Civil War period saw the blossoming of utopian communities throughout the country, involving interesting religious, sexual, racial, and dietary experimentation—attempts, perhaps, to reclaim the innocence beginning to be lost with the rise of industry. Among these were sects such as the Shakers, Oneidans, and Mormons. Joseph Davis, the brother of Confederate president Jefferson Davis, organized an alleged model community of slaves at Davis Bend in Mississippi, cooperative to the degree that outright bondage would allow. In Massachusetts, the interracial Northampton Association of Education and Industry became home to the prophet Sojourner Truth. Frederick Douglass visited from time to time, and he would later write, "The place and the people struck me as the most democratic I had ever met."[5]

With the first fits and starts of modern industrialism came the beginnings of modern cooperation. The National Trades Union, which arose out of early skirmishes between industrial labor and capital, professed a worker-governed economy as its objective. The 1830s occasioned the first "building societies"—essentially joint lending clubs that enabled working families to become homeowners—as well as early co-ops for agricultural marketing and processing. For the rest of the nineteenth century, cooperation and worker organizing went hand in hand. The cooperative workshops and benevolent societies and communes reflected assumptions that have become long lost today.

In 1859, a year before winning the presidential election, Abraham Lincoln made a speech in Wisconsin that outlined a kind of American dream based on *"free* labor." Some people might need to hire themselves out for a little while to get started, he allowed, but all in order to one day own and control the manner and fruits of their labors—a farm, a store, an office, whatever. "If any continue through life in the condition of the hired laborer," Lincoln said, "it is not the fault of the system, but because of either a dependent nature which prefers it, or improvidence, folly, or singular misfortune."[6] Ownership is the path to realizing one's selfhood. Pity the job-holders.

These words, at that time, could not be separated from the question of slavery—labor at its least free. The implication was that working a job for wages lay on a spectrum not far from outright enslavement. The absurd notion of spending one's whole career in jobs, with no ownership over one's work, could illustrate for Lincoln's audiences the injustice of that more extreme version of the same thing. Yet his efforts to secure abolition also helped secure the rise of the job-based industrial economy; the North's victory in the Civil War was a victory of factory capital over plantation capital, and factory owners wanted wage workers.

Lincoln was not the first to imply a continuity between jobs and slavery. It's part of a long legal and philosophical tradition, from the Emperor Justinian and John Locke to Nobel-winning economists, that has regarded the sale of one's labor in an employment contract as akin to being sold into a life of slavery. (Locke described employment as mere "drudgery," just shy enough of slavery to be permissible; the economists refer to it as a kind of self-rental.) In times of legal slavery, even paid work for others could seem too close for comfort. It was obvious to Lincoln, at least, that a prerequisite for economic self-respect was owning and directing the means of one's own livelihood. And when women in the textile mills of Lowell, Massachusetts, went on strike in 1836, a favorite marching song ended:

For I'm so fond of liberty
That I cannot be a slave.[7]

The prevailing ideology nowadays regards getting a job as a celebration-worthy accomplishment and a free choice. It is now the politician's ultimate conversation-stopper; nobody in Washington can get away with arguing against more jobs. A decent job, or a string of them, promises at least the possibility of a decent life. Humane and rewarding jobs surely deserve more credit than Lincoln and Locke allowed them. But how much choice is there, really? Most people feel they need to get a job to secure material necessities, so the choice is already not a matter of *whether*, but *which*. A common criterion for a successful work-life is having made excellent contributions to an undertaking whose purpose and benefits are somebody else's. This would sound altruistic if the path had been chosen without coercion, which is not usually the case. We've forgotten the search for something better, a search that in Lincoln's time was producing remarkable discoveries.

———

Slave-picked cotton from the Southern states, combined with new weaving machines, furnished a profitable and brutal textile industry in England. Charles Dickens recorded the horrors. But the cooperators' favorite chronicler of this period is surely George Jacob Holyoake. In addition to his participant-observer histories of British cooperative enterprise, Holyoake coined the terms *secularism* and *jingoism* and held the distinction of being the last Briton convicted of blasphemy for a public lecture, for which he spent several months in prison.

The catalyst of Holyoake's tale was misused technology. "The rise of machinery was the circumstance that filled the working class with despair," he wrote in his *History of Cooperation*. "The capitalist able to use machinery grew rich, the poor who were displaced by it were brought in great numbers to the poor-house." This was machinery that could have been labor saving and life improving. But the early industrial free-for-all brought about such conditions as fourteen-hour workdays, child labor, and wages conducive to little more than permanent indebtedness. Holyoake held this condition up against the order that preceded it:

> The capitalist was a new feudal lord more cruel than the king
> who reigned by conquest. The old feudal lord had some care for
> his vassal, and provided him with sustenance and dwelling. The
> new lord of capital charges himself with no duty of the kind,
> and does not even acknowledge the laborer's right to live.[8]

Yet from this capitalist class arose Robert Owen, Holyoake's first hero of British cooperation and its first great dead end. A fellow religious skeptic (who frequented spiritualist seances in his later years), Owen spent his early life fulfilling the mythic promise of the self-made industrialist. He was the son of a Welsh saddler, with education only until age ten, and he worked his way into the management of Manchester textile mills. After marrying into wealth, he arranged for the purchase of a mill in New Lanark, Scotland, which he gained substantial control over by 1813. This became the ground of his experimentation.

On New Year's Day in 1816, Owen opened his Institute for the Formation of Character. It took on the education of the mill-workers' children, starting from when they were old enough to walk—unusually early schooling for the period, and soon to be replicated widely. The curriculum avoided books and formal instruction, instead relying on the children's innate curiosity and self-direction. "Thus it came to pass," explains Holyoake, "that the education of members has always been deemed a part of the cooperative scheme among those who understood it."[9]

This was only one of the ways New Lanark modeled an industrialism that served its workers, not just the owners, eschewing private profit for the common good. While mill workers across England and the United States agitated for a ten-hour workday, Owen instituted eight hours. And yet the mill prospered; it seemed to demonstrate that other kinds of industrial orders were possible, attracting visitors as eminent as the tsar of Russia. Owen also established a store where the workers could buy their necessities without the usual markup, together with a system of exchange wherein people could trade an hour of one kind of work for that of another. There was a system for arbitrating conflicts among workers. Today, the New Lanark complex is a UNESCO World Heritage Site.

The crucial component that held this remarkable artifice together, it turned out, was Owen himself. In addition to his entrepreneurial prowess, he proved an effective propagandist, inspiring many imitators but not nearly as much actual replication.

In 1825, he relocated to the United States to found a new New Lanark on the southern tip of Indiana with a settlement called New Harmony—on the grounds of an earlier utopian community of German extraction, Harmonie—but it collapsed upon his departure two years later. His was a kind of cooperation that relied on a skilled paternalist. Yet it helped circulate the notion of cooperative industrialism, even if its reality was so far-fleeting. Attempts to test and perfect variants of Owenism began to spread.

The earliest explicit mention of *cooperation* as an economic system that Holyoake could find was from the period of Owenist enthusiasm. The first issue of a short-lived periodical called the *Economist* declared, on August 27, 1821, "The SECRET IS OUT," and "it is unrestrained COOPERATION, on the part of ALL the members, for EVERY purpose of social life."[10]

———

After decades of Anglophone experiments and dead ends in the wake of Owen, the fervor began to coalesce around a more or less common model that worked. Disparate groups arrived at similar conclusions on their own with the simultaneous isomorphism that tends to occur around consequential discoveries. The most famous site of this discovery was Rochdale, an English town ten miles north of Manchester. To Holyoake, this was the great focal point and turning point for the whole history of cooperation—perhaps because of his own role in it.[11]

Holyoake recounts a speech on cooperation he delivered to Rochdale textile workers in 1843—a year after his blasphemy trouble, a year before the start of the famous store. He spoke about Chartism, a movement by which workers were seeking the vote and other political rights, and he railed against the scourge of debt. Rochdale was a town through which these and other ideas, including Owen's, had long been circulating. It had been home to cooperative experiments already. But the year after Holyoake's visit, a group of twenty-eight workers there—weavers and others associated with the textile trade—arranged to establish a small store on Toad Lane where they could buy decent groceries, clothing, and other goods at reasonable prices. They were the Rochdale Society of Equitable Pioneers. The store opened before the end of 1844 for a few hours a week.

The Rochdale store implemented a specific concoction of the cooperative practices that had been swirling around in different combinations for years. Its member-owners were its customers. They would invest a weekly subscription of two pence, with each member entitled to an equal vote in decision-making. Perhaps the critical innovation was that, as co-owners, they were each entitled to a dividend from the store's profits, proportional to how much they had spent—a system that would come to be called the patronage dividend, or simply the divi. If a member collected it, this could be a windfall; if not, it became a mechanism for savings. There was a strict rule, too, that the store would neither extend nor expect credit. All cash, no debtors.

When compared to Owen's feat, the significance of Rochdale was that it put the beneficiaries—the ones in need—in charge. It wouldn't have happened without them. This system depended on no patriarch for either wisdom or capital. The store's early success spread simply because of the visible effect it had on its members, who "appeared better fed, which was not likely to escape notice among hungry weavers," according to Holyoake. "The children had cleaner faces, and new pinafores or new jackets, and they propagated the source of their new comforts in their little way, and other little children communicated to their parents what they had seen." Whereas Owen wanted to abandon private property to a paternalistic commons, the Rochdale store was a commons that put its members in better stead for a world of property.[12]

At a time, too, when unscrupulous dealers might adulterate flour and soap to the point of danger, the co-op was a means of ensuring quality sourcing—quality of the product itself and the labor practices that produced it. In this, Rochdale prefigured how co-ops would later pioneer the organic and free-trade movements.

My earliest memory of a co-op is of a store my mother shopped at when I was little, where she could get the boxes of organic soy milk that were not yet available in supermarkets.

The mighty Rochdale store, even by Holyoake's cheerful account, had its troubles. Rochdale included its share of "social porcupines, whose quills eternally stick out," "who know that every word has two meanings, and who take always the one you do not intend," "who predict to everybody that the thing must fail, until they make it impossible that it can succeed, and then take credit for their treacherous foresight." And yet. Perhaps the chronicler's most lyric phrases come while meditating on a table that listed the society's quantities of members, funds, revenue, and profits each year, from

1844	28	£28	—	—

to

1876	8,892	£254,000	£305,190	£50,668

"Every figure glows with a light unknown to chemists," he writes. "Every column is a pillar of fire in the night of industry, guiding other wanderers than Israelites out of the wilderness of helplessness from their Egyptian bondage."[13]

Even with such growth, the Rochdale organization would be little better than Owenism if it were yet another impressive but solely historical exception. The difference is that it lives on in one of the ways that mortal cooperators can: institutionally. The Rochdale store began producing offspring within a few years of its founding. New branches opened around town, with services from shoemaking to housing, and copycat co-ops appeared elsewhere. The British Parliament helped clear the legal pathway for this with the Industrial and Provident Societies Act of 1852—again, before the 1856 Joint Stock Companies Act, the founding legislation for public, investor-owned corporations. But, as a cooperative, the Rochdale store wasn't set up to become a rapacious conglomerate, as investor-owners would demand. It would have to grow differently.

What came to be called the Cooperative Wholesale Society began in Manchester, in 1863, through a conspiracy of several hundred local co-ops across northern England, with several Rochdale Pioneers among its leadership.[14] Cooperative wholesales like this had been tried before, but now they had the firm foundation of the Rochdale model to build on. The wholesale's job would be to furnish products for the local co-ops, whether by bulk purchase or through its own factories. It would also aid them with marketing, putting the strength of a national brand behind them. And the wholesale was a co-op, too. Its member-owners were the local cooperative stores that patronized it, and its management was responsible to them, just as the stores were responsible to their own patrons.

This kind of structure is called a federation, or a confederation, or a secondary cooperative—a co-op of co-ops. It's how cooperative endeavors around the world since then have met the challenge of scale, while retaining units small and autonomous enough to be responsive to their members. It's reflected in that sixth cooperative principle of "cooperation among cooperatives," as well as Elinor Ostrom's eighth design principle of nesting commons within a commons.

It was this same Cooperative Wholesale Society whose buildings boasted their grandeur from Warbasse's frontispiece in 1936. Today, its pile of buildings is even more impressive. The CWS has evolved into the Cooperative Group, or the Co-op, a massive consumer federation that includes grocery stores, the Cooperative Bank, the Phone Co-op for telecommunications, an appliance business, insurance, and funeral services. Since 1917, too, it has been a leading sponsor of the Cooperative Party, a political coalition that pursues policies friendly to co-ops. British cooperation has ultimately accompanied, rather than replaced, the investor-owned corporate order. But the breadth of the Co-op's offerings bears witness to that old and comprehensive idea of local co-ops linking into a commonwealth.

———

Simply sharing everything with everyone wasn't what made the Rochdale model work. The Pioneers didn't try reenacting the Acts of the Apostles. What's more formidable is that they struck a balance. The mix of cooperative rules at Rochdale hit a spot where human nature, economics, and neighborliness converged to make a certain kind of business work. In the years since, as cooperation of this sort has spread, there has been research—not enough— to explain the competitive advantages of co-op enterprises, especially in markets not designed to support them. The findings go a little something like this:

- Co-ops can *establish missing markets* by reorganizing supply or demand to meet unmet needs

- *Leaner startup costs* can result from volunteerism and sweat equity

- *Productivity benefits* arise when members experience direct benefits from their co-op's success

- Co-ops offer *protection from exploitation* for members, resulting in greater trust and loyalty

- *Information-sharing* within an organization becomes easier with shared ownership

- Co-ops face a *lower chance of failure*, especially after the startup phase, and greater *resilience in downturns* due to risk adversity and shared sacrifice

- There can be *savings in transaction and contracting costs* through co-ownership among clients[15]

These competitive advantages come with costs of their own. Doing business this way can present barriers to obtaining capital and more demanding forms of governance. A give-and-take between costs and benefits has steered the course of this story—as with that between pragmatism and purpose.

Horace Greeley, founder of the *New-York Tribune*, became one of the nineteenth century's most effective propagandists of cooperation in the United States. He served on various co-op boards, introduced Holyoake's writings to American attention in the *Tribune*, and put the newspaper itself under an employee profit-sharing arrangement. The paper was also an early member of the Associated Press, a co-op for news gathering. Greeley, Colorado, the city where my grandfather got his start in business and where members of my family still live, takes its name from him; the *Tribune*'s agricultural editor founded the settlement in 1870 as Union Colony, a prohibitionist cooperative. Those decades after the Civil War saw a hardening of the US corporate system along with new varieties of agitation for something else. Co-ops, Greeley predicted, would be "the appointed means of rescuing the Labouring Class from dependence, dissipation, prodigality, and need...conducive at once to its material comfort, its intellectual culture, and moral elevation."[16]

Once again that ambition of holistic human improvement repeats itself like a refrain. Cooperation's boosters proposed it as an antidote to the deterministic, one-dimensional class struggle of Karl Marx. A person is more than any class. They promised this kind of business as a means of overcoming drunkenness and other workingmen's temptations. They talked about "emancipation" from wage labor, extending slave liberation from cotton plantations to the textile factories. The same year the Civil War ended, a group of cooperators in Philadelphia announced their store in terms much like Greeley's: "Cooperation aims at elevating men morally, socially, physically, and politically." The poster enjoins its readers, "Be of one mind in support of the truth; have faith in the lovely principle of Cooperation, and you may cast your mountain of woe into the sea of oblivion."

Some of those who fell for the principle fell hard. In an 1868 union newspaper, an iron molder in Troy, New York, confessed, with respect to cooperation, "I have dreamed about it, thought about it in the shop, on the street, at church, in fact, everywhere."[17] Everywhere, the lovely principle was spreading.

This was the period that saw the birth of the modern insurance industry, first through local fraternal organizations and secret societies that people organized to cobble together a safety net. These evolved into cooperative-like mutuals, owned by their policyholders, such as New York Life and Northwestern Mutual, which are still leaders in the US insurance business. Mired in labor conflicts, industrialists such as Andrew Carnegie, John D. Rockefeller, and J. P. Morgan dabbled in employee ownership and profit-sharing.[18] And as family farmers began to see their power wane compared to the influence of big-city industry, they began to create a cooperative system that remains the basis for a lot of the family farming that has managed to persist today.

One can still find Grange halls scattered across the rural United States, active and otherwise, attesting to the difficulties and salves of that time. There are several still operating within an hour's drive of where I live. The National Grange of the Order of Patrons of Husbandry first appeared in 1867, out of the ashes of war, to unite farmers across North-South lines and among the West's scattered settlements. In those halls, farmers learned skills from each other and shared their economic hardships. Grangers organized co-ops for purchasing, processing, credit, and retail, usually following the Rochdale model. One of their mottos was "cooperation in all things." It was an educational, political, and social movement—and in the West, also a colonial one—but its outcomes and underpinnings were consistently cooperative. More co-ops grew out of the later Farmers' Alliance, a multiracial network whose cooperatives broke from the Rochdale system by allowing its cash-strapped members to buy their supplies on credit.

Meanwhile in the cities, with the 1870s came the rise of the Knights of Labor, a cross-industrial national union for which organizing workers also meant organizing co-ops. Just as the Grange did for farmers, it set up cooperative stores for factory workers, as well as worker-owned businesses—mines, foundries, mills, printers, laundries, lumberyards, and more. These put a Knights of Labor label on their products. During the 1880s, at least three hundred such co-ops formed. The Knights joined with farmers to create the People's Party, which waged an insurgency in national politics to break the capitalist grip on government.

This was a prohibitionist, women's-rights, anti-monopoly populism hard to imagine under the rural-urban, red-blue lines that divide the United States today. The principal demand was for a more flexible monetary system than the gold standard, one that would put the supply of credit under the control of small producers, not big bankers. The People's Party elected a local Knights of Labor secretary to the Colorado governor's seat in 1893, and before the year was out, it became the second state to adopt women's suffrage. The populists' basic premise throughout was that opposing entrenched power and creating co-ops went hand in hand.[19]

That strategy was already well known and well practiced among African Americans. W. E. B. Du Bois, the most prominent black intellectual of the period, organized a conference in 1907 called "Economic Cooperation Among Negro Americans" at Atlanta University. The event's resolutions determined, "From the fact that there is among Negroes, as yet, little of that great inequality of wealth distribution which marks modern life, nearly all their economic effort tends toward true economic cooperation."[20] The almost two-hundred-page report details the many forms of the black cooperative economy, broadly conceived, including churches, schools, insurance, banks, secret societies, and more. Among these are formal cooperative businesses, more than 150 of which are listed by name. Co-op lending circles, insurance pools, and stores were a necessity for people whom white-controlled businesses and governments often declined to serve. Cooperation would be an ongoing fascination for Du Bois; in 1918, he organized a Negro Cooperative Guild to help the co-ops unite their efforts. Even as white society opted for the allures and inequities of capitalism, he believed his people could choose another way.

Mutual education was part of it all along. In her more recent survey, political economist Jessica Gordon Nembhard writes, "Every African American–owned cooperative of the past that I have researched, and almost every contemporary cooperative I have studied, began as the result of a study group or depended on purposive training and orientation of members."[21] Whether an individual business thrived or foundered, the effects of that education shaped its participants.

By the time of Du Bois's conference, the populists' surge was over. The crackdown following the 1886 Haymarket riot was the beginning of the end for the Knights of Labor, and the American Federation of Labor that took its place practiced a kind of unionism friendlier to investor-owners and indifferent to cooperation. The People's Party collapsed after it splintered during the 1896 election. There was an attempt to form a Cooperative Union of America, a predecessor of Warbasse's Cooperative League, but it lasted only until 1899. Yet the lovely principle kept on seducing.

One of its remnants sits just ten miles up the road from me. In 1897, a Colorado mining-equipment supplier, Charles Caryl, composed and self-published a utopian drama outlining a system of worker-managed mines in Boulder County meant to swallow the whole country in a cooperative New Era Union. Despite raising substantial capital from New York investors, however, Caryl's scheme failed; he reestablished himself in a spiritualist sect and fled to California. His office is a museum now, open one day a month, in a mountain gulch with a few neighbors left and the towering ruins of the old gold mill. Meanwhile, Maine departmentstore owner Bradford Peck penned another cooperative fantasy called *The World a Department Store*; he thereafter attempted to form a Cooperative Association of America, which fell short of national reach but which at least managed his store under an employee profit-sharing arrangement from 1900 to 1912.[22] It seemed like the cooperative commonwealth might kick off anywhere, and with time, in pieces, it did.

The populists' organizing built the basis of a system that, in the coming century, would generate cooperative agricultural brands like Cabot Creamery, Land O'Lakes, Ocean Spray, and Organic Valley. (Less visible in grocery stores are CHS, the agricultural supply giant, and Genex, the high-tech purveyor of bull semen.) A revived Grange and the Farm Bureau insurance systems kept the Rochdale idea spreading. The US Department of Agriculture established dedicated co-op programs, and acts of Congress in 1914 and 1922 shielded farmers' co-ops from antitrust law.[23] Immigrant communities—perhaps most energetically, Scandinavians in the Upper Midwest—imported cooperative models from the Old World and innovated new ones. Department-store mogul Edward Filene, who first coined the term *credit union*, financed the spread of such co-op banks across the country, starting with his own employees, and lobbied for enabling legislation. A cooperative radio network emerged in the 1920s, the Mutual Broadcasting System, which produced such classic radio dramas as *The Lone Ranger* and *The Shadow*. The more cooperation became a fixture of the economy, the less it drew attention to itself; one could be forgiven for failing to notice that practical, powerful, hardly utopian pockets of a commonwealth had already taken hold.

In 1941, the year Murray Lincoln succeeded Warbasse as its president, the Cooperative League produced a film, *The Co-ops Are Comin'*. It depicted a co-op department store in Columbus, Ohio, a co-op tractor, the co-op hatchery of the Indiana Farm Bureau, and a co-op fertilizer plant challenging a corporate

A recent—and far from complete—map of cooperatives throughout the United States.

monopoly, all bound together with a map of the forty-eight states blanketed in the twin pines logo. Such universality was aspirational, but it represented the mounting reality of an agricultural heartland more and more bound together in cooperative business, if only the commonwealth's momentum would continue. But this momentum, the film contended, would depend on local, informal, mutual education. "Since a cooperative is a miniature democracy," one title card explains, "its strength lies in its informed members who teach themselves through their study groups."[24] Perhaps without the impending war and the corporate juggernaut that followed, those little groups would have been sufficient. The fate of cooperation, anyway, was not merely a question for one or another constituency in the United States. By the time the International Cooperative Alliance first met in London in 1895, a global movement was already discovering itself.

Salinas de Guaranda is an Ecuadorian mountain village most of a day's drive from Quito. It has become a minor destination thanks to its factories that make cheese, chocolate, and textiles. At least part of its appeal is the fact that each of these enterprises is owned by and accountable to Salinas's residents, all through a byzantine organizational structure surrounding their credit union. The village has become an engine for development throughout the region, producing offshoots and replicas. A cooperative hostel hosts visitors. The weekly town meeting takes place in an upper room next to the church on the main square, under the concrete cross mounted on the hill above; the gathering doubles as a prayer meeting. The whole system arose in the 1970s at the instigation of an Italian priest.[25]

Salinas is in some respects an exception—to the usual economic hopelessness of remote mountain towns, to the usual craving for rescue by multinational corporations—and in some respects not. Among impressive co-ops the world over, a story of influence repeats itself, in parallel with the spread of the Rochdale model. The first credit union in the United States, St. Mary's

Salinas.

Bank, was born of a New Hampshire parish in 1908 with the help of Alphonse Desjardins, founder of Quebec's vast credit-union federation, who also mentored Edward Filene. Desjardins, in turn, borrowed the idea from Farmers' Bank of Rustico, founded under the guidance of a Jesuit priest on Prince Edward Island. The largest, most renowned worker cooperative on record is the Mondragon Corporation in the Basque Country in Spain, which employs more than seventy thousand people, most of them co-owners—thanks to another enterprising priest, much like the one in Salinas.[26]

The medieval commons found new expression in modern co-ops. Roman Catholics were not alone in this; secularists, Jews, communists, Buddhists, Protestants, Muslims, and others have formed the cooperative movement as well.[27] But the Catholic contribution has been notably persistent, even if few Catholics know about it. I'm a Catholic myself, and I've never heard this story told in church. One might not expect cooperative democracy from such a monarchic, rigid hierarchy, but it's there. It is a story I had to piece together from inklings in my travels and in books, from stray remarks and unexpected teachers.

When Pope Leo XIII promulgated his 1891 encyclical letter *Rerum Novarum* (or, *Rights and Duties of Capital and Labor*), he regarded his church as standing between a materialist-socialist rock and a robber baron–capitalist hard place. Decades of revolution and class conflict had shaken Europe, cracking many of the church's secular buttresses. Wary of accumulations of power in either business or the state, Leo proposed a third-way solution: double down on private property, but provide for its more widespread distribution. He called for the dispossessed workers of the world to take ownership. "The law," he wrote, "should favor ownership, and its policy should be to induce as many as possible of the people to become owners."[28]

Even while asserting the priority of property, he retained the spirit of that old idea of the universal destination of goods, by which property should be treated somehow as if everything were really everyone's. The encyclical didn't include an explicit embrace of Rochdale-style cooperation but provided a basis for its subsequent adoption. And throughout the Catholic world, in a tremendous variety of ways, people tried to figure out how to put his sketch of a solution into practice. Popularizers of the effort such as Hilaire Belloc and G. K. Chesterton fashioned "distributism" into a subgenre of political philosophy.[29]

At a crowded lunch reception in Melbourne, Australia, a young cooperator working for the local archdiocese pointed me to an elderly man. The man had something he wanted to say. He came close to me and began to speak, and from that noisy scene I recollect only one crucial word: *formation*.

The man's name was Race Mathews. And despite his reference to a theological concept, he confessed to being neither a Catholic nor a believer. For most of his career, before retiring to study the origins of the modern cooperative tradition, he was a politician and official in Australia's Labor Party. He wanted to share his latest discovery.

Formation is a word now used frequently in the Catholic vernacular. It refers to a person's ongoing conversion to Christianity—through prayer, study, and experience. The kind of formation one receives depends on one's outside influences and one's interior choices, and economic life is part of formation, too.

Since the 1980s, Mathews had made a series of visits to Mondragon. This remarkable network of worker co-ops emerged under the shadow of Francisco Franco in the 1950s through the guidance of the one-eyed priest José María Arizmendiarrieta, or simply Arizmendi. It's a system of factories, schools, banks, retailers, and more, all owned and governed by people who work in them. It's a beacon of possibility the world over that democratic business can thrive, employing high tech and large scale, though it has yet to be outdone or replicated.

Mathews's 2009 book, *Jobs of Our Own,* traces Arizmendi's precursors, including *Rerum Novarum* and the distributists. In Mondragon, Mathews saw a practical manifestation of the ideas earlier Catholics had only alluded to, dubbing it "evolved distributism." But only after publishing that book, while studying the Catholic Action and Young Christian Workers movements that influenced Arizmendi, did Mathews zero in on the concept of formation.

Mondragon, he realized, is a monument not only to a particular way of doing business but to a vision for forming the souls who partake in it. Before the first Mondragon cooperative opened in 1956, Arizmendi started a secondary school, financed and co-governed by students' families, in which he and his students developed their plans together over the course of a decade. They tested their ideas relentlessly and creatively through practice, and then adjusted those ideas accordingly. The reasons for Mondragon's success are complex enough to be infinitely open to interpretation, but among them is the view of participants' spiritual development as an end in itself, rather than simply a means toward enacting an abstract economic system. "It has been said that cooperativism is an economic movement that uses the methods of education," Arizmendi once wrote. "This definition can also be modified to affirm that cooperativism is an educational movement that uses the methods of economics."[30] The centrality of this kind of education for Mondragon is hard to overstate.

Mondragon continues to be a uniquely successful model of cooperative industrialism, but as a cooperative expression of Catholic social teaching it is far from alone. The Knights of

Labor's ranks were heavily Catholic, including pro-cooperative leaders such as Terence Powderly, who petitioned Leo XIII for support. Starting in the mid-1930s, through a university extension program, two priests in Nova Scotia seeded the Antigonish movement, which resulted in hundreds of co-ops throughout the region. In the US South, the African American priest Albert J. McKnight became one of the architects of a cooperative system that enabled thousands of black farmers to own land. Meanwhile in New York, the lay-edited Catholic magazine *Jubilee*, active between 1953 and 1967, organized itself as a consumer cooperative, with shares owned by subscribers; this model took inspiration from journalist and children's book author Clare Hutchet Bishop's *All Things in Common*, a lyrical dispatch from among the worker-cooperative industries that appeared throughout France after World War II. Around the world, mission agencies have supported co-ops among poor farmers and craftspeople, enabling them to bring products to global markets on terms more of their own choosing. Catholic Relief Services calls this methodology "integral human development." Among the "interfaith partners" of the fair-trade worker cooperative Equal Exchange are not only Catholic Relief Services but also the Quakers' American Friends Service Committee, the Jewish Fair Trade Project, the Mennonite Central Committee, the Presbyterian Church USA, and the Unitarian Universalist Service Committee.[31]

Few places exemplify the odd bedfellows that cooperation brings together like the northern Italian territories of Tuscany, Trentino, and above all Emilia-Romagna. There, cooperatives organize the timbre and tempo of the whole economy. Italy's two largest grocery-store chains are cooperatives—one owned by its consumers, the other by local retailers. Co-ops control Unipol, one of the largest insurers, whose modern skyscraper towers over the terra-cotta rooftops of Emilia-Romagna's capital, Bologna; they carry out activities as varied as construction, garbage collecting, and producing a best-selling brand of boxed wine. Co-ops can look like the trattoria in the Trastevere neighborhood of Rome run by the community of Sant'Egidio, or a monastery-turned-guesthouse along a canal in Venice; both make a point of

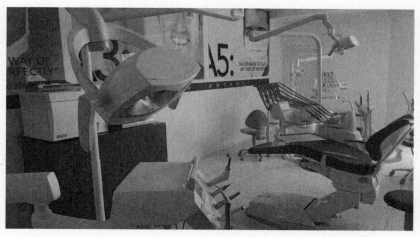

A showroom of dental chairs at a factory for Cefla, a manufacturing cooperative near Bologna.

employing people with disabilities. One can visit a showroom of sophisticated dental chairs at a massive worker-owned factory or buy bonds from a dairy co-op backed by wheels of its Parmesan cheese. Cooperative networks enable small- and medium-size enterprises to remain dominant in a region that exports world-renowned food, automobiles, and packaging equipment. In part because of its culture of cooperatives, Emilia-Romagna has the highest median family income in Italy, with the lowest unemployment rate and the highest participation of women in the workforce.[32] This is the outcome of a curious convergence.

Emilia-Romagna was, starting in the late nineteenth century, a leftist stronghold. Communists and socialists dominated the first national cooperative association, Legacoop, founded in 1886. Catholics formed another association, Confcooperative, in 1919. At a time when the Catholic Church preferred monarchies over democracies, and communists were vying for their own absolutist schemes, in northern Italy both opted to back bottom-up businesses. Today, the two organizations have come to regard their ideological differences as negligible. They have initiated a merger. "The Berlin Wall doesn't exist anymore, but we in Italy realized it only recently," says Gianluca Laurini, a Legacoop official in Bologna. "Ideology aside, a co-op is a co-op."

Cooperative formation, it seems, can outlast its original rationales. It works by a distinct logic and imparts its own lessons, assembling a commonwealth among people and places with little else in common.

———

My flight arrived in Nairobi with the sunrise. It was my first time in the city, my first time in sub-Saharan Africa, and I was still half asleep. But I had an appointment an hour later at a hotel downtown, so I allowed myself no time to come to my senses before getting into a taxi.

In the thick traffic between the airport and the city, I started to look around through the haze of morning. Along the side of the road, buildings came and went among the palm trees and power lines. There were stores, stray hotels, and office buildings that offered no indication of the work done inside. Fashion models watched me go by from billboards, towering over hand-painted mural ads for Safaricom, the telecom company that runs a celebrated text-message payment system called M-Pesa. And then I started seeing storefronts for the Co-operative Bank.[33] As the Nairobi skyline came into view, I saw that name also atop one of the taller buildings. I hadn't come to Kenya because of its cooperatives, nor did I know that I should; I'd come to visit family members who were living at a research station near Mount Kenya. But I had never been to a place where co-ops were so ubiquitous and so vital.

I asked the cab driver about the Co-operative Bank. He told me about *his* cooperative bank, a kind of small credit union among his fellow drivers called a SACCO, or savings and credit cooperative. For these independent workers fending for themselves, the SACCO is their social-safety net, enabling them to cover medical expenses if they get ill and burial expenses when they die. It's also how he got his start as a business owner; with loans from the SACCO he started buying cars and built a small fleet. He told me about the secrets of his business—turnover, not margins—and about the tricky politics that can arise among a group of drivers trying to manage a pool of swirling capital. He'd been president of the SACCO on and off, so he knew all about conflicts between membership and management. As I listened to him talk, I felt I'd never met someone so expert in the mechanics of democracy— along with its contradictions and limits. Cooperation, for him, was a matter of necessity more than choice. He said, "It's a double-edged sword."

Modern cooperation had come to the country as an instrument of exploitation. By the end of the nineteenth century, after honing cooperative business to uplift their own working poor, the British turned it on their colonies. Even by the time of the 1931 Cooperative Societies Ordinance in colonial Kenya, membership was still open only to white settlers, who used their co-ops to organize the export of cash crops grown with African land and African labor.[34] Meanwhile, British colonists in India encouraged farming co-ops, and in British-Mandate Palestine, Jewish settlers from Europe were establishing collective villages on land Arabs had held for centuries.

In Kenya, the white-only system started to change in the 1940s, when the colonial governors reasoned that a middle class of black cooperators could serve as a bulwark against uprisings.

The Cooperative University of Kenya.

Upon independence in 1963, Kenyans turned this means of exploitation into one of liberation; co-ops became the basis of state-sponsored "African socialism" in the country. The official ideology reinterpreted the cooperative system as a return to a precolonial, communal way of life—the economic expression of the new nation's motto, *harambee*, meaning "coming together."

Today, nearly half of Kenya's gross domestic product flows through cooperatives, and the International Labour Organization estimates that 63 percent of the population derives a livelihood from them.[35] The historic dominance of farming co-ops is giving way to the finance sector, which ranges from my driver's small SACCO to the Cooperative Bank, the country's fourth-largest financial institution. Kenyan co-ops organize themselves into a series of federations according to sector and region, which in turn join to form an apex federation, the Cooperative Alliance of Kenya. The International Cooperative Alliance also has a regional office in Nairobi.

On my last day in the city, I caught a ride to the Cooperative University of Kenya, a tranquil campus in the western suburbs. The buildings were painted blue and white. It is in most respects an ordinary business school, with better-dressed-than-average students darting along its sidewalks and lawns between classes on marketing, accounting, and finance. But it's more than that, too.

Esther Gicheru, the school's former director, grew up on a coffee farm, the daughter of co-op members. Her own education began by taking part in her family business. "In cooperative training," she told me, as if channeling the likes of Holyoake and Greeley, "we are not just thinking about disseminating business knowledge and skills. We are thinking about the growth and the advancement of people at all levels, in a way that an ordinary stock company will never do." Now she runs the Institute for Cooperative Development, a new arm of the university dedicated to research. She and her colleagues want to help existing businesses do better, as well as to set up business types less common in the country, such as worker co-ops and housing co-ops.

Only since a law passed in 1997 have Kenyan cooperatives been meaningfully independent from government support and

Esther Gicheru.

control. This was part of a bigger, ambivalent restructuring process at the behest of such institutions as the World Bank, nudging the country away from African socialism and toward global markets. Perhaps only then did Kenya's co-ops have to become true co-ops—truly autonomous and self-managed. Some collapsed under their own unmarketable weight, while others have learned to become more competitive and thrive. The university's job has taken on new significance. "Members used to look at cooperatives as extensions of government," Gicheru said. "Now cooperatives take education very seriously."

Back in downtown Nairobi, in a dense complex of bureaucratic concrete, I visited Nyong'a Hyrine Moraa, chief cooperative officer at the government's Ministry of Industrialization and Enterprise Development. Co-ops used to have the privilege of their own ministry; now, the job of her office is to steer the sector toward habits of mind more conducive to survival under globalization. Every co-op in the country still has to submit its accounts to the reorganized ministry, but no longer can they expect state protection as in times past.

"We try to tell the cooperatives it's not business as usual. It's not like the way they used to do things," Moraa said. "There is need to impress entrepreneurship in anything that they are doing."

Moraa's particular priority was for co-ops to invest in the means of adding value to their products, beyond just churning out raw materials. It's an old problem, dating back to the British system of growing cheap crops in the colonies but keeping the most profitable links of the supply chain at home. Moraa talked about leather, about food processing, about textiles. Yet the vexing paradoxes of the postcolonial condition persist there, as in so many parts of the world. Around half of Kenyans live in poverty; their SACCOs don't give them access to the wealth that the political elite skims off the top. Much of the financing for co-op development comes from agencies abroad, often from the same wealthy countries that compel Kenya to conform its policies to the dictates of global markets. But Moraa was also trying to help Kenya's co-ops leverage each other. Her office, for instance, was connecting farmers in the countryside with affordable, flexible loans from SACCOs in the cities.

As I went on asking about the details of these financing schemes, Moraa grew restless and asked if I had noticed that the office was mostly empty that day. I had; it was. She explained this was because the employees' SACCO was having an election. She had to excuse herself, which she did as she showed me back to the elevator. She needed to go vote.

———

Just as the cooperative idea needed forming by trial and time, co-operators need forming too. Education was among the founding principles of the Rochdale store, and it has remained enshrined in every update of that list. But it is also an easy principle to disregard in the short term, until after a while it is nowhere to be found. The kind of formation I saw available in Nairobi is harder to come by back home. There's no such thing in the United States as a cooperative business school.

Despite representing a sector with significant scale and a distinctive logic, cooperative principles and practices nearly disappeared from economics textbooks after World War II. According to one study, published in 2000, only six of seventeen North American introductory economics texts even mentioned co-ops, and almost always briefly and dismissively.[36] Among twenty leading US MBA programs I polled, not one reported a single course devoted to cooperative enterprise. Several professors of management and economics I queried about cooperative business weren't sure what I was talking about.

This would come as a disappointment to Leland Stanford, the robber-baron founder of Stanford University. Accompanying his 1885 initial endowment were instructions to promote "the right and advantages of association and cooperation." As a US senator, he championed legislation to support worker-owned cooperatives, which he saw as preferable to the investor-owned enterprise that had made him so wealthy. He told the university's first class of students, "Cooperative societies bring forth the best capacities, the best influences of the individual for the benefit of the whole, while the good influences of the many aid the individual."[37] This was guidance that his university, including its elite business school, has almost completely ignored.

The exceptions to this lacuna are generally found not in MBA programs but in the less glamorous discipline of agricultural economics. Since cooperatives are part of US farmers' essential infrastructure, the Department of Agriculture has long supported university research on co-ops, especially at land-grant campuses. Among the most prolific of these programs is the University of Wisconsin–Madison's Center for Cooperatives, established with federal assistance in 1962, whose very existence is required by state law. Yet when the center was running the search for its current faculty director, it had trouble finding qualified candidates. Brent Hueth, the agricultural economist who ended up getting the job, had been studying co-ops largely in isolation. "I pretty much stumbled into it on my own," he says.

What drew him was the recognition that co-ops were uniquely effective in enabling independent farmers to purchase supplies and sell to markets with an economy of scale. "It's not idiosyncratic to the country, it's not one-off," he told me. "There seems to be something fundamental about these sets of markets and these economic environments where the investor-owned model doesn't get the job done."

Keeping the Madison center open and funded hasn't been easy; the co-op sector doesn't have access to the kinds of wealthy benefactors that furnish MBA programs with names and fortunes. "Cooperatives create a lot of wealth, but it doesn't get concentrated in a small number of people," Hueth says. Persuading a democratic co-op to fund university programs can be trickier than luring individual donors with the prospect of leaving a legacy. A co-op MBA program at Canada's St. Mary's University depends on relationships with cooperatives that send their employees to study.

A lot of the co-op business education that does take place nowadays happens in unaccredited academies run by community organizations. The lessons are often experiential and group oriented, evaluated by real-world success. But the formation of a co-op sector of any scale and seriousness will need formal training, too. Melissa Hoover, executive director of the Democracy at Work Institute, a leading promoter of US worker co-ops, can't afford to wait. She needs co-op entrepreneurs, as soon as possible, who know how to work with the nuts and bolts of existing capitalism. "I reject the special-snowflake version of cooperative education," she told me. "Move, people. Go to traditional business schools and politicize your own learning."

The university system itself has origins in cooperation. Europe's early universities emerged from self-governing guilds of scholars, a legacy that lives on in dreaded faculty meetings and committee work. Perhaps this legacy is in need of revival. Some have called for schools to be owned and governed not just by faculty members but by stakeholders ranging from students to custodians. Throughout the United Kingdom in recent years, at pre-university levels, parents and teachers have taken advantage of privatizing reforms to set up cooperative schools that they own and manage together.[38]

When I try to figure out what prompted me to think that the stories of equitable pioneers might be worthy of consideration, I think back to a time in school. My high school math teacher once invited me to chair a committee that would reconsider our public alternative school's admissions policy. This was a touchy subject because our previous policy had been overruled in a big court case. I don't think I'd ever been on a committee before, much less chaired one; who knows why he thought I could. But I did. We met in his classroom in the evenings—including him, parents just out of work, and fellow students. With the school nearly empty and night outside, the building itself seemed to be listening to us. For months, we debated possibilities, then drafted a proposal to better reach underserved neighborhoods in the county. We brought it to the school board. I gave a speech there, and our proposal passed. I guess I got it into my bones then that even a teenager lousy at math, given the chance to help govern, can rise to the occasion.

"With a greater intelligence, and with a better understanding of the principles of cooperation," Leland Stanford said in the 1887 congressional record, "the adoption of them in practice will, in time I imagine, cause most of the industries of the country to be carried on by these cooperative associations."[39] He believed that a bit more of the right kind of research and teaching and forming would usher in a cooperative commonwealth. But despite his best efforts at the university he founded, and those of others since, his supposition remains mainly untested. Those turning to cooperation today have had to rediscover the lovely principles for themselves.

3

The Clock of the World

Disruption

I went to Detroit looking for the concrete, for the tangible stuff I'd heard was there—guerrilla farms carved into abandoned lots, foreclosed homes turned into communes, peeks into the apocalyptic future that other cities might have coming their way when the American dream abandons them, too. Those were there all right. Pedaling among the empty, stately homes and factory ruins at the speed of a borrowed bike, the possibilities were as visible as the wreckage, and in many cases the two were one and the same. It is as good a place as any to pivot this story from the past to the present and its contending futures.

Detroit has long been a place of pilgrimage. It was Motor City, the engine of American car culture, and it was Motown, where the black middle class built a center for entertainment and art between the coasts. Lately, the country has looked to it for other reasons—for the direness of its postindustrial decay, and for its relative emptiness, which is not in fact emptiness at all, but which looks enough like it to beckon the imaginations of pioneers, equitable and otherwise, all vying to be protagonists of the city's inevitable revival. Detroit understands the disruptions of our time with particular acuity. It also knows especially well the new longing for cooperation.

My excuse for the visit was a conference called New Work New Culture, an oblique celebration of Michigan philosopher Frithjof Bergmann's decades-long quest, amid the rise and fall of the auto industry, to transform work from a dead-end chore into a joy. Also in town that week were the Black Farmers and Urban Gardeners Conference and the United Nations representatives investigating home water shutoffs that were part of the city's on-going bankruptcy proceedings.

"Ask what 'new work' is," said one of my hosts at the New Work Field Street Collective house, where I slept on the floor, "and everyone will tell you something different." That was the point. Bergmann found the genesis of good work in how each of us probes our most genuine, most particular desires.

The night I arrived, I met the elder member of the Field Street Collective, Blair Evans, not long since out of prison for Black Panther–era activities. He told stories. He loved all the gadgets he'd been missing out on, and he kept a little video camera hanging from his neck to record the police. In the house, he was teaching younger guys how to craft leather goods, which he'd learned to do while incarcerated. The next day, I met Marcia Lee, a younger woman-about-town who worked for the local Franciscan friars. She let me ride along for a strenuous day in her life of organizing, including a stop at a photo shoot for queer activists and a prayer supper. In between, she told me about her study circle with fellow women of color who were dreaming up co-ops.

How much of this was really working? If something works in what remains of Detroit, surely it can work anywhere. I was ready to see models—replicable innovations I could gather up and share elsewhere. To the model-acquiring frame of mind alone, however, the first day of New Work New Culture was an almost total waste of time.

Under the fluorescent lights of a lecture hall at Wayne State University in midtown Detroit, the invocation came as a volley of African drumming. The discussions that followed were on the

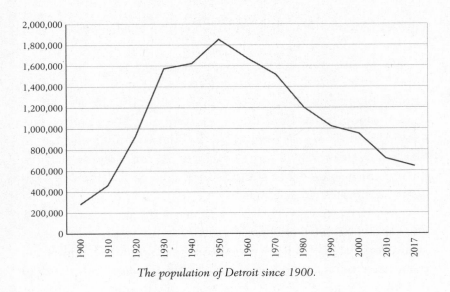

The population of Detroit since 1900.

"new culture" side of things, consisting of fairly general reflections on life and the universe derived from a synthesis of activist idioms, Africana, and plain experience. "If you stand here"—meaning Detroit—"and survive, you learn something about a higher self," said Mama Sandra Simmons, a transfixing woman who introduced herself, among other things, as an ordained minister. "We are warriors, and we are in this together." But the most frequently repeated phrase among speakers was a question: "What time is it on the clock of the world?"

These were the words of Grace Lee Boggs, the mentor of many of the event's organizers. She earned her PhD in philosophy just before the United States entered World War II. A Chinese American herself, she married an African American factory worker and labor organizer, Jimmy Boggs, and fell under the influence of the Trinidadian socialist C. L. R. James. She rejected Soviet communism but joined with the Black Panthers and Malcolm X to build a revolution of local economies, by and for marginalized communities of color. She preached the power of "critical connections" over "critical mass."[1] As the conference proceeded, Boggs remained in the basement of her home, while the rooms above were still being used for organizing. She had strength at her advanced age to see only her closest companions, including Marcia Lee. The following year, a century old, she would pass on to join the ancestors.

"The clock of the world" is a call to notice where we are and where we might go next. Boggs had long used Detroit as a clock that could see into the future, that could predict the crises soon to spread elsewhere and the means of surviving them. Automation came to Detroit's factories long before the internet came for travel agents; the housing bubble was already long-popped by 2008. Her disciples invoked the question less because they expected an answer than to provoke further probing. The best hope was "a way out of no way."

As the day's sessions ended, boxes full of percussion instruments appeared and made their way out among the crowd. Thus began a rising cacophony that took several minutes to resolve into a common beat. I received, and proceeded to shake, an old plastic POM juice bottle half full of sand.

The second day was more like what I'd originally had in mind. A bus tour showcased the gardens in abandoned lots. But back at the conference, attendees grilled Bergmann, who wore a black leather cap over restless gray hair, on the features of his theory. Ideas he'd formed decades ago as an antidote to the auto assembly lines—like living your passion and choosing your own hours—sounded suspiciously like a pitch for the gig-economy hustle that younger people in the room knew too well. Bergmann's liberation was their perpetual insecurity. He reveled in the possibilities of 3D printers for localizing production, but groans came from those who were sick of being told that their rescue was only one more contraption away. To Boggs's big question, gender theorist Kathi Weeks won applause when she replied, "It's quitting time." She didn't trust work enough to entrust her passion to it.[2]

That afternoon I found Bergmann sitting alone, feeling frustrated and misunderstood. So much had changed. The factories weren't the starting point anymore. The vision of new work he'd hoped for had been co-opted in capitalism before a better version got a chance to grow.

Around him, breakout groups held nitty-gritty discussions about financing cooperatives and organizing time-banks. I joined a tour of a state-of-the-art fab-lab, in which "at-risk" youth were making everything from coasters to an electric car with precision mills and, yes, 3D printers. Something to write home about, maybe.

To get back to my inflatable mattress that night, I caught a ride with Tawana Petty. She was an organizer of the conference, an activist and mother with a relentless smile that she said she had learned as part of the emotional labor expected of her while serving fast food. Now, she does research and education on "data justice." I listened from the back seat as she, in the passenger seat, caught up with a visiting friend behind the wheel. She described a moment in which she'd been called to speak before UN representatives about the water crisis. She said she'd felt the ancestors speaking through her, in her, with her. Not blood family, necessarily—for instance, she'd felt the presence of Charity Hicks, a woman who had fought with particular tenacity against the water shutoffs until she was killed by a rogue car. "Charity was there," Petty said.

The utopias of Detroit, as best I could judge, were mostly in the process of being steamrollered by capital, or co-opted when doing so was profitable. The tide was raising some boats and sinking others. The only way for the others was no-way. The error on my part was failing to see enough value in the primary tip or trick or model these holdouts of Detroit had to offer: the stubborn cultivation of faith.

————

There is a simple chart that captures many perils and anxieties of our age in pithy summary. It has come to be called the jaws of the snake.[3] There are two lines. One ventures upward, jagged but steady. That represents the percent increase in US productivity since World War II. The second line follows it almost exactly—at first. This one represents wages, the degree to which most actual producers actually benefit. After rising in unison with the first, around 1970 the second line goes flat; by then private-sector union membership was in freefall. A similar thing happened again

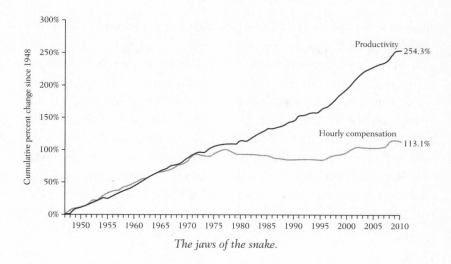

The jaws of the snake.

in 2000, except this time the line that went flat was total private-sector employment; this time, some say, it was automation by software.

The economy keeps getting more efficient and generating more value, but most people are getting a smaller and smaller portion of it. The rest of the value gets siphoned upward to the few and wealthy. More than pleasing customers, more than creating jobs, business keeps getting better at serving the single-minded goal of maximizing shareholder value—the rewards for those who already have excess to invest. Economist Thomas Piketty's best-selling book *Capital in the Twenty-First Century* argued that the returns to investors are careening the world into a new feudalism; his most celebrated critic, twenty-six-year-old MIT graduate student Matthew Rognlie, differed only in stressing that the major share of the phenomenon was in real estate.[4] An uptick in the minimum wage isn't going to fix this. One way or another, wealth is going to the owners—of where we live, where we work, and what we consume.

In between the jaws sit most of us. The lucky ones could go on being peaceably ignorant until the widening jaws clenched a bit in the 2008 financial crisis. Then the nature of the system revealed itself. High finance got bailouts while millions of people around the world, especially those in already precarious situations, got catastrophic losses. Even the new regulations meant to keep this from happening again were tailor-made for big businesses and further squeezed smaller ones. This laid bare the power relations at work; it demonstrated right out in the open which people and which institutions had the capacity to protect their interests and which didn't. Where jobs have returned to replace the ones that disappeared, they have been less predictable, with fewer benefits, fewer of the guarantees that used to accompany employment. Millions of homeowners lost their homes. It was a crisis, yes, but it was also a symptom of celebrated norms. This was the upshot of something we'd been longing for.

———

A favorite aspiration for entrepreneurs today, by their own broken-record account, is disruption. The sign of a promising new enterprise is that it disrupts some industry or cultural habit or human-intensive inefficiency. This talk has become so pervasive that we neglect to notice what the word means—what it means and has meant, for instance, in Detroit. There, Jimmy Boggs saw disruption decades ago, when a brew of robots, racism, and imports from Asia shut down the city's factories, and when what remained of the auto industry fled to the whiter suburbs—consigning that capital of black America into decline and collapse.

The jargon of disruption derives from a more precise academic concept. Harvard Business School professor Clayton Christensen began honing what he came to call "disruptive innovation" in the mid-1990s and early 2000s, referring to how a simple development, often from an oblique end of a market, can refashion the rules of the market in which it operates.[5] In this way, the cheaper, less-mighty cars from Japan took on Detroit's Cadillacs. It's how Kodak invented the first digital camera in the 1970s but, by clinging to film, collapsed into bankruptcy by the hand of its own invention. It's how smartphones have replaced everything from alarm clocks and record collections to asking driving directions from a gas-station attendant. The disrupters can win big. Christensen's peers credited him with discovering a motive force in contemporary capitalism, a sunny successor to the "creative destruction" that Karl Marx, and then Joseph Schumpeter, observed in the industrial age. Thus we deify serial disrupters like Steve Jobs and Elon Musk. But what about the disrupted—those who endure the effects?

In centuries past, among St. Clare's nuns and the Diggers, among the Rochdale Pioneers and the Knights of Labor, cooperative economies have tended to take hold on the receiving end of economic upheavals. What cooperators built then became infrastructure for the new order, more or less in tension with it, a lifeline that enabled people who would otherwise be left behind to survive and flourish. It happened with the monasteries that lasted through the collapse of the Roman Empire, with the urban guilds that bore the costs of caskets in plagues, with the cooperative stores and workshops that helped workers endure the sweatshops that disrupted the guilds.

The disruptions of the early third millennium cascade and intersect. Human civilization's exhaust has caused extreme weather events to grow in frequency and force, together with the long, slow devastation of droughts. These combine with a whack-a-mole world war on terrorism to set off waves of mass migration. Globalized markets let capital flow freely but stop the desperate migrants at the borders. The liberal-democratic consensus that some expected to spread everywhere has buckled as voters around the world elect autocrats.

We've also been living through a disruption of networks. For Silicon Valley, the internet has created the favorite case in point of disruptive innovation. It wasn't walking, talking, sci-fi robots that took the place of travel agents or Borders Books, it was apps—new points of connection that replaced incumbent intermediaries. These connections replace physical assets and "human resources" with creative arrangements of users and their data. McKinsey and Company estimates as many as half of all jobs are vulnerable to existing technologies.[6] Rather than industrial production and distribution—now outsourced to other lands—the apps offer postindustrial matching algorithms. But networked connections can do more than endlessly disrupt us.

Behind so many disruptive tech companies lies an innovation that started with collaboration. Before there was Airbnb, travelers stayed in each other's homes for free with Couchsurfing. While Google and Facebook were disrupting the print advertising industry, an Egyptian Google employee used Facebook to help set off the popular uprising that brought down the regime of Hosni Mubarak. Car sharing, crowdfunding, social networks—these are things that people previously turned to co-ops to do. The collaborative possibilities of the internet are cooperative possibilities, too. The trouble is, as finance goes on becoming an ever-larger portion of the economy as a whole, outside investors' money has become easier and cheaper for new companies to access than that of customers or employees.[7] Maverick businesses that a generation or two ago might have had little choice than cooperation now find investors willing to buy in and take over before they bother considering other options. Awash in investor capital, most ambitious entrepreneurs seem oblivious to the prospect of funding and growing businesses grounded in the communities they serve. But not all have.

The new equitable pioneers don't tend to salivate at the thought of disruption the way startup bros do. Disruption sounds great to investors whose money lets them hover above the economic fray. But when you're accountable to fellow members, to others struggling to get by, there's not much to like about wiping away the basis of their livelihoods. Less exposed to risk and less inclined to panic, financial co-ops and credit unions kept up deposits and kept lending after the 2008 crisis hit.[8] While others were disrupting, cooperators have been innovating in their own fashion.

The 1960s counterculture produced famous consumer-owned grocery stores like Brooklyn's Park Slope Food Co-op: by the turn of the millennium, co-ops like these had helped build the global fair-trade movement for goods like coffee and chocolate, a much-needed feat of counterglobalization. The 1960s and 1970s saw a more buttoned-up kind of cooperation as well, such as when Seattle banker Dee Hock convinced Bank of America to spin off its credit-card franchise into a bank-owned cooperative, Visa. The

Vanguard Group meanwhile bypassed Wall Street's gatekeepers with a low-cost, consumer-owned mutual fund. In Italy, so-called social cooperatives transformed the care industry through shared ownership by both caregivers and their clients. Social co-ops also specialize in employing people with disabilities and criminal records; when painter Mark Bradford created his installation for the US pavilion at the 2017 Venice Biennale, he partnered with a social co-op through which local inmates grow produce and make crafts. Since it opened in 1985, Cooperative Home Care Associates in the Bronx has become the country's largest worker co-op—signaling promise for more in the fast-growing care sector—and it's now a certified, public-benefit-seeking B Corp on top of that. Japanese housewives in search of decent milk built a consumer co-op conglomerate. Indian sex workers used co-ops to establish more bearable standards in an underground industry. When Argentina's economy collapsed in 2001, workers took over factories that owners tried to close and started running them for themselves. Aided by tax perks, employee-stock ownership plans expanded to transfer corporate profits to millions of US workers.[9] New cooperators are appearing alongside the disruptions, the artificial and natural ones alike.

Hurricane Sandy struck New York City on October 29, 2012—an event ambiguously attributable to climate change, worsened in turn by the city's human inequities. It nearly washed away the Rockaway Peninsula, a narrow strip of land on the southeastern end of Queens, home to over one hundred thousand people. Structures that once stood near the beach could be found in pieces blocks away, alongside overturned cars and other hefty debris. A long strip of storefronts burned down in an electrical fire. Public apartment towers stood dark, without electricity or heat. Because of the mold growing in their flooded basements, residents couldn't return home. Yet thousands of New Yorkers joined in the recovery effort, there and in other coastal areas. The most sudden, remarkable volunteer-wrangling operation was Occupy Sandy, an undertaking of organizers who had been sharing things in common at Occupy Wall Street a year earlier. Within days, they had furnished a complex system of intake forms, trainings,

mold-remediation equipment, and distribution centers for donated supplies. Before long they were creating co-ops, too.

The following June, in the cramped upper room of a church
building in Far Rockaway, I attended a graduation ceremony for
WORCs, or Worker-Owned Rockaway Cooperatives. Occupy veterans had teamed up with five aspiring co-op businesses from the
neighborhood for a twelve-week program. In the making were a
panadería, a "people's market" for fresh groceries, a *pupuseria*, an
entertainment company, and a construction crew. Among them
was Brendan Martin, offering encouragement and footing the bill,
young for an executive director and wearing street clothes. After
working in high finance, he moved to Argentina and formed the
Working World, which began by making hundreds of loans to cooperative businesses there. The organization was beginning to expand back into the United States, starting with disruption zones
like this one, with the Occupiers' help.

"We've done a lot of protesting in the last few years, but this
has been a way to create alternative structures," one of the volunteers told me at the time. She would soon be among the Occupy
veterans to make a pilgrimage to Detroit, searching for guidance
on what to do next. When they got back, they could be heard asking each other, "What time is it on the clock of the world?"

Occupy's co-op affinity was only part of a revival in the United
States during the Great Recession. Move-your-money campaigns
turned disgust with the big banks into new accounts at credit
unions. Real estate investment co-ops organized to turn the tide
of urban gentrification. But the most fervent hope was reserved
for worker co-ops. The New York City Network of Worker Cooperatives was founded in 2009; it became part of the US Federation of Worker Cooperatives, which was itself only five years
old then. NYC NOWC, pronounced "nick knock," proved an
effective lobbyist, and by 2014, its coalition had convinced the
city council to fund $1.2 million in worker co-op development,
particularly in immigrant communities—which has since grown
to millions more. Former Occupy Sandy organizers joined NYC
NOWC's fledgling staff. In Cleveland, a group of local "an-
chor institutions" like hospitals and universities helped create

worker-owned laundry and green-energy co-ops; the allied Democracy Collaborative used this and other examples as the basis
for national-scale transition plans. Madison, Wisconsin, voted to
fund worker co-ops in late 2014; Oakland, Austin, Minneapolis,
Newark, and other cities got on board in various ways. By 2017,
Bernie Sanders was leading a group of Democratic senators and
representatives to propose federal legislation on behalf of worker-
owned businesses. Some embattled labor unions seemed ready to
turn back to their roots with a newfound interest in co-ops, too.
Alongside the NCBA and other older co-op organizations, these
efforts tended to coalesce around the youthful, intersectional, diverse umbrella of the New Economy Coalition—founded around
the time of the 2008 crash. They considered themselves part of a
wider "solidarity economy."[10]

It was in 2008, too, that Bank of America cut its line of credit
to Republic Windows and Doors, a factory on Chicago's Goose
Island. Production was set to end, but some of the workers refused to leave, and their occupation became a national totem.
President-elect Barack Obama said then, "What's happening to
them is reflective of what's happening across this economy." A legal settlement required the bankers to compensate the workers,

*Armando Robles in the New Era Windows Cooperative office, with the factory
floor behind him.*

and another company tried to buy the factory but failed to keep it afloat. Then one of the original worker-occupiers, union-local president Armando Robles, met Brendan Martin and invited the Working World to get involved. It was a case much like those Martin had seen among the recovered factories in Argentina. A group of workers, with the support of their union, formed New Era Windows Cooperative and borrowed more than $1 million through the Working World. Now they have their own factory, and they're making windows at a profit again.[11]

"To me, it's the next step for any union," Robles told me when I visited the new factory. "Instead of losing members, try to help them to maintain their jobs, create co-ops, and give them the tools they need."

New Era is an isolated case, but it's also a scalable model—no lock-ins required. More than half of US employers are businesses owned by baby boomers set to retire in the coming generation. Project Equity, an Oakland nonprofit that assists in such conversions, estimates that 85 percent of those businesses don't have a succession plan, and many will have trouble finding an outside buyer. Selling to their employees might be the best option in a lot of those cases, if only the owners—and the employees—knew that there might be another way.

———

When I moved to Colorado in the summer of 2015, I found that the cooperative revival was happening there, too. A group called the Community Wealth Building Network was meeting monthly in Denver office buildings, wrangling funders and policymakers to support cooperative models. The Rocky Mountain Employee Ownership Center was targeting retirement-ready business owners for conversion, and the Rocky Mountain Farmers Union started bringing its agricultural co-op experience to urban service workers. But some of the most seismic action was happening on the roads.

On the morning of Labor Day Sunday in 2016, the parking lot behind the Communication Workers of America Local 7777 office filled up with cars. Some already had the black or green paint of Green Taxi Cooperative, its name inscribed in the typeface of a Wild West saloon. But many were unmarked, or bore the branding of one of Denver's other cab companies, for whom their drivers were working even after putting down the $2,000 investment to become member-owners of Green Taxi. Some hadn't yet quit Uber. All eight hundred slots for Green Taxi members had been filled, and there was demand for more, but only around 150 members were driving for the co-op so far. The rest were waiting, working for other companies, keeping their status as co-owners of a competing business quiet and biding their time to see if this would really work. The largest taxi company in the Denver metro area was still mostly secret.

"I've never heard of a meeting on the Sunday before Labor Day," Sheila Lieder, the local's political director, told the assembly of about ninety co-owners, nearly all of whom were born and raised in places where Labor Day does not exist. Green Taxi's drivers came from thirty-seven countries, I was told, especially East African ones. At a time when the taxi industry here and virtually everywhere was facing an existential disruption from Silicon Valley apps, these immigrant workers self-funded a third way. They hoped that without bosses skimming profits they'd be able to take home enough to make driving a decent living in the age of apps, with a company and an app of their own.

"When we talk about the company, that's you," Abdi Buni, the board president, reminded his co-owners, "and when we talk about the drivers, that's also you."

With the backing of Communication Workers of America, including an office Green Taxi rented in the union hall's basement, Buni and his fellow founders had been clearing regulatory hurdles since 2014. The company's slow, quiet start began when the office opened on July 1, 2016; the first cars hit the streets later that month. It was part of an international surge of taxi co-ops trying to turn the industry's disruption-by-app into an opportunity for worker ownership—in suburban Virginia, in Seoul, throughout Europe, and beyond. For the Denver taxi scene, Green Taxi was game changing. For members, it was a better deal.

"I paid extra to use the owners' license before," said Kidist Belayneh, who has been driving taxis about half of the six years since she moved to Denver from Ethiopia. "Now I'm an owner. We don't pay extra." She was one of just a handful of women in the room.

The main business of that Sunday meeting was to vote on a legally inert but rhetorically meaningful amendment to Green Taxi's bylaws, which would emphasize that "members" were indeed "owners." These drivers were sticklers for detail. Some had driven for the two other smaller co-ops formed in recent years, Union Taxi and Mile High Cab, which allowed members to lease cars to nonmembers. Green Taxi set out to be different; all the drivers would be member-owners. "We need documentation of legal ownership," one of them said from among the ranks. "That's why I came from my other company." Another allowed me a glimpse at his stock certificate.

The first shouting match broke out over the books. Green Taxi lost its first bookkeeper, and the board had been slower than it had promised in delivering the financials to members. The hired accountant made excuses, insisting that any profits would go back to the members and that they should be patient, but a few loud voices pressed on. "This is our money and our company," one interjected. "This is not just some job." The uproar was so intense I wondered if some were paid disrupters from other companies they still worked for. Members got up to speak, alternating between declarations of loyalty and surges of defiance, then counteraccusations against the malcontents who wouldn't stop driving for Uber. In exasperation, one man stood up and said to the board what migrant workers aren't supposed to say out loud in America, that America is anything other than the hilltop Promised Land: "I came from Ethiopia sixteen years ago to make money so I can go back to Ethiopia. You're supposed to help me make money so I can go home." At last the board treasurer offered to show anyone who wanted to see it the bank ledger on his phone.

"This is democracy," Buni repeated, attempting to moderate— as if consoling himself, telling himself that the voice of the people will somehow lead to the good.

One of Green Taxi Cooperative's early member meetings.

Green Taxi's biggest problem, however, was not there in the room. In a car-culture city, the backbone of the taxi industry was the $55.57 flat-rate fare between the airport—nestled in the high prairie, far from everything—and downtown Denver. According to how the airport granted permits, in proportion to market share, Green Taxi's eight hundred members should have entitled the company to about one-third of the 301 available slots. So far, it had received only twenty. But with eight hundred drivers, according to Buni, twenty airport permits wouldn't be enough to keep the business afloat. What's more, the airport was planning to change the whole system, just as Green Taxi organized to claim its market share. The airport's website had a notice about an impending contract bid for taxi companies, replacing the permits. This could reshape the city's taxi business and make or break Green Taxi's plan to cooperativize—and unionize, with CWA—one-third of the market.

The airport's new regime affected only taxi companies, but it had everything to do with the influx of apps. Unlike taxis, Uber and Lyft drivers faced no restrictions on their airport usage. They often drove nicer cars and spoke better English; they were more likely to be white. In December 2014, the app drivers made

10,822 trips through the airport, compared to 30,535 by taxis. A year later, for the first time, app-based airport trips exceeded the taxis, and they'd done so every month since. As taxi companies prepared to fight among themselves under the still-unpublished new rules, Silicon Valley's expansion proceeded unrestrained— even welcomed by the relevant authorities. Rumors were flying about an insider deal, and nobody at Green Taxi seemed to be in on it.

"I have really deep concerns about how this is being done," Lieder told the drivers. She said she'd been trying to reach people all over government about it and not hearing back. "Something stinks about this."

Proceedings continued to the bylaws, and some complained that they'd never seen any. (They were on the internal website, but not where you'd expect.) A debate broke out about whether the members not yet driving for the co-op or paying dues should be allowed to vote. This necessitated a break, five minutes of intermingled talk, shouting, a bit of shoving, and laughter. It wasn't all hard feelings. But it was tense. I heard grumbling that the board might have rigged its own election—which came, it turns out, from a candidate who lost.

Jason Wiener, Green Taxi's counsel and a rising-star lawyer for the region's social-enterprise sector, tried to clarify things. He broke down the provisions of the bylaws about who could vote. The members almost made it to voting on the ownership amendment, but they didn't. They decided to table it for later. That was the closest thing to a decision made all day—for some, their first decision as business owners.

Despite whatever powers come with ownership, so much was out of the drivers' control, and the anxieties of futility seemed to be bearing down on them hard. They were fighting for slots at the all-important airport, and they were only a tiny player in the global scramble for control over the future of logistics. Wiener counseled more patience. "What you're trying to do is not easy," he said. "Try to see the long arc." He fielded more questions about the bylaws. It wasn't much longer before the three-hour meeting ambiguously ended.

A day earlier, I attempted to hail a Green Taxi for a short ride using the company's new mobile app. I was far from downtown Denver, and it took a few minutes before the app found me a driver from the skeleton fleet. While I waited, I scrolled through the Twitter feed of Autocab International, the company that created Green Taxi's app, "the No. 1 largest supplier of taxi booking and dispatch systems in the world." Recent posts included pictures of a workshop held in the United Kingdom about how to beat Uber, as well as links to news articles reporting new tests of self-driving cars, self-driving trucks, self-driving mini-buses. Also, alongside a broken link: "Crisis management is our specialty."

While Green Taxi's drivers scrambled to protect their livelihoods, Uber and Tesla and Google were tooling up to automate them. I asked Buni about this. He said, "We're really trying to feed a family for the next day. When it happens, we'll make a plan"— that is, crisis management, for the foreseeable future. To that end, he and his crisis-ridden co-owners pooled more than $1.5 million to put one-third of Denver's taxi industry under worker control. Self-driving cars hadn't come to the city's roads yet, but Wall Street's anticipation of them was fueling investment in the big apps, which put pressure on the taxi market and motivated so many drivers to set off on their own. The disruption was already happening, and Green Taxi had been born of it.

———

In the beginning, before Uber and Lyft and even checkered taxicabs, there was sharing. At least that's the story according to Dominik Wind, a German environmental activist with a genial smile and a penchant for conspiracy theories. Years ago, out of curiosity, Wind visited Samoa for half a year; he found that people shared tools, provisions, and sexual partners with their neighbors. Less encumbered by industrial civilization, they appeared to share with an ease and forthrightness long forgotten in the world Wind knew back home.

Wind and I got to know each other in Paris while splitting a stranger's apartment that we found through Airbnb. It was 2014, and thanks to apps like that, such apps were on the rise in urban centers.[12] The internet was making it possible again for people to share resources such as cars, homes, and time—bringing us together, for a price. Capitalism's creative destruction may have ravaged our communities for centuries with salvos of individualism, competition, and mistrust, but now it was ready to sell the benefits of community back to us on our smartphones.

Without owning any guestrooms of its own, Airbnb was by then more valuable than Hyatt; Zipcar, which rents cars by the hour, had been bought by the international car-rental company Avis Budget. The sharing economy was also changing the way at least some people worked. Online labor brokers such as Amazon's Mechanical Turk enticed hundreds of thousands of people to take up digital piecework—data entry, transcribing audio, running errands—without expectation of paid leave, health insurance, or even a minimum wage. But it was also alluringly permissionless—no application process, no fixed hours, no managers. Compared to the rest of the global economy, these companies remained small potatoes, but they seemed like portents of a shift that we'd soon be taking for granted before we had the chance to question it.

The occasion that brought Wind and me to Paris was Oui-Share Fest, an annual gathering for the sharing economy held in a red circus tent, on an adjoining strip of AstroTurf, and aboard a boat floating in the nearby Canal Saint-Martin. That year's theme, the Age of Communities, was broad enough to welcome all sides of the sharing phenomenon: venture capitalists alongside black markets, slow foodies alongside big data.

Paris is not Detroit, but here was another conference meant to ascertain the time on the clock of the world, to confront widespread disruption with critical connections.

The first morning of the three-day event began with an invitation for everyone to stand up and hug three people around them. Forms of sharing spread across domains freely; a conversation about startups could quickly pivot to one about polyamory or the universe. The same words came out over and over: *trust, community, network, passion, collaboration,* and a good deal of *love.* As a Brazilian entrepreneur put it, "Why don't we talk about love in big companies?"

It wasn't so clear, however, how far the sharing economy they were supposed to be building would bend toward justice. This sharing was not the kind of sharing that co-ops had been doing for generations. Cooperative models were alluded to occasionally. But for the moment, challenging corporate control with shared ownership and shared governance wasn't really on the table. When the sharing evangelist and consultant Rachel Botsman showed slides of Arab Spring crowds, those scenes served as an analogy, not a recommended course of action. She described sharers as "insurgents" against old-fashioned hierarchical businesses, engaged in "revolution," "democratizing," and of course "disruption."

Disruption came up at OuiShare Fest a lot. Just as Airbnb disrupted the hotel industry, the sharing startups present were poised to undermine more industries in short order. One could sense a general din of cheerfulness, as the startup boosters and organic farmers alike expected an imminent and inevitable disintegration of the economic establishment and a triumphant future of sharing ready to take its place. We heard little, however, about the effects that disrupting major industries might have on those people less well-equipped than the entrepreneurial class to adapt, about how workers on sharing apps usually lack what used to be standard benefits and rights of employment.[13] At this all-English conference in Paris, the kinds of people most likely to be disrupted were not around to speak.

Surely an economy built on sharing could be for the good. Sharing enables ordinary people to buy less, connect to one another more, and retain the value they generate in their own communities. But sharing could also make us even more reliant on corporate whims, allowing companies to dictate how, why, when, and what we share, extracting the highest fees they can get for themselves in the process. That's what was happening already in Paris. That's why, in Denver, cabbies had to form Green Taxi.

In a network economy, the power lies with whomever controls the points of connection—the web servers and databases and terms of use. The old means of production matter less. A sharing elite was well on the way to establishing itself; by the time I went to OuiShare Fest, the sharing sector built on venture capital and gray-area labor was a multibillion-dollar business. The idea of a real sharing economy based on shared ownership and shared governance remained mostly an afterthought.

Silicon Valley was already giving up on the language of "sharing." The word left companies too vulnerable to criticism, and even they could recognize it wasn't very accurate. Uber became part of the "on demand" economy; Mechanical Turk was mere "crowdsourcing." In the years to come, though, the young organizers behind OuiShare kept on being OuiShare, kept trying to hold the tensions between big business and the hope of business models that might actually be collaborative, that might actually share. They formed partnerships with an older generation of cooperative companies, including a large mutual insurer, to support the upstarts and ground their work in the legacy of pre-digital sharing. They schemed about entering politics.

In the United States I've noticed a particular chasm between the entrepreneurs and the protesters, between those building functional enterprises and those who feel the inadequacy of the status quo in their bones. Maybe it's because, for certain can-do types, there's simply so much investment capital going around that questioning the system would mean giving up too much; we've become victims of our own success, unable to see beyond the particular business models with which we so marvelously disrupt. Maybe it's also because protest becomes a habit that's hard to break.

I remember Grace Lee Boggs warning about this when she spoke to a roomful of New York's activist intelligentsia in late 2013. "Think about the people, not just the system," she said. "If you only look at the crimes of the system, you aren't looking at the people, and you won't meet their needs."

In international circles like OuiShare, I've found this kind of critical-constructive sensibility to be more common than it is at home.

It was through OuiShare, for instance, that I learned about SMart—*Société Mutuelle pour Artistes*—an organization of more than seventy-five thousand workers in eight European countries. Together they turn the precarity of sharing-economy gig work on its head by creating a support infrastructure of their own. In Belgium, SMart members can process their gig income through the organization, which then pays them as salaried workers, making them eligible for more public services, even while keeping the autonomy and flexibility of freelancing. They share a variety of digital tools for invoicing and collaborating. The organization pays members for their jobs promptly, out of the general cash flow, regardless of when the client pays up. SMart began as a Belgian nonprofit, but as it spread abroad, it found cooperative ownership to be more appropriate, and now the whole network has gone co-op. It binds many thousands of workers into a common enterprise, a togetherness that eases the path to independent, experimental work-lives. Julek Jurowicz, SMart's founder, described it to me as "a solidarity mechanism."

Jurowicz has deep-set eyes and short, gray hair. Between sessions at OuiShare, he explained how SMart got its start with the case of an undocumented immigrant—his wife, who came to Belgium from the Czech Republic to work in the film industry. Jurowicz accumulated enough bureaucratic expertise that artist friends started coming for help, followed by strangers, until he realized he needed to form an organization. That was back in 1998. The problems of an undocumented immigrant have since become a condition of the masses. SMart brought to OuiShare the reminder that precarious, uncertain work is nothing new, although it may be shifting from marginal to ubiquitous.[14] As destabilizing tremors spread with each subsequent disruption, so do the contrivances among those determined to take back control, or at least to take more control over their lives than they could have had before.

Among those who cluster around OuiShare, the corps of elite organizational scientists are the New Zealanders, in particular the members of Enspiral. They're best known for an app called Loomio, a collaboration and decision-making tool initially derived from the assembly process at the Occupy Wellington encampment in 2011. This activist invention is now used by schools, political parties, and businesses around the world. Whereas a discussion in a Facebook group usually just leads to more endless discussion, feeding more data to the algorithms, Loomio's polls and proposals steer discussions toward actual accomplishments.

From 2003 to 2010, Enspiral was just a name used by Joshua Vial, an Australian software developer living in Wellington, for his personal consulting business. By 2010, he was trying to spend less time on paid work and more on volunteer projects; he turned Enspiral into a vessel to help others do the same—sharing gig opportunities and freeing hours for good works. It then grew to more than forty core members, as well as about 250 "contributors" who are participants in the network, and fifteen small companies called "ventures," of which Loomio is one. Many members are techies of some sort, but people of any profession can join, in principle. Vial stepped down from its board. He's now, more or less, just another member.

New Zealand has the world's largest cooperative economy as a percentage of GDP, thanks mostly to hulking dairy co-ops. After incorporating as a worker cooperative, however, the Loomio team discovered it was the country's only one. Enspiral's structure is less easy to categorize—a standard limited-liability company that calls itself a foundation and operates as a co-op.

I visited Wellington expecting to find a group of people bound by managing shared *things*—for instance, working space and budgets and businesses. And I saw some of that. But Enspiral's power lies less with the stuff it manages than the connections it enables. It links like-minded people and groups, and they pool some of their money for whatever they want to invest in together. Members and contributors spoke about their friendships, their mutual encouragement, and the way the community responds to requests for help. Enspiral is, no more and no less, a network—one that has evolved to meet the needs of an often alienated, isolated network society.

Enspiral serves as a financially lean, but anecdotally essential, connective fiber among its independent workers and small companies. Enspiralites pass jobs around to help stabilize the ups and downs of freelancing, as Vial started the network to do, but now they also fund one another's business experiments and assist one another if things go sour. They hold retreats twice a year. They're relying less and less on the Robin Hood strategy of taking corporate contracts to pay for volunteer time; instead, they're creating their own jobs and companies with do-gooding built in. Enspiral-affiliated ventures, along with Loomio, have included ActionStation, an online organizing tool; Scoop, an alternative-news source; and Chalkle, an education community.

I spent a morning with Vial in a conference room at Enspiral Dev Academy, a web-developer boot camp he opened in 2014. He gave me a tour of the network on his laptop. Enspiralites work at several co-working spaces across town—and, increasingly, outside Wellington—but the space that most unites them is a cluster of online tools. Some are commercial, such as GitHub and Slack; the most important ones had to be custom-built. There's an internal bookkeeping system at my.enspiral.com, and at cobudget.co, they've created a tool that helps contributors and members allocate funds for each other's projects and other worthy causes. Loomio serves as the network's official decision-making mechanism.[15]

As Vial showed me the various tools and tasks, I asked questions about how they prevent bad actors. What if someone wants to rig a decision on Cobudget to get money for his or her project? What if the project is a sham? He replied with a shrug. "It's a high-trust network," he said. "We don't try to optimize for low-trust situations." An almost universal characteristic among the Enspiralites is an enthusiasm for interpersonal processes and a systemic manner of describing them.

A short walk from the Dev Academy and up the elevator of a downtown office building is a drab half-floor of co-working rooms that are the closest thing to Enspiral's headquarters. There I met Alanna Krause, an immigrant from California who encountered Enspiral early in its transition to collectivity. She became, among other things, the "bossless leadership geek" at Loomio and an Enspiral board member. She and some of her co-workers relayed the litany of ways the network works for its members.

"Somebody's laptop gets stolen, we buy them a new one," Krause told me. "Somebody's house burns down, we pay their rent. Somebody's organization has to downsize, the other ones will hire those people." They also cover one another's therapy sessions, when needed. And the result of this safety net, she thinks, is "actual innovation." When you know someone has your back, it's easier to take risks.

From the other side of the world, seeing Enspiral's work-life mix lent some vindication to Frithjof Bergmann's theories, which were so hard to hear in disruption-worn Detroit. When equality is its premise, perhaps work really need not be segregated from life, from the ambitions and needs of our actual selves. Back home in Colorado, I've started to see that kind of vindication as well, again in the form of a real sharing economy.

————

There's a local talisman around Boulder known as Niwot's Curse—to the effect that the beauty of the place, the gentle weather and soaring rocks, would draw people in and those people would destroy the beauty that drew them. The curse's namesake was a peaceable Arapaho chief from Boulder Valley who died of wounds suffered in the 1864 Sand Creek Massacre, on the east end of Colorado, conducted by an especially genocidal militia of white settlers.

Boulder's present residents interpret his words in a variety of ways. For some, especially the older-timers, it's a rebuke against the plentiful newcomers fleeing from the coasts, along with the traffic and construction projects they bring. For the newcomers, it evokes the discovery that here in flyover country, the cost of living turns out to be no lower than back on the coasts. And thus the curse is also a hypocrisy, one familiar among liberal utopias: the counterculture and inclusivity that attract so many new settlers have priced out any inclusive countercultures to come.

Part of any curse is the curse of forever trying to lift it. Here, we keep at it. That's why, after midnight on the first Wednesday of 2017, the city council passed a measure that enabled housing cooperatives to form in Boulder's neighborhoods.[16]

I first saw the curse at work almost two years earlier, soon after moving to Boulder for a job. It was at another city council meeting, where the subject of debate was an occupancy limit that prevented more than three or four unrelated people from sharing a single house—and in particular, whether the city should start actually, aggressively enforcing it. Angry homeowners, especially from around the student ghetto of University Hill, called for a crackdown. But far outnumbering them was an organized bloc of mainly young, illicit over-occupants, together with allies from the three legal co-op houses.

Almost a hundred people spoke that night in the public comments, but the phrase I remember most vividly was from a woman who pleaded before the council, "You're legislating isolation!"

It was a statement about family. A family of two grandparents, two parents, and six grandkids could, by right of law, share a house that ten people unconnected by blood could not—even if they considered their housemates their family, even if their biological families had turned them out, as was the case for several speakers that night, generally on account of their gender identities. This was a claim to the right of intentional community, the right that so many monastics, artist colonies, friends, and co-workers have shared. Those words rebuked the regime of detached houses with yards and strip malls, which James Howard Kunstler has suggested make America less "worth defending."[17] This system of thought requires each person or couple to consistently earn the money sufficient for a house, a car or two, a lawn, however many batches of child care and higher education they dare to commit themselves to through procreation, and so on. The cooperators, in contrast, shared their calculations of how drastically their electric, gas, and water consumption paled in comparison to the average Coloradan. This enabled them to take risks with their work, to be artists and entrepreneurs and activists. As I listened, I remembered the stories of an old friend (we met in a housing co-op in college) who grew up in the Boulder of another era, raised by the members of his family's Marxist commune.

In the debate about occupancy limits, speakers were beginning to coalesce around co-ops as a solution. The council could create a pathway to legalization for those affordable, over-occupied homes by enabling them to become bona fide, above-ground, registered cooperatives, governed and in many cases owned by their residents. This would mean replacing an existing, decades-old co-op ordinance so cumbersome that the only legal co-ops had to be formed as exceptions to it. By injecting the mutual and community responsibility that cooperative principles require, perhaps the over-occupiers could stem the fears of their neighbors. Boulder would get a cheap and bottom-up way of creating the affordable housing that had otherwise been so elusive.

And so I watched from a cautious newcomer's distance as the organizing took place, a campaign of mobilization and persuasion. A group of cooperators led it, under the aegis of the Boulder Community Housing Association. Some of their neighbors supported them, and packs of retirees, longing for co-ops of their own, joined the cause, too. Together they drafted ordinance proposals, held public events, helped elect friendly city-council candidates, kept saturating council meetings, concocted social-media memes, saturated more meetings, collected public data into spreadsheets and graphs, wrote letters, got their friends to write letters, got me to write letters, invited council members over for visits, and sometimes rested—all the stuff you're supposed to do in a good, local democracy. The opposition formed the Boulder Neighborhood Alliance, led by homeowners intent on preserving their town more or less as-was, despite its actual residents. They took out ads demonizing the young and tried to get some of the illegal co-ops evicted. People lost their homes. Yet the democracy seemed to be working. At the International Summit of Cooperatives in Quebec, I met the head of the Canadian co-op housing association, and when he heard where I lived, he asked about the effort, knowingly, and wanted to hear how things were going. As someone usually drawn to lost causes, I surprised myself by saying that things were going pretty well.

The style of co-op housing then being sought in Boulder—packing big houses with a dozen or so people—is only one form that housing co-ops might take. On the north end of town, there was a group putting together a community land trust, an arrangement that places the land under a home or apartment permanently off the market, reducing the dwelling's speculative value and thus its cost of use. Down in Denver, some Catholic Workers I knew were trying to set up cooperative tiny-house villages for the homeless. In other parts of the country residents of manufactured home parks were organizing to buy and own their parks cooperatively. Some of New York City's most exclusive, expensive apartment buildings are co-ops, but so are many affordable buildings, true to the model's roots among immigrant networks and labor unions. The policy for packed houses on the table in Boulder was just a start, a wedge in the door.

I arrived half an hour early for the final, fateful city council meeting, that January night in 2017, but early was late. There was already a potluck underway in the lobby, full of co-op stir-fries and salvaged baked goods. I ran into a woman I knew from church with her little son and daughter, who unbeknownst to me used to live in one of the co-ops. She told me I shouldn't wait to go upstairs to sign up to speak in the public comment, which I'd been asked to do. There, an enormous line snaked around the stadium seating—enough chairs for most Tuesday nights but not this one. I joined the end of the line and began talking with the man in front of me, a retired sociologist at my university wearing a colorful knit sweater, who turned out to be the uncle of my aforementioned friend, one of whose tasks in the Marxist commune was to take care of that friend, when he was a baby, on Monday mornings.

Before getting to co-ops, the council passed a mainly symbolic measure to declare Boulder a "sanctuary city," defying the tide of deportations that was soon to come under President Donald Trump. This seemed promising; if co-ops thereafter failed to find sanctuary also, the hypocrisy might cause Chief Niwot to strike from his grave.

Eighty-eight people signed up to speak at public comment. We got two minutes each. Some organized so as to pool their time as a continuous presentation of charts and figures in defense of the right density limits and resident caps and square-footage-per-person, so that affordable co-ops would actually be possible. A few residents spoke of fears about their neighborhoods and their property values; some outright demanded fewer people and fewer jobs in town. But the vast majority stood in favor, testifying as residents, neighbors, and experts to the benefits of co-ops. Again, they said a lot about family.

This time, the testimony that stuck with me most was from a resident of Rad-ish Collective, a co-op whose floor once harbored me during a visit before I moved to town. The speaker first clarified their gender pronoun as "they" after the mayor referred to them as "she," then proceeded to call for triage. Referring to the numerous stories we'd heard of co-ops as places of refuge for those who could afford nothing else, as pockets of economic, ethnic, sexual, and gender diversity, they suggested the council members think of themselves for the moment as doctors. Which case takes precedence—the papercut or the trauma, the property values or the displacement?

Some speakers later, around eleven-thirty that night, my turn to step forward came, which is worth mentioning only because it gave me the chance to see the council members up close. I don't think it was solely my remarks on the self-regulating capacities of the cooperative model that left them rubbing their faces, out of fatigue, into such frightening contortions that they reappeared to me when I finally got into bed later that night.

The decision finally came through, 7–2, at one o'clock in the morning. The co-op ordinance passed, mainly in the form that the Boulder Community Housing Association had been calling for. The compromises necessary for passage still resulted in a list of provisions long and specific enough to risk making impossible the very formations they were supposed to enable. Just barely, they supported the kinds of co-ops that already existed underground in Boulder, while leaving little room for much-needed innovation. But there was some flexibility—two hundred square feet per person, plus the option for rental, nonprofit, and equity co-ops. The cooperators' victory was complete enough that they might be tempted to think they'd dodged Niwot's Curse, at least for the moment, and vanquished a demon of affluent-liberal hypocrisy. For their opponents, however, this outcome was the curse's meaning precisely. Despite its cooperative guise, this was disruption.

4

Gold Rush

Money

The octogenarian artist Mary Frank traces her earliest debts to the prehistoric images in books that her mother kept around the house. Their shadows have reappeared throughout her sculptures, paintings, and photographs. But she knows none of their creators' names; there is no address where she can send a royalty check. The best repayment she can offer is the work of her own hands, and so she works.

Those of us who came of age in the millennial period have learned to think about debt and money quite otherwise. Debt does not motivate so much as it inhibits and stigmatizes. We accumulate it in order to have an education, to make a home, to pay for medical necessities. Servicing debts can prevent us from doing work we believe in, compelling us into better-paying livelihoods that might compromise our values. Our lenders' identities seem as obscure as those of ancient artists, as they trade our debts on veiled secondary markets, but the sums we owe are as precise as they are daunting. The collection agencies won't let us forget them. These debts haunt lives.

The creditors that Frank can name are those who have motivated and influenced her. She talks about studying dance under

the legendary, demanding choreographer Martha Graham, about
El Greco and Marcel Proust and Gerard Manley Hopkins, about
a pair of Guggenheim fellowships, about the writer Peter Mat-
thiessen, her departed friend, and about music. When she was
broke, she'd trade pictures for things she needed. ("Dentists, you
know, have great art collections.") As time went on, her debts
grew larger and even harder to quantify. She lost her two children;
all the world's children came to feel like hers. The first thing she
always wants to show me are her brochures promoting low-cost
solar cookers in regions where women would otherwise have to
cook over flames fueled by scarce wood or poisonous garbage. "I
feel a debt to the sun," she says.

That's very different from the debt arrangements many people depend on, which determine who can have access to what
and how. Nonwhite communities in the United States, to which
banks had in the past refused to extend credit, became targets
for predatory lending before the 2008 crash; new financial "products" and government bailouts ensured that the banks won regardless of what happened to the lives of borrowers. Debt also
maintains the international pecking order—subtler than armies,
though no less vicious. From Athens to Bangkok, globe-spanning
lending agencies dangle new loans (needed to pay old ones) as rewards for slashing public services and lowering trade barriers that
might protect local economies. Whether through dollar bills or
the International Monetary Fund, rule by debt is as omnipresent
as sunlight.

It now seems quaint to refer to the time when premodern
Christian, Jewish, and Muslim civilizations were united in their
prohibitions of usury—the definition of which could range from
merely the charging of any interest at all to the most abusive lending. We might ridicule the medieval metaphysicians' trepidation
about money begetting money through interest, or the Islamic
banks that devise techniques to avoid interest-charging today.
But as more people break the silence and shame of their financial indebtedness, perhaps we're forced to recognize that those
forebears had a point. Those religious traditions—built on notions
of sin, fealty, and mercy—regarded debt as a precious and sacred

thing to be handled with care. They insisted on clarifying the difference between the debts worth having and those that are not.[1] They regarded debt not just as a transaction but as a relationship.

Consider, for instance, Salish Sea Cooperative Finance. It began with a series of intergenerational meetings in Washington state, where the Gen Xers present began to grasp just how much student debt was crippling recent college graduates. The respective groups got over their mutual resentments—the jadedness of the young, the affluence of their elders—and designed a cooperative that would refinance the graduates' debts under less burdensome terms. After the refinancing, rather than leaving the borrowers to fend for themselves, the model calls on the lenders to be mentors and help the borrowers find the sources of income they'll need.

The benefits go both ways. "My partner and I were never burdened with student debt, and so we feel obligated to help those who are," says Rose Hughes, who is both an architect of Salish Sea Cooperative Finance and an investor-member in it. "We also get to network with younger people who are doing fascinating things to help our society."

In the process, says borrower-member Erika Lundahl (accumulated student debt: more than $16,000), "the people with capital are taking some systematic responsibility for student debt and the effect it has on society as a whole." When organized like this, financial institutions can resemble the loans that happen among friends and family. They can incline us toward trusting each other more, rather than giving up on trust and entrusting our economic lives to markets alone.

Hughes's involvement in alternative finance brought her into the twilight zone of trying to develop community-oriented institutions around existing financial regulations. "All the rules are written assuming a profit motive is what drives everything." And there's consistently a bias, she says, "for the benefit of the lender, not the borrower."

The cooperative tradition has tried to play by different rules, to preserve democracy by making sure lenders remain lenders, rather than becoming bosses. "Our model has been to rent capital from the outside and give it no control," says Rink Dickinson, a founder of the fair-trade worker cooperative Equal Exchange. His company generates returns for investors that back it, but the more than one hundred workers don't give up governing power. When Loomio raised nearly half a million dollars in 2016, it did the same thing. It sold redeemable preference shares, which entitled investors to a return based on revenue, but no voting rights.[2] For co-op savvy lenders, this is a smart investment; the people who are in control of the business, the member-owners, have a direct stake in seeing it succeed.

Entire systems of finance can be, and have been, built on this approach. Credit unions and other cooperative banks hold money and provide loans, but they do so on behalf of the same people doing the depositing and the borrowing. Here, debt is a relationship among members of a community, rather than one between a bank's customers and its investor-owners. Typically, credit union members are individuals, and there are about 114 million total memberships in nearly six thousand credit unions in the United States. But some cooperative banks are themselves made up of the cooperative businesses that use them. One such institution is CoBank, headquartered on the southern end of Denver, whose assets total more than $100 billion.[3] It is an outgrowth of the national Farm Credit System, designed over the course of the past century to serve the critical agricultural co-op sector. As co-ops flourish, they need their own kind of finance, and they design it in their own image.

The debt worth having, cooperativism holds, is the kind that allows us to be more fully ourselves, that we use with our freedom rather than our servitude. It resembles Frank's anonymous, ancient artists—who live on not by collecting royalties and enforcing constraints, but through the flourishing of their debtors.

Money itself is a kind of debt. It appears from nothing through bank loans, according to rules that governments set. People who have lived among multiple currencies, or collapsing currencies, know from experience that money is no stable thing, that its value can vanish overnight. That's why, when it comes to monetary policy, average Argentinians and Ecuadorians today can talk circles around average North Americans, who have lived through decades of well-behaved dollars. Here, we mistake money for a constant, for something real and stable, rather than a complex of fickle debt relations. But that can change. The old populist farmers demanded more democratic means of money creation, and now tempestuous digital currencies have come to represent billions of dollars in value. People tired of banknotes, or simply seeking to keep their money under their control, are setting up alternatives to state-issued tender.

From the Brixton Pound, in an immigrant neighborhood of London, to Ithaca Hours and BerkShares in the northeastern United States, local currency schemes are turning up even in currency monocultures. Some peg the unit of value to the dollar or the pound, whereas others work as equalizing time-banks, pegging value to an hour of a person's life. The point is that the community of users can decide how it works, a capacity that distant central banks don't allow. Money itself could become cooperative, if meaningful democracy held sway over its issuance and nature. New technologies are helping such schemes proliferate, thanks to tools with such inviting names as Common Good (a payment system) and Main St. Market (a cooperative market app co-owned by local currencies).

The most effectual developments, however, have been in service of more ambivalent purposes. In times of flux like this, it's easy to lose sight of the basics—those nagging questions of ownership and governance that the cooperative tradition continually insists on posing.

––––––

The Bitcoin Center NYC, the self-described "center of the Bitcoin revolution," used to inhabit a retail storefront on Manhattan's Broad Street, a block from the New York Stock Exchange. The staff of an Asian-infused kosher steak house next door shooed loitering Bitcoiners from the sidewalk, indifferent to the revolution allegedly underway. Inside the Bitcoin Center, two small tables off to one side housed a menagerie of internet-age extraction equipment: Bitcoin mining machines. They resembled boxy desktop computers, only larger and without screens or keyboards attached. During a visit I paid to the center in November 2014, only one of them, the CoinTerra TerraMiner IV, was in use, emitting a purr of white noise. But the thing was still pretty much dead weight.

The TerraMiner IV rested on the table horizontally, encased in black metal, with rack-mounts and two stainless steel grates on either end that looked like the eyeholes of a deep-sea diver. The grates covered fans that cooled its array of application-specific integrated circuits, or ASICs—advanced chips that do little else but churn through the complex cryptographic math. In return for their calculations, miners earn payouts of new bitcoins from the network, plus transaction fees from users. (Capitalized *Bitcoin* is the system; *bitcoin* is the unit of currency.) Like mining precious metals, mining cryptocurrencies can be lucrative. But this Terra-Miner IV had little hope of reward.

At just about a year old, the miner represented a particularly rapid and fateful instance of the obsolescence that awaits every gizmo that alights on the cutting edge. Because of competition from faster, sleeker models already on the network, it could no longer mine enough bitcoins to pay for the electricity it burned. CoinTerra, the TerraMiner IV's maker, filed for bankruptcy in early 2015. Like a used-up gold mine, the machine lent even the Bitcoin Center's busiest evenings the sensation of a ghost town.

Bitcoin was supposed to usher in a new global economy— gold for the internet age—and mining it was supposed to be an act of democracy. On February 11, 2009, Bitcoin's pseudonymous creator, Satoshi Nakamoto, announced his invention in an online forum by explaining, "The root problem with conventional currency is all the trust that's required to make it work."[4] This was just as the financial giants were breaching the world's trust. At the time, only a month after Bitcoin's initial "genesis block" went online, users could mine with an ordinary computer, though doing so was technically difficult and barely lucrative. But the citizen-miners could also choose which version of the software to run, a kind of voting power over the future of the network.

This was unquestionably a breakthrough. For the first time, the technology underlying Bitcoin made possible a secure, decentralized, open-source financial network. Users wouldn't have to trust any bank or government, just the software. Boosters announced that financial freedom would soon be at the fingertips of the previously under-banked, and people anywhere in the world could send money over the internet with negligible overhead. Nakamoto prophesied in that 2009 forum post, "It takes advantage of the nature of information being easy to spread but hard to stifle."

In essence, Bitcoin is a list, held in common among its users— a list of transactions, a record of which account holds what. The list is called a blockchain. The list's value lies in its security and reliability. Enthusiasts like to emphasize the impressive math involved in keeping the system secure, but what holds the whole thing together just as much is game theory—the assumption that users are rational actors and won't blow up their own virtual wealth. As much as Bitcoin is a feat of cryptography, it's also an experiment in anthropology. And to a remarkable degree it works. Despite countless hacks and crashes and human foibles that have befallen the infrastructure around it, the core hasn't cracked.

The first converts were tech-savvy utopians, whose bitcoins went from being worth just cents to hundreds of dollars; many believed that the old financial industry's days were numbered. Traffickers looking for a discreet way to transact for drugs, weapons, and the like came soon after. An industry of magazines and websites appeared to simultaneously report on and promote the new currency. A Bitcoin-based charity in Florida bought a nine-acre forest as a sanctuary for the homeless; *Wired* deemed Bitcoin "the great equalizer" for its potential to put financial services in the hands of the poor. It also attracted the interest of such innovation-hungry investors as the Winklevoss twins, Mark Zuckerberg's old nemeses. Bill Gates called it "better than currency." But soon the Bitcoin revolution began to look more and more like the system it was intended to replace—except perhaps more centralized, less egalitarian, and similarly clogged with unseemly interests.[5]

As the value of bitcoins swelled against the dollar over the course of 2013, a mining arms race began. People realized that their computers' graphics chips were better suited to Bitcoin's mining algorithms than standard CPUs, so they built specialized machines overloaded with graphics processors, which increased their chances of reaping a reward. Starting in the first months of that year, ASICs arrived. Before long, the lone miner with a regular computer was a lost cause, unable to compete with the new mining syndicates, or "pools." Multimillion-dollar data centers appeared in places around the world with the most profitable combination of cold weather and cheap electricity—forty-five thousand miners in a Swedish helicopter hangar, for instance, or twenty million watts in the Republic of Georgia. Together, Bitcoin's miners amount to many times more computing power than the combined output of the world's top five hundred supercomputers. Processing and protecting the billions of dollars' worth of bitcoins in circulation requires hundreds of millions of dollars in electricity each year, plus the carbon emissions to match.

The prospects for democracy in the system grew dimmer still. By the middle of 2014, the largest mining pools came within reach of a 50 percent market share—making it possible for them to endanger the whole system by falsifying transactions. What prevented them from actually doing so, apparently, was that it

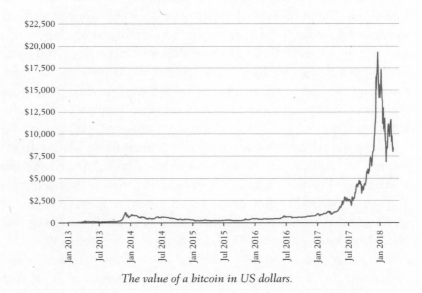

The value of a bitcoin in US dollars.

would reduce confidence in the value of the bitcoins they invest so much to mine. They also started preventing changes to the Bitcoin software that would lessen their dominance. In pursuit of trustless money, a distributed network of users had to trust a mysterious oligarchy of capital-intensive miners.

A certain style of evangelistic piety prevails in the Bitcoin "space," as participants in the burgeoning industry tend to call it. (From the "wallet" software used to manage accounts to the "coins" in virtual circulation, cryptocurrency jargon relies on the most physical of metaphors.) Optimism is the dominant idiom among enthusiasts, but at times it has seemed to rest less on any genuine belief than on an anxiety not to see their bitcoins further depreciate.

"Some of the New York Bitcoin Center guys are pretty religious," said Tim Swanson, an early analyst who had written two self-published e-books on cryptocurrencies. Before that, while living in China, he built his own graphics-chip miners. But Swanson grew increasingly skeptical that Bitcoin would unsettle the existing finance megaliths. "You have centralization without the benefits of centralization," he told me. He calculated that the cost of bringing Bitcoin services to the developing world would wipe away the savings from the system's low transaction costs. By the time I met the TerraMiner IV, Bitcoin wealth was distributed far more unequally than in the conventional economy. Users were probably more than 90 percent male.[6]

Entrusting money to algorithms, it turns out, was no guarantee of a better result than managing it with institutions and people. Nakamoto's longing for money free from trust simply shifted the location of that trust. The blockchain technology at work in Bitcoin is flexible; it can be rearranged for cooperation rather than competition, for reputation tracking rather than anonymity, for democracy rather than oligarchy. Some early experiments along these lines, among the hundreds of "altcoins," did away with intensive mining altogether. But unlike Bitcoin, they were short on financing and evangelists. A lot of the people I knew who had been around for the early days of cryptocurrency—software hackers who became overnight whizzes in monetary theory—were soon building

Bitcoin-like systems for the very banks they thought they would utterly disrupt. Other imperatives took over.

I remember this shift in priorities becoming especially evident one evening at the Bitcoin Center. In a cluttered corner of the room, the notorious hacker-troll Weev, recently released from prison and veering into full-on neo-Nazism, was tinkering on a laptop; "Living off my bitcoins," he told me when I asked what he was up to. Attendees drifted around him eating pizza and sipping rum-and-Cokes. As the evening began winding down, a middle-aged woman with a pearl necklace visible beneath her trench coat approached a shaggy-haired staffer standing next to the miners. She was from Harlem; the only name she cared to give was "Ms. E."

"What is this Bitcoin?" she asked the staffer, who embarked on a long explanation of Bitcoin as a "layer" on the internet for finance, a valuable contribution to the work taking place in the towers around them. He was far from done when Ms. E started to look like she was ready to leave.

"I thought I would come in here and find someone who was gonna replace these banks," she said, gesturing out the window to Broad Street. "We need to distribute the wealth, you know what I'm saying? I thought this was something for the small people."

———

I first heard about Bitcoin in 2012, but I wasn't interested. I don't tend to get excited about money for its own sake—to a fault. (A dollar of the stuff then would be worth hundreds of dollars now.) I didn't start paying attention until a visit to San Francisco in January 2014, when Joel Dietz and Anthony D'Onofrio cornered me at a downtown pop-up cafe run by war veterans and explained to me that this new kind of money was about a lot more than money.

Dietz was an old friend; I'd seen his brooding genius pass through phases as a theologian, a linguist, a coder, and a tea aficionado. D'Onofrio was new to me; he turned out to be a serial visionary, too, who at the time was in the cannabis-edibles business. His partner, pregnant, sat quietly nearby while we talked.

Just a few weeks earlier, a nineteen-year-old Russian Canadian named Vitalik Buterin had published a proposal for what he called Ethereum.[7] What Bitcoin was for money, Ethereum would be for everything else. It turns out that the basic idea of an ironclad list with no single caretaker—the blockchain—has an enormous range of potential applications. Rather than listing transactions, for instance, it can list contracts and enforce them computationally, resulting in an autonomous legal system without courts or cops. A blockchain of websites could be the basis of a more secure kind of internet.

"It's an operating system for society," D'Onofrio said.

Before long, coders were sketching out prototypes for what they called decentralized autonomous organizations, or DAOs— entities made up of Ethereum "smart contracts." One might code a constitution for a nongeographic country that people can choose to join, pay taxes to, receive benefits from, and cast votes in—and whose rules they would then have to obey. One could design a transnational microlending program or a new kind of credit score. In an online video, Dietz and a friend demonstrated how to code a simple marriage contract. The world's next social contracts, the successors to the Declaration of the Rights of Man and the US Constitution, could be written on Ethereum's protocol. The cooperatives of the future, too, might be built with smart contracts, inscribing co-ownership and co-governance for vast networks with a freer hand than local laws allow. Or, as Buterin sometimes joked at the time, it could be used to create Skynet, the armed robot network in the *Terminator* movies determined to exterminate its human creators.[8] Ethereum could go either way.

During those early months of trying to follow the hackers rallying around Buterin's idea, including run-ins with the savant himself, the word *blockchain* would repeat in my head at night, like a divine incantation. The universal ledger, that arbiter of value—the sensation of seeing into a future of all-seeing lists, revealing and yet hiding. Everything is a transaction, in every corner of our lives.

In a Reddit discussion about an early article I wrote on Ethe-reum, Buterin explained:

> Lately I have become much more comfortable with the idea of computer-controlled systems for one simple reason: our world is already computer controlled. The computer in question is the universe with its laws of physics and humans provide the inputs to this great multisig by manipulating their body parts.[9]

In midsummer 2014, back in the Bay Area, I rode a friend's rickety bike to Hacker Dojo, a member-run hackerspace not far from the Googleplex in Mountain View. An office-park storefront opens into an expanding series of rooms with clusters of people, mostly white and Asian young men, staring into their individual screens, but at least breathing the same air. At the door, you're met not by a receptionist, but by a computer asking for your email address. When you give it, you're told the rules. Among their dis-tinctions: everywhere and everything is "100 Percent Communal," but it is "Not a Public Facility." Naps are okay, but sleeping is not.

Hacker Dojo was host to an event that night in which one could find some features of the new order being worked out, one of the first gatherings of the area's Ethereum Meetup group. Steve Randy Waldman, a coder and economics blogger, spoke to a room of about twenty enthusiasts. He talked about the coop-erative and fraternal organizations that, a century ago, provided insurance and other benefits to millions of Americans. Many of these mutual-support networks have fallen away in an age of mo-bility and frayed communities, but he believed blockchains could bring them back.

Waldman said he hoped to see DAOs that are "designed as strategic actors." By collecting dues and holding members respon-sible to contracts, a DAO could be a means of organizing new kinds of labor unions or fostering disciplined consumer activism, which had failed to appear in online social media so far. What if, rather than just indicating on Facebook that you plan to par-ticipate in a protest, you joined a group of people contractually bound to do so? Could smart contracts bring back solidarity?

It was a statement of digital possibilities but also, intentionally or not, a testament to what the digital world had lost. Waldman cited such pre-internet curiosities as in-person meetings, distinctive clothing, even religious belief—"a powerful engineering tool, and we should take it seriously." He talked about orders such as the Freemasons and Elks in the past tense, as sources of inspiration for the DAOs to come. But three-fourths of the way through his talk, one of the engineers present—middle-aged, with a thick beard and large glasses—raised his hand and declared himself a real-life Freemason.

"We're still around!" he insisted. He later interrupted the discussions on technical feasibility and implementation with stories of real-life good deeds done through his lodge, offline.

Ethereum went live in 2015. Its underlying currency, ether, soon became second only to bitcoin on the crypto-markets, with a total value in the billions of dollars. Walmart is using Ethereum to manage supply chains, and J. P. Morgan is writing smart contracts to automate transactions. A coalition of US credit unions is building a "CU Ledger" to manage member identities. Some people are trying to craft the perfect co-ops or other sorts of egalitarian DAOs, but they're not making money like the ones concocting blockchain ledgers for big, old banks.[10]

A year into Ethereum's life, the system hit trouble. A glitch in the code enabled a hacker to siphon millions of dollars' worth of ether from a flagship DAO known simply as "the DAO." Thus, a basic dilemma for a world built of code: must the code be honored, glitches and hackers and all, or do the intentions behind the code matter? By and large, the "community" chose the latter—it chose human intention and opted to wipe away the hack. At least for the moment, the system was young and flexible enough for there to be a choice. It was an improvisation but also the harbinger of a whole new kind of governance.[11]

That was only the start. People are building companies with this stuff now, funding themselves with made-up crypto-tokens that they sell to contributors and users, who hope to cash out in a windfall of speculative magic. These initial coin offerings, or ICOs, have re-created a little-regulated free-for-all like the

pre–Great Depression stock markets, before government oversight ruined the dangerous fun. They have democratic potential
but mostly anarcho-capitalist adoption. Blockchains will become
what we use them for, and we will become creatures of those
uses.

One of those nights visiting Silicon Valley, I stopped by Joel
Dietz's house for the meeting of a group that called itself the
Cryptocommons. The house itself had a name, the Love Nest,
having become home to a shifting cast of residents who shared
Joel's interests in blockchains, art, and "exponential" relationships. Dietz wore a black T-shirt bearing the white circle that
represented his current project, Swarm, a prototype for crypto-
crowdfunding, still so new as to be of ambiguous legality; it would
later be resurrected as a "cooperative ownership platform for
real assets." Vitalik Buterin's cousin Anastasia arrived late. The
speaker that evening was Eric Smalls, a Stanford undergrad, on
leave from school to work on his drone startup. He talked about
Leland Stanford's interest in co-ops and Dunbar's Number and
the burning of the Library of Alexandria as "a single point of failure." He quoted Angela Davis and proposed abolishing prisons
and replacing them with blockchain-based reputation systems.
Then autopoesis and systems theory. Everything.

I never did catch the name of the guy there who remarked,
"I'm interested in freedom as a product to be built."

When I'm among groups like this, I get an irrepressible impulse
to start drafting rules and social systems of my own in code. Code is
precise, needing no interpretation except how the computer reads
it. No corruptible judges or juries; perfect transparency. Here is a
routine in the Python programming language, for instance, for adding a new member to a virtual community:

```
def addMember(person, votes):
    if len(MEMBERS) == votes:
        MEMBERS.append(person)
```

These lines define a function, addMember, that, upon being fed
the name of a person and a number of votes, adds that name to

the membership list when the number of votes equals the number of names already on the list. Simple, but pure.

Industrial cooperation first arose among those with the gall to tinker with the habitual social algorithms of their time. They found value where others couldn't see it. They were system-makers, but the systems would only work when they accounted for the human beings involved—the selfish urges, the bonds of trust, the capacity to choose. Now that kind of stumbling, iterative tinkering is happening again, remaking society from lines of code.

———

Being underground is not a condition Enric Duran always takes literally, but one late-January night in 2015, I followed him from one basement to another. At a hackerspace under a tiny library just south of Paris, he met a group of activists from across France and then journeyed with them by bus and Métro to another meeting place, in an old palace on the north end of the city. The main floor looked like an art gallery, with white walls and sensitive acoustics, but the basement below was like a cave, full of costumes and scientific instruments and exposed masonry. There, Duran arranged chairs in a circle for the dozen or so people who had come. As they were settling in and discussing which language they'd speak, a woman from upstairs, attending an event about open licenses for scientific research, peeked in through the doorway. She pointed Duran out to her friend—trying, barely, to contain herself. After the meeting was over, she came right up to him and said, "You're the bank robber!"

Although little known in the United States, Duran's name, or at least his reputation, is easy to come by among the activist and hacktivist sets in Western Europe. I'd been hearing about him for years. I'd been told that if I wanted to see a real, living model of the ideas others were just talking about, I should find him. Other people said that his latest scheme would probably go nowhere. Mutual friends connected us over encrypted email, and I followed him around Paris, day and night, for the better part of a week.

In that basement, Duran held court. The thirty-eight-year-old, nearly two-year fugitive had a space between his two front teeth, grizzly hair, and a matching beard—black except for stray grays mixed in throughout. He wore a white sweatshirt. His presence was discreet and stilted, yet it carried authority in the room. While others made small talk he looked off elsewhere, but his attention became total as soon as the conversation turned to the matter on his mind and the opportunity to collaborate.

He had gathered the group to describe his latest undertaking, FairCoop, which gradually revealed itself to be no less than a whole new kind of global financial system. With it, he said, cooperatives around the world would be able to trade, fund one another's growth, redistribute wealth, and make collective decisions. They would hack currency markets to fund themselves while replacing competitive capitalism with cooperation. He proceeded to reel off the names of its sprawling component parts: FairMarket, FairCredit, Fairtoearth, the Global South Fund, and so on. "We will be able to make exchanges with no government controls," he promised in broken English. To get the project going, he had hijacked a Bitcoin-like cryptocurrency called FairCoin.

The French activists indulged him with questions based on whatever hazy grasp of it they could manage—some political, some technical. How does FairCoin relate to FairCredit? What can you buy in the FairMarket? How many faircoins go into each fund, and what are they for? Most of these came from the men, all more or less young, who stroked their chins as they listened. Most of the women left before it was over. Duran's voice was never other than monotone, but his responses nonetheless sang a kind of rhapsody. The answers to a lot of the various what-if questions were some variation of "We can decide."

The only reason the group would even consider this bewildering set of possibilities was that Duran was, in fact, the bank robber. He rejects that term for himself, but he doesn't deny that he expropriated several hundred thousand euros from Spanish banks during the lead-up to the 2008 financial crisis. He then used the momentum from his heist to organize the Catalan Integral

Enric Duran at work in Paris.

Cooperative—or CIC, pronounced "seek"—a network of cooperatives functioning throughout the separatist region of Catalonia, in northeast Spain, which the activists in Paris were attempting to replicate across France. Even if it meant years of living underground, in hiding from the law, his undertakings tended to work. Perhaps even this one.

Long before messing with banks, Enric Duran connected people. As a teenager he was a professional table-tennis player and helped restructure the Catalan competition circuit. He turned his attention to larger injustices in his early twenties, when he read Erich Fromm's diagnosis of materialist society and Henry David Thoreau's call to disobedience. This was the late 1990s, high times for what is alternately called the global-justice or anti-globalization movement. The Zapatistas had set up autonomous zones in southern Mexico, and just weeks before Y2K, activists with limbs locked together and faces in masks shut down the World Trade Organization meeting in Seattle. According to Northeastern University anthropologist Jeffrey Juris, in Barcelona "Enric was at the center of organizing everything."[12] People called him *el hombre conectado*.

Duran helped organize the Catalan contingent for protests at the 2000 World Bank and International Monetary Fund meetings in Prague; a cop there whacked him on the head in the streets. He called for ending reliance on oil and for canceling the debts of poor countries. He was then living on a small allowance from his father, a pharmacist, until using the remainder of it to help set up a cooperative infoshop in Barcelona called Infospai in 2003. He'd hoped to support himself with Infospai, but it was soon plagued with money problems, like the projects of so many activist groups around him. They needed streams of revenue that capitalism was unlikely to provide.

Duran had been studying the nature of money, which he came to see as an instrument of global debt servitude on behalf of financial elites, carrying the stain of their usurious dealings wherever it went. He became convinced that big banks were the chief causes of injustice in the world. But, he thought, maybe they could be a solution, too.

An entrepreneur friend of his first suggested the idea of borrowing money from banks and not giving it back. At first they talked about organizing a mass action, involving many borrowers, or else just making a fictional film about it. But after the friend died in a car accident, Duran decided to act by himself. In the fall of 2005, he began setting up companies on paper and applying for loans. Soon he had a mortgage from Caixa Terrassa worth €201,000, nearly $310,000 at the time. It was the first of sixty-eight acts of borrowing, from car loans to credit cards, involving thirty-nine banks. The loans, he says, totaled around €492,000—€360,000, not including interest and fees along the way. That was more than $500,000.

For almost three years, Duran proceeded. "My strategy was completely systematic," he wrote in his testimony, *Abolish the Banks*, "as if my actions were part of an assembly line in a Fordist production system."[13] He'd carry a briefcase to meetings with bankers, though he couldn't bring himself to wear a tie. For a single item—say, a video camera—he'd get the same loan from multiple banks. As he acquired more cash, he funded groups around him that he knew and trusted. He backed the Degrowth March, a mass bicycle ride around Catalonia organized in opposition to the logic of economic growth, and equipped Infospai with a TV studio.

The beginning of the end came in the summer of 2007. Duran says he noticed signs of the mortgage crisis forming in the United States and decided that it was time to prepare for going public. For the next year, he assembled a collective to produce a newspaper detailing the evils of banks and what he had done to trick them. The people who helped organize the Degrowth March provided a ready-made distribution network throughout Catalonia. He selected a date: September 17, 2008.

The timing was pretty amazing. On September 15, Lehman Brothers filed for bankruptcy, marking beyond doubt the arrival of a global chain reaction. That morning Duran flew from Barcelona to Lisbon, Portugal, and then the next day from Lisbon to São Paulo, Brazil, where his friend Lirca was living. On the seventeenth, volunteers across Catalonia handed out two hundred thousand copies of Duran's newspaper, *Crisis*. Until then, most of them had no idea what news they'd be spreading. The international media picked up the story, and Duran became known as the Robin Hood of the banks.

He came to refer to this as his "public action." All along he'd planned it that way—a spectacle, but one that would create networks for other projects. "This is not the story of one action," he said. "It is a process of building an alternative economic system."

In Brazil, Duran set up a website for supporters to discuss the next move. At first, the plan was to mount a mass debt strike. People around the world started organizing to renege on their loans, but the scale of participation necessary to hurt the banks seemed overwhelming, and the plan was scuttled. In the last months of 2008, Duran, Lirca, and their friends pivoted toward another proposal—the Integral Cooperative and, eventually, the Integral Revolution.

Like the bank action, the idea was both political and practical. Infospai, despite its money troubles, taught him that there were certain benefits to organizing as a cooperative. The Spanish government normally exacted a hefty self-employment tax for independent workers—on the order of about \$315 per month, plus a percentage of income—but if one could claim one's work as taking place within a cooperative, the tax didn't apply. Amid the crisis, people were losing their jobs, and the tax made it hard for them to pick up gigs on the side to get by—unless they were willing to join together as a cooperative. Duran wasn't planning a traditional cooperative business, owned and operated by its workers or by those who use its services. Instead, he wanted to create a co-op umbrella under which people could live and work on their own terms, in all sorts of ways. The idea was to help people out and radicalize them at the same time. The rich use tax loopholes to their advantage; he realized that cooperators could do the same.

Duran looked around for more parts to connect to his system. He knew about a group of alternative currencies that had started forming in Catalan towns called *ecoxarxes*, or eco-networks; the first, by coincidence, began the day after Bitcoin went online in 2009. These currencies reflected shared interests and values, but they lacked a unifying structure. Duran proposed to connect them through this new cooperative, and their users became another gateway into what he was hatching.

He and his friends adopted the word *integral*, which is used for "whole wheat" in Spanish and Catalan, to connote the totality, synthesis, and variety of the project. It emboldened Duran, and he began making promises of his return to Catalonia. He devoted much of the remaining money from his loans to a second newspaper, *We Can!* Whereas *Crisis* had focused on the problems of the banking system, *We Can!* would be about solutions. The front page declared, "We can live without capitalism. We can be the change that we want!" It outlined the vision Duran and his friends had been developing for the Integral Cooperative. On March 17, 2009, exactly six months after *Crisis*, 350,000 copies of *We Can!* appeared throughout Spain. The same day, Duran surfaced on the campus of the University of Barcelona, and he was promptly arrested. Several banks had filed complaints against him. The Spanish prosecutor called for an eight-year prison sentence.

Duran was thrown into jail, but he went free two months later after a donor posted his bail. Thus began almost four years of freedom and organizing with his friends. They made sure to set up the cooperative legal structure at the outset, so that the tax benefits could draw people into the system. Then the priority was to arrange for necessities: food from farmers, housing in squats and communes, health care by natural and affordable means. By early 2010, the Catalan Integral Cooperative was real, with commissions and monthly assemblies. The following year, when protesters occupied city squares across Spain to rail against austerity and corruption, participants entered the co-op's ranks. Replica organizations began to emerge in other regions of Spain and in France, and then Greece. None of the money from Duran's loans actually went to forming the CIC, but it grew with his notoriety, his networks, and his fervid activity.

––––––––

After months among the Bitcoiners, my time in hiding with Duran came as a relief and a release. A lot of it was due to the fact that, although he shared their complaints about the money system and their hope for decentralized ledgers, he had cooperativism. He had that basic concern for accountable ownership and governance, even though what he was building looked little like any cooperative before it. Rather than setting out to turn more and more parts of life into trustless transactions, he wanted more trust. The CIC reminded me of those cutout diagrams of the Earth's geology. The hard, crusty outer layers offered newcomers specific services they could join and benefit from, requiring little knowledge of what was happening beneath for their use. The newcomers could stay there. But that could also be a step closer to the center, where members found more services and more trust—a molten, liquid, shared commons where formal transactions are less necessary. It's far from the rock-solid, transactional paradise at the heart of planet Bitcoin. Start with usefulness, lead toward community.

One rainy night in Paris, I was in the middle of articulating some long-winded question about "the commons," trying to ascertain where Duran stood in some theoretical debate or other, when he interrupted me. "I don't want to build commons for people who talk about the commons," he said. "I want to build commons for commoners."

That stuck with me. It humbled me, for one thing. And it was also a lesson and warning about cooperativism in general: none of it is worth much of anything unless it is of use.

———

A few blocks from Antoni Gaudí's ever-unfinished basilica, the Sagrada Família, I found Aurea Social, a three-story former health spa that since 2012 has served as the Barcelona headquarters of the CIC. Past the sliding glass doors and the reception desk was a hallway where products made by members were on display—soaps, children's clothes, wooden toys and bird feeders, a solar-powered reflective cooker. There were brochures for Espai de l'Harmonia, a hostel and wellness center, where one could receive Reiki treatments or take aikido lessons. Beyond, there was a small library, a Bitcoin ATM, and offices used by some of the seventy-five people who received stipends for the work they did to keep the CIC running. On certain days, Aurea Social hosted a market with produce

Weighing out products at the Catalan Supply Center.

fresh from the Catalan Supply Center—the co-op's distribution warehouse in a town an hour or so to the south, which provided markets throughout the region with thousands of pounds of goods each month, most of which came from CIC farmers and producers.

Joel Mòrist, a member of the CIC's public-facing Communication Commission, greeted me when I arrived. He loves Jack Kerouac but more resembles Walt Whitman and Slavoj Žižek—almost a dead ringer for the latter, with similar spasms of gesticulation and cleverness. His left eye is lazy, though no less wild. He's a filmmaker. He displayed reverence toward little but Enric, speaking of him in a running joke as an absent god, perhaps soon to return. And he went on to tell me the history of the CIC, starting with the first inklings of civilization—the first bosses, the first priests, the first armies, the first money, and the first debt. He sketched on small scraps of paper an explanation of usury-based money and the need for another way.

Each of the enterprises advertised at Aurea Social operates more or less independently while being, to varying degrees, linked to the CIC. When I visited in 2015, the CIC consisted of 674 different projects spread across Catalonia, with 954 people working on them.[14] The CIC provided these projects with a legal umbrella, as far as taxes and incorporation were concerned. Their members traded with one another in ecos, the unit of alternative currency from among the Catalan eco-networks. They shared health workers, legal experts, software developers, scientists, and babysitters. They financed one another with the CIC's half-million-dollar annual budget, a crowdfunding platform, and an interest-free investment bank called Casx. (In Catalan, x makes a "sh" sound.) To be part of the CIC, projects needed to be managed by consensus and to follow certain basic principles such as transparency and sustainability. Once the assembly admitted a new project, its income could run through the CIC accounting office, where a portion went toward funding the shared infrastructure. Any participant could benefit from the services and help decide how the common pool would be used.

Affiliates might choose to live in an affiliated block of apartments in Barcelona, or at Lung Ta, a farming commune with tepees and yurts and stone circles and horses, where residents organized themselves into "families" according to their alignments with respect to Mayan astrology. Others moved to Calafou, a "postcapitalist ecoindustrial colony" in the ruins of a century-old factory town, which Duran and a few others purchased after he found it for sale on the internet. (Further details about my visit to Calafou cannot appear here because this book isn't published under an open license, a requirement the colony's assembly had for press wishing to cover it.) Not far from there, a group of anarchists operated a bar and screen-printing studio in a building that once belonged to the CNT, the anarcho-syndicalist union that ran collectivized factories and militias during the civil war of the 1930s, orchestrating what was almost assuredly the modern world's largest experiment in functional anarchy. Like the CNT, the CIC was making a new world in the shell of the old—so the utopian mantra goes—and, to a degree that is not at all utopian, creating livelihoods for themselves in a place where livelihoods were not at all easy to come by.

For years Spain had been sunk in a perpetual downturn, with an unemployment rate exceeding 20 percent for the general population and hovering around 50 percent for those under twenty-five. The exasperation gave rise to Podemos, a new populist political party that opposed austerity policies and, when I visited, was poised to displace the establishment. But the less-noticed sides of this uprising were movements like the CIC, working closer to the ground and reshaping the structure of everyday life. These cooperators were done seeking steady, full-time jobs along the lines of Mondragon. More industrial bureaucracy churning out consumer goods en masse was not the point. I asked once if they had taken lessons from those famous cooperatives in a nearby, also-separatist region of Spain; the reply I got was a glance to the effect of "Why would we bother?" They wanted a fuller kind of freedom than that.

The office of the CIC's five-member Economic Commission, on the first floor of Aurea Social, didn't look like the usual accounting office. A flock of paper birds hanging from the ceiling flew toward the whiteboard, which covered one wall and read,

"All you need is love." The opposite wall was covered with art made by children. The staff members' computers ran an open-source Linux operating system and the custom software that the IT Commission developed for them, which they used to process the incomes of the CIC's cooperative projects, handle the payment of dues, and disperse the remainder to project members upon request.

If the taxman ever came to CIC members, there was a script: they would say that they're volunteers for a cooperative, and then point him in the direction of the Economic Commission, which could provide the proper documentation. Officially, there was no such thing as the CIC; it operated through a series of legal entities established for various purposes in the organization. Insiders referred to their system, and the tax benefits that went with it, as "fiscal disobedience," or "juridical forms," or simply "the tool."

Accounting took place both in euros and in ecos, which had become the CIC's native currency. Ecos don't require high-tech software like Bitcoin, just a simple mutual-credit ledger. Whereas Bitcoin is supposed to bypass central authorities and flawed human beings, ecos depend on a community of people who trust one another. Anybody with one of the several thousand accounts can log in to the web interface of the Community Exchange System, a package of open-source software first developed in South Africa. There, users can see everyone else's balances and transfer ecos from one account to another. The measure of wealth, too, is upside down. It's not frowned upon to have a low balance or to be a bit in debt; rather, it's troublesome when someone's balance ventures too far from zero in either direction and stays there. Because interest is nonexistent, having lots of ecos sitting around won't do any good. Creditworthiness in the system comes not from accumulation but from use, from achieving a balance between contribution and consumption.

The CIC's answer to the Federal Reserve is the Social Currency Monitoring Commission, whose job it is to contact members not making many transactions and to help them figure out how they can meet more of their needs within the system. If someone wants pants, say, and she can't buy any in ecos nearby, she can try to persuade a tailor to accept them. But the tailor, in turn, will accept ecos only to the extent that he, too, can get something he needs with ecos. This forces people to work together across urban-rural divides, connecting punks with hippies, farmers with hackers, bakers with scientists. It's a process of assembling an economy like a puzzle. The currency is not just a medium of exchange; it's a measure of the CIC's independence from usurious finance.

A word I often heard around the CIC was *autogestió*. People used it with an affection similar to the way Americans talk about "self-sufficiency," but without the screw-everyone-else individualism. They translated it as "self-management," though what they meant was more community than self. This ethic was more cherished in the CIC than any particular legal loophole; the tax benefits merely drew people in. The more they could self-manage how they eat, sleep, learn, and work, the closer the Integral Revolution had come.

About an hour's drive east toward the coast, one of the CIC's punks lived in a tiny medieval town with a death-metal name, Ultramort. Raquel Benedicto wore a black *Clockwork Orange* hoodie and had dyed-red hair. There were rings all over her ears.

Raquel Benedicto and Joel Mòrist on the roof of Aurea Social.

Her nose was pierced at the bridge and septum. She said she had to avoid street protests, because when cops attack her she fights back, and she couldn't risk that now that she was a mother.

With her brother, who returned after years of food service and surfing in the British Isles, she started the town's only restaurant, Restaurant Terra, at the end of 2014. It was a CIC project through and through: meals could be paid for in ecos, and it regularly played host to regional assemblies. Members of the local forestry cooperative, which used a donkey to help carry away logs, came to her to collect their pay. In the back, Benedicto started a nursery school for local kids, including her son, Roc.

Benedicto met Duran during the 15M movement's occupation in 2011. She was already pissed off, but he showed her something to do with it—"something real," she said. She began working with the CIC in the Welcome Commission, learning the Integral logic by teaching others, and by talking as much as she could with Duran. Soon, she was on the Coordination Commission, the group that orchestrates the assemblies and helps the other commissions collaborate better. But her new focus was running the restaurant. "I'm starting to do what I want, finally," she told me.

Duran and Benedicto were often in touch, but she had to be careful. The police once took her phone, and they'd interrogated her friends about his whereabouts. Now she put her phone in another room when she talked about him and encrypted her email. Benedicto was also one of the people who kept the CIC running in Duran's absence, who ensured that it no longer needed him.

I got to witness the CIC's annual weekend-long assembly, devoted to planning the coming year's budget. Sixty or so people sat in a circle in Aurea Social's large back room, with spreadsheets projected above them. A woman breast-fed in the back, while semi-supervised older children had the run of the rest of the building. Benedicto took notes on her Linux-loaded laptop as debates came and went about how to reorganize the commissions more effectively, about who would get paid and how. That weekend they also decided to end EcoBasic, a cautious hybrid currency backed by euros that the CIC had been using—a decision that brought them one step away from fiat money and closer

Assembly at Aurea Social.

to pure social currency. In the fatigue and frustration of it all, one could be forgiven for failing to appreciate the miracle that this many people, in an organization this size, were making detailed and consequential decisions by consensus.

Over the minutiae, too, hung the looming prospect that whatever local decisions they made were part of a model for something bigger. During an argument about whether Zapatista coffee constituted a basic need, I noticed that a web developer in the assembly was quietly writing an encrypted email to Duran about changes to the FairCoin website, the public face of the CIC's new, global stepchild. Most people there at least knew about it, but only a few were ready at this point to let it distract them from their particular projects.

"Enric thinks about something and everybody starts to tremble," Benedicto told me during a break. "No, no—we've got a lot of stuff to do, and now you want to do that, really?"

————

In France, I found that Duran was filling his days and nights with as much activity on behalf of Integralism as his underground condition allowed. He was out and about, passing police officers on the street without a flinch, changing where he lived and worked from time to time in order not to be found too easily. He shared his whereabouts on a need-to-know basis. Perhaps the strangest thing about his daily existence was its steadiness, and the lack of apparent anxiety or self-doubt about the scale of his ambition.

"I feel that I have these capacities," he told me plainly.

One overcast day in Paris, following an afternoon meeting with a developer working on the FairMarket website, Duran set off to one of the hackerspaces he frequents, one whose WiFi configuration he knew would let him send email over a VPN, which can obscure one's location. He was sending an update to the more than ten thousand people on his mailing list. After that was done, he went to meet with a French credit-union executive at the office of a think tank. Her skepticism about FairCoop didn't faze him in the least. Although the discussion seemed to go nowhere, his only thought afterward was about how best to put her networks to use. At around midnight, he introduced FairCoop to the heads of OuiShare in the back of their co-working space. In order to continue the conversation later, he showed them how to use a secure chat program.

Following the cryptography lesson, we went back to the Airbnb apartment that we were sharing, and he sat down with his computer. There he worked until 4:30 in the morning—eating the occasional cookie, smiling every now and then at whatever email or forum thread had his attention, and typing back by hunt-and-peck. All day and all night, a second laptop in the room emitted a glow as the FairCoin wallet program ran on it, helping to keep the currency's decentralized network secure. He slept four or five hours, usually. No cigarettes, no coffee, rarely any beer. He's not a cook. He makes one want to care for him like a mother.

Duran was attempting his third great hack. The first was the "public action"—hacking the financial system to benefit activists. The second was the CIC and its "fiscal disobedience"—hacking the legal system to invent a new kind of cooperative. The third was FairCoop—hacking a currency to fund a global financial system. Being on the run from the law made this task no easier.

Duran's trial was slated to begin in February 2013. But by that time, it didn't seem like it would be much of a trial at all. None of the defense's proposed witnesses had been approved to testify; the authorities didn't want the courtroom to become a stage for political theater. A few days before the first proceedings, Duran went underground again. (The English word he uses for his condition is *clandestinity*.) At first he shut himself away in a house in Catalonia, but when that became too restrictive, he left for France, where he'd be farther from the Spanish police and less recognizable in public.

With not much else to do, he began learning all he could about cryptocurrencies. Friends of his had already been building Bitcoin-related software. Calafou had been a center for Bitcoin development; Vitalik Buterin spent time there while developing the ideas behind Ethereum. But Duran noticed the market-adulating speculation that tended to pervade the cryptocurrency scene and wondered whether the technology could be used for better ends. "I was thinking about how to hack something like this to fund the Integral Revolution," he recalled.

Among the hundreds of Bitcoin clones out there, each with its particular tweaks to the code, Duran found FairCoin. A pseudonymous developer had announced it in March 2014 and gave coins to whomever wanted them. Duran liked the name. Part of what supposedly made FairCoin fair was that it didn't rely on Bitcoin's proof-of-work algorithm, which rewards the miners who have warehouses full of machines that do nothing but guzzle electricity and churn out math. Instead, faircoins were distributed with what seemed like a spirit of fairness. But the whole thing looked like a scam; the currency went through a quick boom-and-bust cycle, after which the developer disappeared, apparently quite a bit wealthier.[15]

The total value of faircoins peaked in mid-April that year at more than $1 million. Halfway through the subsequent free fall, on April 21, Duran made an announcement on the FairCoin forum thread and on Reddit: he had begun buying faircoins. "Building the success of FairCoin should be something collective," he wrote. "FairCoin should become the coin of fair-trade." Between April and September, Duran used the stash of bitcoins he'd been surviving on to buy around ten million faircoins—20 percent of the entire supply. For most of that time, the coin was close to worthless, abandoned by its community. He then teamed up with Thomas König, an especially earnest web developer in Austria, who tweaked FairCoin's code, fixing security problems. They began experimenting with ways to replace the competitive mechanisms FairCoin had inherited from Bitcoin with more cooperative ones designed to fit into the FairCoop structure. By the end of September, CIC members started to invest in faircoins, and the value shot up again to fifteen times what it had been while Duran was buying them in the summer.

Just as the CIC was more than its patchwork of local currencies, FairCoop was much more than FairCoin. Duran intended FairCoop to be a financial network, governed by its member cooperatives. They could sell their products in the FairMarket, trade with one another using FairCredit, and finance their growth with FairFunding. They could buy in at GetFairCoin.net and cash out with Fairtoearth.com. It was meant to be for the whole world what the CIC was in Catalonia. He had laid out the beginnings of a structure, in the shape of a tree—councils and commissions, markets and exchanges, each seeded with faircoins. One fund's job was to build software for the ecosystem, and another's was to redistribute wealth to the Global South. Bolstered by a $13,800 grant from the cosmetics maker Lush (thanks to a friend from his global-justice days), Duran was spending every waking hour enlisting everyone he knew to help make FairCoop something useful for postcapitalists everywhere.

The trick to making this hack work was as much a matter of organizing as it was of tech. The more that local cooperatives became part of the network and used its tools, the more faircoins would be worth in cryptocurrency markets, where wide adoption helps make a coin valuable. To build the community, therefore, was simultaneously to finance it. If the price of faircoins reached the price of bitcoins now, for instance, Duran's initial investment would be worth billions.

The plan has since far out-earned his bank loans. At the end of our time together, Duran sent me some faircoin to cover his share of the apartment we stayed in; during the cryptocurrency boom of 2017, with shady ICOs and crypto-millionaires blowing up everywhere, that reimbursement multiplied to one hundred times its original value. New collaborators were flocking to Fair-Coop to be part of at least one corner of this inflationary universe that was engineering something that wasn't ruthlessly speculative. Organizations around the world were starting to accept fair-coin for purchases and donations. By then, the FairCoin team had implemented a new algorithm to help stabilize the system; as opposed to Bitcoin's proof-of-work mechanism, they called it proof-of-cooperation.

This remains a risky game. The value of a cryptocurrency can be gone as quickly as it appears. But Duran didn't see the currency as the kind of salvific software that tech culture trains us to expect, one that will correct human imperfection if we hand ourselves over to its algorithms. He wanted to use it to create trust among people, not to replace trust with a superior technology. "If you are not creating new cultural relations," he told me, "you're not changing anything." Just as CIC members tried to make their cooperative stronger than any one legal structure, he hoped to see FairCoop become strong enough to be able to outgrow FairCoin altogether.

For all the plan's manic complexity, it was also a plain and simple extension of the logic of Duran's previous endeavors: cheat capitalism to fund the movement, take what already exists and recombine it. But even this unlikely track record was no guarantee. In the hackerspace basement-cave in Paris, while attempting to on-board the French Integralists for his new project, Duran added, as if it were no problem at all, "We don't know if this is going to work."

He needed to find partners, to arrange meetings, to carry out the various tasks a new enterprise demands, and doing so in the confines of clandestinity put daily constraints on an undertaking that would be difficult enough on its own. Jail would be worse, of course, but he was tired of hiding. The bank robber was ready to be a banker.

5

Slow Computing

Platforms

W ell-meaning people have, for a good many years now, been
forming a "consciousness" about where their food comes
from, who produces it, and how. This gets tedious. But
it's also sensible, given how important food is in our lives. Perhaps computers deserve similar conscientiousness. They are constant companions; they shape our experience. Many of us entrust
to them our private lives, our lives' work, and much of the time
we spend carrying those out. Perhaps we owe our computer-lives
some extra tedium, too.

Several winters ago, after a decade of MacBooks, I put myself
at the mercy of this supposition. I bought a newly obsolete laptop
PC. I cleared the hard drive, replacing the obligatory Windows
with Ubuntu, a free, open-source operating system managed by a
UK-based company (founded by a South African) and a large network of volunteers. It's one of the more user-friendly variants of
GNU/Linux, which emerged after 1991, when Linus Torvalds, a
student at the University of Helsinki, wrote his own version of Unix,
a then-popular operating system that AT&T invented in the 1970s.
He released it under the GNU General Public License, which made
it legally available for the world to use and modify. Linux now runs

many of the internet's servers, most supercomputers, and Google's Android mobile operating system. Despite its scale, the original amateurism of Linux is alive and well; once, when a student was helping me set up my computer for a lecture at his college, he told me that he'd helped design the icons on my desktop.

I couldn't afford for my new consciousness to become a huge time-suck. I had work to do, and collaborators who wouldn't put up with weird .odt and .ogg file-types. I had to install some extra utilities on the command-line to get the touchpad and my printer to work properly. There were moments when I feared that with a single click or an *rm -f* command I would break everything. But it never happened. Within hours, in fact, Ubuntu was working about as smoothly as Mac OS ever had—which is to say, with occasional hiccups, both unexpected and chronic. For years, the same vague "system program problem detected" error message recurred every time I turned on the computer, until a system update replaced it with another glitch; some programs have an erratic relationship with my printer. The free-and-open software for complex tasks, like vector graphics and video editing, is still catching up with features the commercial versions had years ago. But it's surprising how little all this bothers me.

More than reducing the literal tempo, the slow-food movement has sought values-oriented economies and thicker communities. Similarly, though my computer is for the most part very speedy and able, slow computing means slowing down enough to compute in community. This turns annoyances into pleasures, just as one learns to appreciate unhygienic soil, disorderly farmers' markets, and inconvenient seasons. The software I use now lacks the veneer of flawlessness that Apple products provide; it is quite clearly a work in progress, forever under construction by programmers who notice a need and share their fixes with everyone. But early on, I found that the glitches felt different than they used to. What would have driven me crazy on a MacBook didn't upset me anymore. No longer could I curse some abstract corporation somewhere. With community-made software, there's no one to blame but us. We're not perfect, but we're working on it.

I do most of my writing in Emacs, a program in active development since the mid-1970s that runs on a text-only terminal screen. (Try it: in Mac OS X, open the Terminal app and type "emacs," and then Enter.) Like produce grown the old-fashioned way, Emacs invites one into connection and continuity with the past. It requires knowledge of ancient keystrokes involving ctrl-x and alt-x. There are no fonts or wizards. But it displays multiple files side by side and plays Tetris. To get the formatting I need, I write in Markdown, a simple set of human-readable tricks. *This* gives me italics, for instance, and I can use [this](URL) to indicate a link. With a few lines of code borrowed from the internet, I taught my ever-extendable Emacs to convert its text files to the .docx files that my editors expect. Anthropologist Christopher M. Kelty, in his study of the free-software movement, describes creating these sorts of Emacs scripts as "one of the joys of my avocational life."[1]

My cloud resides in a co-location center in the Chelsea neighborhood of Manhattan, on a server managed by May First/People Link, a "democratic membership organization"—a cooperative, essentially—to which I belong. May First is based in the United States and Mexico; governance is bilingual. When I was first deciding whether to join, I went to visit May First's founders, Jamie McClelland and Alfredo Lopez, at their office in Sunset Park, Brooklyn, where we spent a few hours discussing our technological preferences and life stories. I learned that they pay a premium to keep the servers in the city, rather than in some far-off data center. It's important for them to have physical access in case something goes haywire. They like to keep our data close.

I joined May First about a year after Edward Snowden's leaks, when it became clearer how the National Security Agency had deputized corporate cloud services for blanket surveillance. I'm not sure if I do anything especially worth spying on, but I figured I'd try to opt out. The May First team has a record of resistance to snooping law-enforcement agencies; McClelland more recently told me about the security system they'd built around the servers, which relays its data outside US borders. After that, we chatted about our travel plans for the coming months, in case they'd overlap. Try doing that with the folks who run your Gmail.

Now my calendars, contacts, and backup files all sync with an open-source program called NextCloud, which McClelland maintains on the May First servers. None of that information about me churns through Google anymore. NextCloud is like an adolescent lovechild of Dropbox, Google Drive, Google Calendar, and Google Contacts—plus whatever other apps people create as plug-ins. A hobby of mine is trolling programmers on Twitter to get them to make more.

My new cloud mostly works. For a while the sync client on my laptop was hanging and had to be restarted sometimes; I posted a bug report on the developers' forums, and before long an update put a stop to it. Then syncing contacts began to crash Thunderbird, my open-source email program; eventually I found a thread in another online forum that helped me fix it. One way or another, someone in the vast and geeky community figures out a solution. We always do.

Such faith, however, should not be mistaken for a cure-all. Like sipping fair-trade coffee and tending a community-garden plot, my commitments to Emacs and May First produce limited macroeconomic effect. "Goldman Sachs doesn't care if you're raising chickens," political theorist Jodi Dean once remarked.[2] Google doesn't care if I'm using Emacs. But I care, and I like it. More important, there's an economy at work in this noodling. Economies can spread.

Tech companies expect us to participate in their networks without really knowing how they work. We're transparent about every detail of our lives with them, while they're private about what they do with it. Community-based software operates on a different logic. Because nobody owns it, it's harder to become fabulously wealthy from keeping secrets. Transparency is the default. People make these programs because they need them, not because they think they can manipulate someone to want them. Instead of relying on rich kids in a Googleplex somewhere, slow computing works best when we're employing people like Jamie McClelland to adapt open tools to local needs. He's my farmer; May First is my community-supported agriculture, my CSA.

Still, to those interested in some consciousness-raising about the machines with which we spend so much of our lives, there's a need for more than my acts of piety—there's a need for better business models, models accountable to users more than the whims of capital markets, that reward contributions to the commons more than tricks that make data of public import artificially scarce and the data of our private lives surreptitiously profitable. Business models matter all the more as the internet graduates from being a mere toy, trick, or convenience to a basic substrate of the economy.

———

The conventional wisdom of twentieth-century industrialism offered little reason to expect that volunteerism and information-sharing would help form the basis of the next economic infrastructure. Yet they have. The products of free, open-source software—that is, an economy of pure sharing and collaborating—serve as the less-visible skeleton beneath the corporate-controlled, user-facing internet. Linux and Unix servers host more than half of all websites.[3] Commercial search engines, including Google, rely on the unpaid contributions of self-governing Wikipedia editors, and e-commerce is possible thanks to the open encryption protocol Secure Sockets Layer. These work precisely because their inner workings are public, for all to see.

The story began with a hack. In order to protect the code-sharing habits of early hacker culture, and to protect them from the proprietary urges of corporations and universities, a geek at MIT named Richard Stallman inaugurated the free-software movement with the GNU General Public License. This and other "copyleft" licenses turned the law against itself; they employed an author's copyright privileges in order to preserve the code as a commons, free for anyone else to use, adapt, and improve. Subsequently, legal scholar Lawrence Lessig translated this same hack to non-software cultural production through the array of Creative Commons licenses.[4] Now, thanks to Creative Commons, a descendant of Stallman's hack is a built-in option when you upload a video on YouTube.

Alongside such legal hacks have been clusters of social ones. Theodore Roszak, best known for coining the term *counterculture* in the late 1960s, published a book in 1986 on what he called the "cult of information." By the early 1970s, those whom Roszak dubbed "guerrilla hackers" had begun to appear at the intersection of the West Coast's tech industry and radical subculture. They had their own publication, the *People's Computer Company Newsletter*, and a mostly theoretical network (with only one actual node, in a Berkeley record store) called Community Memory. Their propaganda described the computer as a "radical social artifact" that would usher in a "direct democracy of information"—"actively free ('open') information," of course.[5]

This was the culture out of which arose such icons as Steve Wozniak, inventor of the Apple computer, and the *Whole Earth Catalog*, which hyped the digital revolution with all that newsprint and mail-order could muster. Like the unMonastery, these guerrilla hackers blended the old with the new, the ancient with the post-industrial. Although their projects often relied on state or corporate subsidies, they envisioned their efforts as apolitical, wrapped in the "safe neutrality" of information, as Roszak put it. With the power of information, they imagined, old-fashioned political and economic power wouldn't be needed anymore. Meanwhile, Wozniak's "homebrew" gadget grew into Steve Jobs's Wall Street behemoth, which now holds more cash reserves than the US Treasury.

Alongside its proprietary tendencies, the Bay Area tech culture still provides leaven for experiments in social organization. Pop-up [freespace] sites have turned unused downtown storefronts into drop-in hackathons—before the founders moved the model to refugee camps in Greece and Africa. In the gentrifying Mission District, there is the famous (and notorious) hackerspace Noisebridge, together with the original location of its feminist rejoinder, Double Union. On the Oakland side of the border with Berkeley, a cavernous nightclub-turned-community-center called the Omni Commons is home to Sudo Room, a hackerspace with an anarchist bent, and Counter Culture Labs, where civilian scientists tinker with donated instruments and synthesize new forms of vegan cheese. And of course there is Burning Man, the Bay

Sign at a 2014 [freespace] storefront on Market Street in San Francisco.

Area's annual sojourn into the barren Nevada desert that manages to be both free and expensive, open and exclusive, all at once.

Hacker experiments turn into systems and workflows, then ways of life, then corporations. Git, for instance, is a program Linus Torvalds designed to manage the deluge of code contributions for Linux from all over the world; now it's the basis of GitHub, a corporate social network and project manager that determines the pecking order of coders. The more than a thousand developers who work on Debian, an important version of Linux, govern themselves through procedures and elected positions outlined in their Debian Constitution. They have created a republic for code, and my computer runs on it.

Inspired by such communities, tech-industry consultants promote new management philosophies with such names as Holacracy, Agile, and Teal.[6] These feats of dynamic, distributed workflow seem to outstrip the democracy of most big, established cooperatives nowadays, which tend to have carbon-copied their hierarchies from industrial-age bureaucracies. Techie capitalism can appear to be out-cooperating the co-ops.

For instance, Holacracy: borrowing a name from Arthur Koestler's concept of the holon—"a whole that is part of a larger whole"—it proposes to replace the top-down hierarchy of the industrial corporation with the free flow of an open-source project. There is some hierarchy in Holacracy—officially capitalized, a registered trademark of the company HolacracyOne—but, rather than the metaphor of a pyramid, the system relies on nested "circles." Rather than a single job description, each worker can hold any number of carefully specified "roles," within which the worker has authority to make relevant decisions, whether the CEO likes them or not. For bosses used to command-and-control, Holacracy means giving up the power to micromanage. Meetings are short and highly regimented. Rather than mouthing off at will, the people formerly called managers have to trust the process and the code-like rules that define it. The system has been implemented partly or fully in various corners of the tech industry—for instance, at Zappos and Medium—though in investor-oriented settings like these, it has a tendency to implode.[7]

Maybe the contradictions become too easily apparent. Although Holacracy grants even the lowliest employees autonomy in their domain, that autonomy must always accord with the rules of the game, with the overriding purpose of the company. The purpose is everything in Holacracy. And, for most sizable tech companies, that purpose is to furnish wealth for investors. Self-determination gets dangled before people but then yanked away as soon as it might really matter.

Despite tech culture's clever hacks of intellectual-property law and organizational charts, it has left the basic accountability of the firm mostly unscathed—in particular, its ownership structure and its profits. Companies have exhibited some cooperative tendencies in their use of employee stock options to lure talent to early startups, and this has meant windfalls for some, but investor control takes over before long. This system benefits mostly a fairly small set of insiders, leaving little for the commoners.

As elements of Stallman's free-software movement went mainstream under the moniker "open source" in the late 1990s, advocates such as Eric Raymond and Tim O'Reilly rebranded code-sharing as friendly to corporate value-capture.[8] Large open-source projects operated under the guidance of foundations controlled and funded by representatives of corporations that benefit from the community-developed code. The effects can be quite congenial. Thanks to Creative Commons, a vast archive of user-generated photos is available for public use through Flickr, which was acquired by Yahoo in 2005; the power of Git wasn't fully apparent until GitHub put it on a proprietary cloud with a friendly interface. But this same pattern of adaptation is what allows Google to redeploy the Linux kernel as Android, the world's most popular mobile operating system and perhaps the most successful corporate surveillance tool ever invented.

Free and open-source software communities have also remained troublingly homogeneous. A 2017 GitHub study found that only 3 percent of open-source contributors identified as female and 16 percent as ethnic minorities where they lived. Theories for why this is the case vary, because open-source cultures often self-identify as meritocratic and open to anyone. Yet in order to contribute, a person must either be paid to do so or have surplus leisure hours—a surplus some are less likely to have than others.[9] Slow computing takes time.

Thus, the marvelous digital commons may actually amplify inequalities in the surrounding society, while funneling the profits to corporations. This doesn't seem to disturb many rank-and-file coders, who participate precisely because they already reap benefits from the corporate system. But if commoners cannot obtain the means of survival through the commons, that commons is actually an enclosure.

By the mid-1980s, Roszak was already speaking of "hopeful democratic spirits like the guerrilla hackers" in the past tense. "Such minimal and marginal uses of the computer," he wrote, "are simply dwarfed into insignificance by its predominant applications, many of which seriously endanger our freedom and survival." Even then he recognized the digitalization of education as a privatization scheme, and the near absence of worker organizing in the tech sector, and the unchecked information-gathering capacities of the National Security Agency. He stressed that the response was not merely a parade of better apps, or nobler ideals, but fairer and stronger forms of association.

"Making the democratic most of the Information Age," Roszak wrote, "is a matter not only of technology but also of the social organization of that technology."[10]

The modes of social organization have been shifting. Industries that once built, distributed, and sold things are giving way to a new breed of business models, which go by the allegedly neutral, blank-slate name *platforms*. These platforms are multi-sided markets that connect people—to rent spare rooms, to share news, to do jobs—reaping fees from our transactions and artificial intelligence from the data of our use. They are finding their way into ever more areas of our lives. In 2016, as many as 24 percent of US adults reported earning income over online platforms. The ever-shuffling list of the most valuable companies in the world now is consistently top-heavy with platforms, from Apple and Google's Alphabet in the United States to Alibaba and Tencent in China.[11] Co-ops, which once specialized in the art of connection, are facing disruption by platforms, too. And as platforms coalesce into the new regime, it matters more than ever how these things are owned and governed.

———

When Jean-François Millet unveiled his painting *The Gleaners* in 1857, a critic of the time expressed repulsion at the three women in the foreground for their "gigantic and pretentious ugliness."[12] Each is bent toward the ground to a different degree, each gathering the stray wheat left by the landowner's appointed army of harvesters, who are working under the eyes of a foreman on a horse in the background. The women don't have much. They're in a shadow, compared to the light on the official operation behind them. It's not evident whether they'll find enough of the leftover grain to make a decent loaf of bread.

Before we were farmers, we were gatherers. Gathering became gleaning when agriculture gave rise to landowning, leaving out the non-owners. Gleaning was the original welfare. This principle was a basic feature of the medieval European economy, when a small minority owned the land and most people had to live by what they could glean and gather. It remains the motive force in the underground economies that support billions of people on this planet, those who survive on cash and knock-offs rather than stock markets and brand names. The platform business models taking over the internet are making more of us gleaners again.

We share the stories of our lives, the data of our relationships, and the news that interests us. Maybe this is a practice that we enter willingly. It can even be a joy; we see a real friend's face, we reconnect after years, we spot opportunities that would otherwise go missed. We can find paying work online without the day-to-day drudgery of a job. These platforms have given us so much. They seem to make anything possible. Like the great cathedrals and castles once were, they are our world's cosmic glue. Increasingly, such sharing is requisite for maintaining relationships and obtaining employment. But this means we have less and less choice. Although the interfaces are organized to help us feel in charge and in control, the reality is like that of Millet's women picking at the edges of the field. We see only tiny scraps of the information about ourselves and our "friends" that is available to the lords of the platforms. We think we are getting something for free while we give away our valuable data. We think we are in some sense members of a digital commons while we relinquish our ownership rights. At least Millet's gleaners knew that's what they were.

Ubiquitous platforms like Facebook and Google gather reams of data about users and offer it for sale to advertisers and others. We know this, to an extent. But our data is also the business of the ride-sharing apps, the office productivity apps, and the apps that use us to train the intelligence of other apps, along with data brokers whose names we'll never know but who trade in the stuff of our lives. Users supply a growing surveillance economy based on targeted advertising and pricing, which, intentionally or not, can bleed into discrimination of vulnerable populations. The prospect that one's online activity can affect a credit rating, or find its way into the database of a spy agency, has already dampened the free speech that the internet otherwise might enable. We users might feel like customers, but to these companies' investor-owners, we are both workers and product. ("My consumers are they not my producers?" mused James Joyce, prefiguratively.) Although Facebook, for instance, may insist that users retain ownership of their data, immense and unintelligible service agreements grant the platform such sweeping rights over that data as to render user ownership close to meaningless. Because of this—because of us—such platform companies can be among the most valuable in the world with only tens of thousands of formal employees, rather than the hundreds of thousands that a major car manufacturer commands, or Walmart's millions.[13]

In between the aristocratic employees and the gleaning peasant users, platforms hire legions of online freelancers for piecework tasks. These people are the leading edge of a growing workforce that is permanently part-time, gig-to-gig—part empowered freelancer, part exile from the rights and benefits that once accompanied employment.[14] Their offline lives, too, can start to feel like a kind of piecework. Rochelle LaPlante, once a social worker, began a second career on Amazon's Mechanical Turk platform in 2012, doing tasks to help support her family, such as moderating offensive images and taking academic surveys. With this came new habits of mind. She told me, "You go to the grocery store and see a candy bar, and you think, *Is that worth two surveys?*" The piecework mentality is spreading, with little legal restraint, from Amazon's newer Flex delivery platform to countless other contenders beckoning an underemployed workforce into ephemeral gigs.

These are the sounds of a social contract shifting. New rules are taking hold, even if it is happening in ways and places that many of us don't see. The implicit rules that can be gotten away with on platforms now could stick around for generations.

The active ingredient that has brought the platform economy to life is venture-capital financing. Most people can be forgiven for not knowing much about it, because it's not for them. It's a trick almost exclusively available to privileged subcultures in a small number of highly networked urban tech hubs, unknown to virtually everyone else who might want to get a business going.

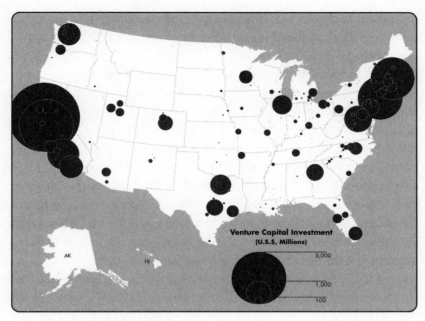

Venture Capital Investment
(U.S.$, Millions)

5,000

1,000

100

The availability and lack of venture capital in the United States.

When a startup is still just an idea or a minimal prototype, venture capitalists can inject large sums of money for a chunk of ownership. The VCs do that for a lot of startups, most of which don't pan out. But for those that do, the VCs expect profits to make up for not only that investment but also the ones that fail. Such payouts don't come from sustainable, linear growth. They come from the "unicorns"—companies that can swallow entire industries. As markets, not just products, platforms are well suited to this. Their game is often winner-takes-all. And as they win, VCs steer their platforms toward a hallowed "exit" event—either an acquisition by a bigger company or an initial public offering on public markets. In the exit, we the users are part of what is being sold.

I've started to hear a story on repeat from apparently successful founders of tech companies: Their startup had a great idea, and users thought it was great, too, so it became worth something. Investors offered fast money in exchange for stock. The founders liked a lot of the investors as people and valued their advice. Some became real-life friends. But before long, the founders discovered that their companies were no longer built around that original idea, or even around the users it could serve. The whole point had become to extract gigantic returns for shareholders—and to disguise that fact from users. The great idea, together with the users it attracted, became a commodity.

Young people with clever ideas, but not a lot of business experience, get drawn in. Their mentors and accelerators groom them to be what investors want to see. For some, it works. But most good ideas are not that rare, monopoly-scale unicorn that disrupts the world and delivers the huge returns investors need to keep lavishing the next new startups with easy money. It's not enough for a platform to be merely useful or profitable; investment funds need commodities, not communities.

Consider Paul Allen—not the billionaire who co-founded Microsoft, but the one who brought the world Ancestry.com, the genealogy platform. Allen and his co-founder started with CD-ROMs in 1990 and then started making websites later that decade. They owned nearly the whole company and were soon turning a profit. They raised millions of dollars from investors, moved the headquarters from Utah to San Francisco, and by Y2K, they were edging toward being one of the top ten web properties in the world.

Then there was an aborted public offering and a sequence of deals—deals that Allen now admits he didn't fully understand. The slice of shares he owned grew smaller, and he finally left the company and its board in 2002, watching as Ancestry endured the vicissitudes of various private-equity buyers and sellers. He's still proud of what the platform he helped build offers its users, but he has grown philosophical as he watches the current investor-owners squeeze the company for whatever they can get—even eliminating troves of users' family memories in the process.

"If you ask me what modern invention has led to the most inequality in modern civilization," Allen told me, "the answer I'd give is the modern corporation."

The seven cooperative principles actually overlap in places with the social contracts of the online economy. "Voluntary and open membership" is a default practice among platforms, which typically enable anyone (with access to requisite technology) to create an account; "autonomy and independence" are values that platform owners assert when skirting local regulations, even while proclaiming a well-meaning "concern for community." There is much "cooperation" among platform companies, such as through API protocols and standards-setting organizations such as the World Wide Web Consortium. Practices of "education, training, and information" happen around platforms, too—whether in online forums and in-person meetups—resembling the kind of mutual education that cooperatives might encourage among members.

The resonance, however, only goes so far. Cooperative principles two and three—democratic governance and ownership, crucially—are absent from the dominant platforms. Online user-experience design seeks to divert users' attention from matters of governance and ownership, such as by rendering opaque how apparently free services squeeze out revenue. Consultation with users on changes to features or policies is superficial, when it happens at all.

In place of meaningful self-governance, the internet has hackers. They're the Jedi knights, the mysterious rogues who supposedly keep the system both honest and a little dangerous—a check on the powerful, a symbol that ordinary people can still have control. To hack is to manipulate a system as an outsider, to be unconfined by law or decorum, to find whatever back doors might lead the way to a break-in or a fix. Some hackers end up in jail for years, while others get big paychecks from companies and governments. This fringe identity has become an aspired-to corporate norm. The address of Facebook's headquarters is 1 Hacker Way.

I wonder if my generation, the first generation of "digital natives," is a generation of hackers. Many of us have never had the feeling that our supposed democracies are listening to us; we glean sporadic work from organizations that gobble up the value we produce for those at the top. We have to hack to get by. Maybe we can at least hack better than whoever is in charge—though they have hackers of their own now. We become so used to hacking into the back doors that we forget there could be any other way.

Who wants to hack forever? What would it mean to open up the front door—to an online economy where *democracy* actually means democracy and technology does its part to help, where we can spend less time hacking and hustling and more time getting better at being human? Tech won't do it for us, because it can't, because the forms that it takes depend on how we organize ourselves.

———

By her early twenties, Brianna Wettlaufer was an executive at iStock, a fast-growing platform for stock photos and multimedia. But at meeting after meeting, Wettlaufer began to feel conflicted. She was caught in the middle. The imperatives coming from the company's investor-owners compelled managers like her to keep cutting what they paid the independent artists whom the company claimed to represent. She's a photographer herself; this mattered to her. The same restless frustration with lousy systems that powered Wettlaufer's climb up the corporate ladder finally compelled her to leave iStock and, with others, start her own company. They were able to pool a bit over $1 million, thanks to a windfall from iStock's sale to Getty Images, and they lent it to the project. Wettlaufer moved from Los Angeles back home to Victoria, Canada. Stocksy United went online in 2013, incorporated as a cooperative.

The result was a different kind of platform business. Rather than seeking growth at all costs, like at Wettlaufer's old job, Stocksy United managers have to ask the photographers and videographers when they're ready to add new members. Fair pay and excellent work are the top priorities. That's why Stocksy has been able to retain some of the world's best stock artists, in dozens of countries, and attract lucrative clients in a competitive market. Wettlaufer and the other early lenders have long since been paid back; the company doubled its revenue in 2015 to $7.9 million, and hit $10.7 million the following year. Now, as CEO, Wettlaufer has little difficulty championing artistic quality and fair treatment for artists at company meetings: the artists are her bosses.

Margaret Vincent, senior counsel of Stocksy United, and CEO Brianna Wettlaufer.

Wettlaufer is her own boss, too. Stocksy United, like many of its aspiring peers, is a multi-stakeholder cooperative. The company's bylaws balance the interests of three classes: artists, employees, and advisers like Wettlaufer, who retain unique powers. Once, over lunch, Wettlaufer and her co-worker Nuno Silva allowed me a glimpse at the members' internal website, where they debate company decisions in forums and vote on major decisions. Silva scrolled through an annual report—the long version, the version meant for members' eyes only. It was a work of elegance and care and attention to detail. Wettlaufer's accountability to her members is not only economic, it is aesthetic.

Stocksy United was a pioneer in bringing a cooperative model into the new platform economy. Wettlaufer and her team did it in isolation; cooperation helped solve a problem they had. But they were not alone.

The Spanish collective Las Indias distinguished platforms as one category of cooperative in a 2011 blog post. In 2012, the Italian federation Legacoop promulgated a manifesto for "Cooperative Commons," stressing the need for cooperative business models to manage the growing stores of data that users feed to online platforms. That year, too, a soft-spoken German entrepreneur named Felix Weth founded a fair-trade, online marketplace called Fairmondo, cooperatively owned by its buyers, sellers, and workers alike. By October 2014, Janelle Orsi of the Sustainable Economies Law Center, in Oakland, promulgated a cartoon video online that called for "the next sharing economy"—a sharing of cooperative ownership. Orsi was also helping to design the bylaws for Loconomics Cooperative, a gig platform owned by gig workers. Small web-development shops were finding worker-ownership a congenial means of attracting talent and distinguishing themselves in a crowded industry.[15]

Three people I met in Paris at OuiShareFest that summer were gesturing in the same directions during the months afterward. Venture capitalist Lisa Gansky had been nudging sharing-economy startups to understand and imitate cooperative tradition. Neal Gorenflo of the online newsletter *Shareable* commissioned me to write an article about a handful of entrepreneurs already trying to share more than just stuff—to share ownership of companies themselves. Media scholar Trebor Scholz was organizing the latest of his conferences on digital labor at The New School in New York City that November. There, the talk among platform workers, labor activists, and scholars mostly dwelled on the dismal standards that had come to prevail for online labor, illustrated through international research studies and the stories of workers. But from time to time, a pointed question would come up among the workers present: What if *we* owned the platforms? How would *we* set the rules?

It was one of those moments of simultaneity that happen when the conditions are ripe, when lots of people land on a particular set of ideas at about the same time. The following month, December 2014, I published my article for *Shareable*, and Scholz posted an essay online whose title posed a choice: "Platform Cooperativism vs. the Sharing Economy."[16] Thus he gave a name to the idea that lots of people around us had been more or less thinking—a many-syllabled name, but it worked, and it stuck. This was platform cooperativism, this was #platformcoop.

Scholz and I teamed up. We started meeting with groups at the front lines of the platform economy, including the National Domestic Workers Alliance, whose cleaning and service workers were seeing their conditions decline with new apps, and another, the Freelancers Union. I called upon the lessons I'd learned from Enric Duran, from the unMonastery, from Kenya. The following November, we put on another conference at The New School. We brought in a cast of investors, CEOs, organizers, critics, and platform workers. Entrepreneurs showcased their actually existing platform co-ops—many encountering each other for the first time. More than one thousand people came to take part. Others began organizing events in Barcelona, Melbourne, Mexico City, London, Brussels, and beyond. The idea was becoming a movement.

Platform cooperativism was an invitation to a broad range of possibilities, to bringing online the art of what business ethicist Marjorie Kelly calls "ownership design." We welcomed developments like when Managed by Q, an investor-backed gig platform for office cleaning, opted to share 5 percent of the company with its workers.[17] But when we called something a platform co-op, outright, we meant *co-op*, in the same way the International Cooperative Alliance and the global sector means it, seven principles and all—*co-op* the way Mondragon means it, the way the Rochdale Pioneers meant it. But rather than sharing ownership among neighbors or co-workers, these were sharing it over the internet.

Early on, lots of people came into this effort craving an instant co-op Uber replica—the same world-disrupting unicorn, except a nice, cooperative version. But we had to realize that Uber came out of a particular kind of ecosystem in Silicon Valley, of accelerators and investors and Burning Man camps and tech schools. To do things cooperatively, we'd need to undertake the patient work of building another kind of ecosystem. Scholz began forming a Platform Cooperativism Consortium to wrangle the various organizations involved, while I took to mapping the network in an online directory, the Internet of Ownership.[18] I noticed that the ownership designs appearing among the baby platform co-ops weren't just copying what was out there already. They challenged some of the basic business models of the internet, as well as some long-held habits in the global co-op movement so far.

———

My slow computing runs into a lot of dead ends. I can control my operating system, the programs on my machines, even the cloud tools I use to manage my personal data. But once I run into public platforms, once I need to connect with others and do things together, it's over. I'm stuck. This is where my personal piety doesn't help. If I want to do slow computing over networks, sensitive to the communities and value chains I'm interacting with, I need platform cooperativism. I need platform co-ops.

There are too few of them. Most that do exist are still getting their start. Except for a few cases here and there, in a few parts of the world, life in the platform co-op stack remains mostly a feat of imagination, a possible future based on projects of the present that may or may not succeed. As some do, it will be easier for more to as well. For now, we're building on each other.

As I write, some of the time at least, I'm listening to music I've never heard of on Resonate. So far, the beta-version player mostly works, and the music keeps being better than I expect. It's a streaming-music co-op, co-owned by its listeners, musicians, developers, and more. Each time I listen to something, a tiny bit of money goes to the musicians who created it. The more I listen, the more I pay, until my ninth stream of a song, when it's mine for good. I wish I had such decent fair-trade options for more of the stuff I might want to buy. I wish more of the networks I spend hours on each day were designed so well to serve the people they connect.

There may be networked cooperators around you already. The car-sharing nonprofit in my town, for instance, benefits from the software that the Canadian cooperative Modo developed to help its members schedule their reservations. Modo was founded back in 1997. And also well before there was any talk of platform co-ops, in 2008, the High Plains Food Cooperative began making grocery deliveries to Colorado's Front Range from farms as far away as Kansas, coordinating its long-distance orders online. But these pose little threat to the giants.

I can keep my calendars, contacts, and email with May First, but a lot of a day's work for me still involves feeding data into Facebook Groups, Google Docs, and Slack channels, all for the sake of collaborating. There needs to be another way. This is a kind of holy grail for today's guerrilla hackers—an antidote to the surveillance addiction that plagues so much of our online lives. Tim Berners-Lee, who invented the World Wide Web, is working on this problem with researchers at MIT, as are countless blockchain startups. But cooperatives could be especially well suited to offering data a trustworthy home, one free from acquisitive investor-owners—a collaborative cloud that is truly ours.

In 2013, a collective of artists developed the prototype website commodify.us, inviting people to download their data from Facebook, re-upload it to their site, and allow it to be sold, on the users' own terms, through third-party data markets. (From the FAQ: "Is this for real? Yes.") That's something like the idea behind TheGoodData, a London-based co-op that obtains members' data through a browser plug-in, then sells it off in transparent ways and reinvests the proceeds in microloan programs abroad. Farmers are doing something similar. The vast reams of data that modern farm machines churn out are of growing interest to investor-backed companies. The Growers Agricultural Data Cooperative builds on the long cooperative legacy of US farmers, using a platform called AgXchange to protect their data, process it, and return it to them in forms that can help them do their jobs better. And then there's MIDATA, a project of Swiss scientists. It offers member-owners a safe place to store their personal, valuable medical data, enabling them to choose who can have access to what information. The co-op covers its costs by allowing members' data—with members' permission—to be used for medical-research studies, though it doesn't allow members to earn income directly, for fear of creating perverse incentives. Opting out of a surveillance economy need not require commodifying ourselves.[19]

At a meeting on an old aircraft carrier floating in the San Francisco Bay, I learned that a group of community colleges was planning to introduce their students to gig work on platforms as an employment opportunity. This was troubling not only because many online labor brokerages ignore such protections as minimum wage, sick days, and basic insurance; it struck me as a poor pedagogical choice. On platforms, workers see only the user-facing side, and they don't really learn, as in a good internship, how the business works. In the end, mercifully, none of the corporate platforms would adopt the federal Americans with Disabilities Act standards that the colleges required. But we found them a platform that would: Loconomics.

Loconomics Cooperative is the creation, principally, of Joshua Danielson, a San Francisco entrepreneur with an MBA and some coding chops. Its member-owners are independent professionals—personal trainers, dog walkers, housekeepers, and the like—whose clients can schedule and pay for appointments through a website or mobile app. The members help determine how the platform works, the standards it sets, and what it does with surpluses. Without conventional financing, it was having trouble reaching critical mass. An influx of community-college students has begun to change that.

Higher education is becoming a fruitful breeding ground for platform co-ops, just as it helped build older co-ops like the Online Computer Library Center, or OCLC, which grew out of Ohio universities in the 1960s. Researchers at Stanford have been building Daemo, a platform for worker-governed crowdsourcing, and a group of my students at the University of Colorado designed a student-run gig co-op. Through cooperation, universities can do business, education, and public service all at once.

Platform co-ops have found other patrons as well. The labor union SEIU-United Healthcare Workers West attempted to develop a platform for home-care nurses, and in New York the Robin Hood Foundation supported Up & Go, a platform for home-cleaning worker cooperatives, built by a tech co-op in collaboration with the home cleaners who use it. The Cooperative Management Group, a development consultancy, helped organize the Golf Ball Divers Alliance, a co-op of independent divers who recover balls from golf-course lakes and resell them online.

And more. LibreTaxi and Arcade City are trying to replace closed apps like Uber and Lyft with open protocols that would be well-suited for driver co-ops. Fairbnb, with founders spread across Europe, plans to challenge Airbnb by offering benefits to local organizations. Savvy Cooperative is a platform co-owned by patients who earn income by providing insights to researchers and companies on their own terms. Word Jammers is a cooperative of copywriters who grew frustrated with the existing crowdsourcing platforms they were using and decided to strike out on their own. The founders of both Savvy and Word Jammers live with chronic conditions, and their concern for the standards of platform work stem from experiences of being differently abled. They know, better than most, that the dominant online economy wasn't designed with them in mind.

Some platform users are already serving as trainers for their robot replacements. Uber drivers feed their data to the future self-driving cars, and Google's algorithms learn every time a website asks us to identify the street signs in a reCAPTCHA quiz. Artificial intelligence should be a wonderful thing, but so far the bulk of it is being owned and controlled by a few big-data giants. That's why a group of researchers in the United States and India has proposed "cooperative models for training artificial intelligence"—enabling trainers to receive benefits through shared ownership.[20] Yet these are still only models, and they're competing against up-and-running juggernauts. For now, platform cooperativism can claim little more than a set of modest experiments in slow computing. They hold prospects, but not much strength. They're not challenging the internet monopolies or their owners yet, and they won't without the means available to let them thrive.

———

What would it take so that a can-do group of pioneers—people with a need to meet or an idea to share with the world—might conclude that the best, easiest way to build their business is by practicing democracy?

This is not an abstraction for me. It's a question I return to several times a week in the exchanges I have with entrepreneurs building or contemplating platform co-ops. We're the blind leading the blind. Consider, for instance, the founder of one very promising startup, with extensive personal and professional knowledge of her target market, plus the do-or-die attitude that's nearly prerequisite for bringing something new and excellent into the world. Nothing should be able to stop her, but starting a co-op might.

At first, on the phone, I want to apologize. We're not there yet. It would probably be easier for her company to get going with a big chunk of venture capital, which she could get if she wanted. There have been offers. She's going after a sector massively vulnerable to disruption. But she doesn't want that. She already thinks of her future users like family, like community, and going co-op is the only thing that makes sense to her. It's the only way she thinks the business will be its best self. The offers haven't changed her mind, thank goodness; this is the way equitable pioneers are.

Still, the founder needs financing. What can I say? Platform co-ops can't easily absorb the free-flowing capital in Silicon Valley or Silicon Alley; VCs want ownership and control. Knowing co-op history, though, makes me confident. Financing gets figured out. When farmers formed cooperative processing plants and national brands, they set up cooperative banks to finance bigger, better ones. As urban workers formed cooperative stores and workshops to help them survive the industrial system, they created credit unions and mutual insurance companies. Co-ops have financed skyscrapers and nuclear power plants. Mondragon's Father Arizmendi insisted that co-ops have a responsibility to capitalize: "A cooperativism without the structural ability to attract and assimilate capital at the level of the demands of industrial productivity is a transitory solution, an obsolete formula."[21]

We're starting to figure out how to do this for platform co-ops. Even the VCs are starting to notice the limits of their existing models. The New York firm Union Square Ventures, for instance, has been an unlikely friend of platform cooperativism. USV partner Brad Burnham spoke at the first New School conference; he envisions a new generation of less risky "skinny platforms" that are less centralized and share their benefits more widely. "We can generate a return participating in that," he said in 2015, "and we think that's what we should be doing."[22] Still, he can't imagine investing directly in co-ops.

There need to be other ways. Co-ops were the original crowdfunding. They were how people got together and financed a business to do things nobody else would do for them. Online crowdfunding borrows this idea, but platforms such as Kickstarter and GoFundMe subtract the co-ownership and mutual accountability of their cooperative predecessors. Platform co-ops are trying to bring this back. One of the earliest platform co-ops of all, Snowdrift.coop, is honing a model for helping its co-owners crowdfund free-and-open projects for the commons that nobody will own. Seedbloom, based in Berlin, enables backers of a new project to become its co-owners—a kind of "equity crowdfunding." It ran the initial membership drive for Resonate, which uses blockchain tech as well, and which later raised $1 million in tokens through a cooperative blockchain project called RChain. The total value of RChain's Ethereum-based crowd-sale tokens has reached over $800 million; while proposing to develop a sophisticated, next-generation protocol, founder Greg Meredith modeled RChain's co-op structure on old-fashioned REI.

A healthy financing buffet needs more than crowdfunding. Purpose Ventures is a new venture fund designed to enable companies to remain "steward-owned" and purpose-oriented—rather than forever seeking an exit that turns the company into a commodity. In order to do that, its young founders have created a model much like an old cooperative bank, a network of mutually supporting enterprises. On a local scale, such financing networks are forming through co-ops such as Uptima Business Bootcamp, a group of member-owned accelerators starting in the Bay Area, and Work Hard PGH in Pittsburgh.

We even have robots. Robin Hood Cooperative, incorporated in Finland, is a kind of hedge fund that earns revenue by investing in stock markets on the advice of the Parasite, a piece of software that mimics the behavior of successful investors; in addition to delivering returns to members, a portion of the co-op's profits go toward supporting commons-oriented projects.

A growing part of the platform co-op surge comes from the older, bigger co-ops themselves. National co-op associations, up to the International Cooperative Alliance, have started speaking up about the need to take on the challenge of platforms. But mobilizing the sector's strength won't be easy. Credit unions and mutual insurers have their own venture capital funds, but they're mostly just doing speculative deals, not seeding new co-ops. They're creating websites and mobile apps for what were once offline services, but they're not generating meaningful alternatives in the connective economy of platforms. Rarely do they take advantage of open-source software or the worker-owned software companies that are becoming widespread. They prefer to play catch-up with the overcapitalized competition. Managers contend their conservatism is in their members' interests, and perhaps it is. It's also a consequence of regulation. After Internet Archive founder Brewster Kahle attempted to start an Internet Archive Federal Credit Union in 2011—an ambitious attempt to scale up credit unionism for the internet age—the effort finally foundered on the rocks of the hefty regulations that credit unions now face.[23] But I think most of the problem is a lack of imagination.

This I would like to change. I want to bridge the gap between the existing, hiding commonwealth of co-ops and the glittery tech startups that get all the fanfare now.

What if startups could aim for an exit to co-op—selling the company to its users or employees, rather than to more investors? What would an incubator or accelerator designed just for co-ops look like? The worry that haunts me is that the founders I work with can't afford to wait for the answers.

A verdant platform co-op ecosystem, meanwhile, will need more than financing. It will need forms of education that train owners, not just workers. Some of these might be versions of the unaccredited tech boot camps that promise to produce coders in a matter of weeks, like the Enspiral Dev Academy that I visited in New Zealand. Some might look like the degree-granting institution that Leland Stanford envisioned for the university that became the corporate training-ground for Silicon Valley. But education also happens through culture. Cooperative tech will need festivals more inclusive than Burning Man, journalism less gaga for startup bros than *Wired*, and a geography that doesn't concentrate the gains into unaffordable places like Mountain View and Palo Alto. A group of women founders has called for a new culture of "zebra" startups, as opposed to the unicorns that VCs covet. Zebras are real, they say, whereas unicorns are imaginary; zebras run in herds and care for each other, but unicorns always seem to be alone.

We're sorting out that culture as we go. In our platform co-op email and social-media groups, we push each other to be more inclusive, more transparent. With the start of each new platform co-op project comes the discussion of which collaboration tools to use. Loomio is a common place to begin, as it's made by a co-op, and it's good for making early decisions in small groups, but the need for more synchronous chatter blows open the debate about whether to use Slack or one of its open-source copycats, such as Mattermost and Rocket.Chat. Should we track our contributions on a spreadsheet, or should we set up our own crypto-token in Ethereum? How many stakeholder classes can we fathom to include, and how do we balance their relative power? Do we incorporate as a co-op now, or run the thing informally through someone's PayPal account for a while? The passion for process among these cooperators, many of whom never meet in person, can turn fatal. I've seen it doom promising projects. But some get far enough to see the process start to work.

Such agonies may soon subside. Tools are beginning to appear that fit platform co-ops' particular needs. Drutopia is a web-hosting co-op for building websites with the open-source Drupal codebase. A company friendly to the movement, Open Collective, lets co-ops get started without the trouble of formal incorporation. It displays members' contributions and shared expenses so openly that the public front end is the same as the administrators' back end. Starting up is getting easier. And platform co-ops need not be breathlessly radical at every turn; even if they mostly work the way other tech companies do, if their ownership and accountability point to participants more than to capital, that's radical in itself.

Platform cooperativism's early advocates have tended to be partisans of the free, open-source software movement. Some platform founders have held to free-software licenses as an article of faith, but others have opted for the user-friendliness of more proprietary platforms for the sake of their user-members. Still others have found options in between. In his 2010 *Telekommunist Manifesto*, for instance, Dmytri Kleiner outlined a proposal for a Peer Production License, which altered the Creative Commons Attribution-NonCommercial-ShareAlike license by adding a clause that permits commercial use by worker-owned enterprises that distribute surpluses solely to the value-producers.

Say Linux were licensed this way; Google couldn't use it for free anymore, but a worker-owned company developing mobile devices could. Lost is the mainstreaming effect of corporate adoption, but the value conjured by peer-producers would be not so easily grabbed away. Such licenses could help keep the lords' hands out of the commons. Startups wanting to use the code would have an incentive to go co-op. A few projects, such as the interpreters' co-op Guerrilla Translation and CoopCycle, a platform for bike courier co-ops, have adopted this license as a general policy, though it remains largely untested in practice.[24]

Code-sharing, meanwhile, has already begun to take hold as a growth strategy for co-ops. When people in the United Kingdom expressed interest in opening the Fairmondo marketplace for their country, the German company didn't simply expand across borders to achieve scale as an end in itself, like an investor-owned corporation would; instead the Germans and the British are building two separate co-ops that both use and contribute to the same open-source codebase. As more local Fairmondos form, the more collaborators they'll have for improving the software, scaling their product by replication rather than just conglomeration. In such ways, platform cooperativism could add a fairer, more explicit economic layer to open-source culture. It's an antidote to being dependent, even parasitic, on an investor-oriented economy. It's also a way to freshen the old cooperative tradition with the verve of open-source.[25]

There are no fixed rules to this. We're learning. But our slow computing can't go too slowly, because the disruptions keep coming, and the stakes for those being disrupted are too high. We need all the allies we can get.

For years now, well-meaning politicians have found themselves in the position of trying to say no to the onrush of digital disruptions, in various and generally futile ways, as they attempt to retain appropriate say over transportation systems and labor relations, and to keep local wealth under local control. Now policymakers can say yes to platform cooperativism.

New York City council member Maria del Carmen Arroyo had already helped secure funding for worker co-ops when she agreed to take part in the 2015 platform co-op conference. In a statement beforehand, she wrote that platform cooperativism "can put the public in greater control of the internet, which can often feel like an abyss we are powerless over." Another city council member, Brad Lander, showed up at the last minute to share his plans for open data. Municipal and national politicians have come to Scholz and me, among others, in search of policies to consider and evidence they will work. The city of Barcelona has taken steps to enshrine platform cooperativism into its economic strategies. After Austin, Texas, required Uber and Lyft drivers to perform standard safety screenings, the companies pulled their services from the city in May 2015, and the city council aided in the formation of a new co-op taxi company and a nonprofit ride-sharing app; the replacements worked so well that Uber and Lyft paid millions of dollars in lobbying to force their way back before Austin became an example. Meanwhile, UK Labour Party leader Jeremy Corbyn issued a "Digital Democracy Manifesto" that included "platform cooperatives" among its eight planks.[26]

The challenge of such digital democracy goes beyond local tweaks. So must co-ops. When a platform serves the role of organizing and enabling the transactions throughout an entire sector of the economy, it should be regarded as a public service. Just as the monopolies of connective railroads inspired the US antitrust laws of a century ago, a recognition is growing that we need new laws and new will for enforcement to regulate the emerging online utilities.[27] Enabling transitions to more democratic ownership designs may be a way to help these companies better self-regulate, rather than inviting more stifling regulatory regimes.

It's also necessary to look beyond the virtual platforms to their material substrates. This means considering the human conditions surrounding the mineral extraction and assembly of the hardware on which platforms depend. Notably, Britain's Phone Co-op promotes the Fairphone, a Dutch smartphone built with decent working conditions and conflict-free minerals, and the Indonesian co-op KDIM is building its own locally produced smartphone. In the United States, where the large internet-service providers are among the country's most hated companies, cooperative and city-owned ISPs have already shown that there's a faster, cheaper, accountable alternative. Some neighbors built their own internet co-op in the mountains west of me, where the big companies wouldn't invest, and to the east the city of Longmont offers service that blows away my corporate connection speeds. These options are so good that in many states, industry lobbyists have preemptively banned them.[28]

A democratic internet will require more than clever startups and impressive founders. It needs not just platforms but infrastructure. And it needs not just a future but a history.

On November 7, 1918, newspapers across the United States put out extra editions announcing that the Great War was over. Germany had finally backed down. Trading stopped at the New York Stock Exchange; church bells rang. The only trouble: it was four days early.

This feat of unity in falsehood was the doing of the E. W. Scripps Company's United Press wire service, which the offending papers relied on for news they couldn't gather on their own. Along with William Randolph Hearst's International News Service, it was a challenger to the older, more exclusive wire service,

Associated Press. The urge to compete lured UP and INS to sensational, even truth-bending habits.

Newspaper-editor-turned-historian Victor Rosewater, writing in 1930, deemed this a systemic problem. He charged the two upstart wire services with preferring salacious headlines to dispassionate reportage, which the Associated Press excelled in providing. "No obstructive neutral policy stood in the way," he observed. And thus the 1918 incident: "Overzeal gave the United Press the unrelished role of sponsoring and disseminating that greatest of false news items, the spurious premature report of World War truce."[29]

The difference between the upstarts and AP was not merely in their age or their relationships with the New York news establishment. They had different ownership structures. Whereas UP and INS were the creations of towering newspaper magnates, AP was a cooperative—jointly owned (to various degrees, depending on the era) by the newspapers it served. And even today, in the freshly polarized, sensationalized media environment the internet has nourished, AP has continued to excel in what it does best: boring, reliable, factual news.

AP's origins lie in unrecorded conspiracies among New York City newspapermen between 1846 and 1848. Their papers were fierce competitors, but they were stuck. If they all used the new telegraph lines separately, there wouldn't be enough lines. So the competitors had no choice but to cooperate—to import news from Europe via undersea cables, to co-sponsor horse-borne dispatches from the Mexican front, to circulate one another's reporting. The New York papers shared ownership and control of the enterprise, and they sold their dispatches to other organizations beyond the docks of the Hudson.[30]

The temptations to hoard this news-gathering resource were immense, and their defeat came only gradually, over the course of a century. Early on, Upton Sinclair called AP "the most powerful and most sinister monopoly in America." After a scandal resulted in its relocation to Chicago in 1897, the Illinois Supreme Court ruled against AP's restrictions on membership as anti-competitive, and in 1900, the company came back to New York, which had more permissive laws for cooperative associations. But it would take a wartime Justice Department investigation, and a 1945 Supreme Court ruling, to turn AP from an exclusive guild into a true, open-membership co-op. (Its British sister, the Press Association, had operated under this stipulation all along.)

Despite its rocky history and plentiful shortcomings, AP has been an irreplaceable fixture of the US media system. More than half of the world's population sees its reports every day, the company says. And it owes its uniqueness and stature in no small part to its cooperative advantages.

AP allows its members to reduce the cost of reportage, giving them access to reports from more than 250 teams around the world. The wide range of political outlooks that its members hold ensure something as close to neutrality as journalism can hope for; it's an overlapping consensus that inclines toward facts. The company's business model depends not on virality and click-bait, unlike most customer-facing publications, but on trustworthiness. It does what many news organizations claim to do but can't quite accomplish—insulating news-gathering from news-selling.

We have new media fixtures now. When I was starting out as a reporter, tweets were my AP. They were how I got the latest news from places where I couldn't afford to travel, raw and apparently immediate. I fell for Twitter first during Cairo's Tahrir Square uprising in 2011, before the likes of Anderson Cooper got there. Like AP, too, it has become the means by which media outlets today speak with each other and share news. Twitter CEO Jack Dorsey has called it the "people's news network"—but it's not.[31] It's a creature of Wall Street, a commodity for the highest bidder.

This became especially clear in the fall of 2016, when headlines announced that Twitter might be up for sale. Prospective buyers as various as Verizon, Google, Salesforce, Microsoft, and Disney circled overhead. By the measure of Wall Street, the company wasn't doing well. The user-base wasn't growing quickly enough. The $14 billion-or-so valuation wasn't enough to satisfy investors' monopolistic expectations, especially not those who'd bought in when the valuation was closer to $40 billion.

Tell that to the users, though. From Black Lives Matter activists to Donald Trump, Twitter has become a vital public square, truly a network of its people (and its many bots). It's also a network of networks; TV news anchors show their Twitter handles next to their names on-screen. The company has even been on-and-off profitable—pretty good by internet standards. So, in an article for the *Guardian*, I proposed an option that wasn't being talked about: What if Twitter were sold to the users who rely on it?[32] The article conjured the image of the Green Bay Packers, a top football team that has stayed in a smallish city, kept ads in its stadium to a minimum, and maintained moderate ticket prices—thanks to its nonprofit, fan-owned structure, dating to the 1920s. While a Packers game was on in a Northwoods Wisconsin bar, I once asked a woman there why she liked the team; once she got over the idiocy of my question, she talked about her various family members who were co-owners.

Usually when I publish such off-kilter suggestions as the *Guardian* article, little comes of it. Not so this time. Twitter users responded by fantasizing about what they would do if they were to #BuyTwitter—step up the spam and abuse policies, re-open the API data, charge reasonable fees for use. Albert Wenger, a partner at Union Square Ventures, tweeted, "I would contribute to this idea by @ntnsndr in a heartbeat." (USV was an early Twitter investor.) Hundreds of people joined Loomio and Slack groups to discuss the idea; many had already been involved in platform co-op networks. They shared online petitions that attracted thousands more. Soon #BuyTwitter was being discussed in *Wired*, *Der Spiegel*, the *Financial Times*, *Vanity Fair*, and dozens of other outlets. Participants' strategies diverged; some wanted to focus on starting co-op competitors for Twitter and others wanted to take on Twitter directly. Both proceeded. An investment club formed to take on the former challenge, and those interested in the latter began looking, among the petition signers, for holders of TWTR stock.

That December, together with willing shareholders, several of us drafted a proposal for the next Twitter annual meeting. It was modest; it merely asked that the company commission "a report on the nature and feasibility of selling the platform to its users via a cooperative or similar structure with broad-based ownership and accountability mechanisms"—a report, that's all. We tried to make the case that the company and its shareholders would be best served by such a transition. We referred to AP. We did so as a way of insisting that this kind of buyout wouldn't be an act of giving up or cutting losses. A people's network can be more fully itself if it's owned like one.

Twitter's lawyers filed an objection, trying to get the proposal barred, alleging vagueness and purposeful misleading. On March 10, 2017, the Securities and Exchange Commission dismissed the claim. When Twitter's official proxy statement came out in advance of the May 22 shareholder meeting, it included our proposal—together with a letter of opposition from the company.[33]

A young Bay Area co-op veteran with a campaign-strategy consultancy, Danny Spitzberg, stepped up to lead the effort, coordinating volunteers to build websites and friendly organizations to persuade shareholders, all along plastering Twitter with chick-in-a-half-shell emojis. He took on the trolls. Lots of us considered the campaign more stunt than serious, but Spitzberg was serious, and his seriousness rubbed off. Major co-op organizations stepped in to vouch for the idea, including the International Co-operative Alliance, the National Cooperative Business Association, and Co-operatives UK. The way this kind of corporate ballot is stacked with proxy votes and institutional investors, winning a full majority hardly seemed feasible; influential shareholders feared that even commissioning a study would spook the markets. We aimed to reach even just 3 percent—itself, not an easy reach—which would be enough to resubmit a proposal in the future.

The day of the shareholder meeting at the Twitter headquarters in San Francisco, Spitzberg was there, along with our main shareholder activist, Jim McRitchie. McRitchie, a straight-talking corporate governance expert, read the proposal through his gray goatee, which inspired a subsequent sheriff meme. Jack Dorsey and other senior executives were there in the room listening. We won nearly 5 percent of the vote.

That day another subgroup of #BuyTwitter, instigated by Vermont cooperator Matthew Cropp, announced the existence of Social.coop. It hosted a server for Mastodon, a new open-source, "fediverse" alternative to Twitter. Social.coop, as the domain suggested, was a cooperative managed by its users. Rather than being controlled by any one company, a federated social network like Mastodon is made up of interconnected nodes; users choose which node to trust with their data, and through the network they can interact with users on other nodes without everyone consigning everything they post to a central hub. Like sending email from gmail.com to someone at yahoo.com, users can communicate with the full network regardless of their host. The technology for doing this has been around for a while. I'd used one example of it, GNU Social, through my May First membership. But these hadn't taken off. Companies looking to profit from surveillance and monopoly don't see enough value in a technology made for privacy and distributed ownership. Social.coop was our small attempt to change that. Social.coop members were soon making decisions on Loomio and managing money on Open Collective. The fledgling platform co-op ecosystem made this small, simple startup easy. Backed by cooperation, the federated technology now had an economy to make it work.

One night in New York City, at the late-2016 platform co-op conference, one of the speakers introduced me to his friend, a man with a warm smile and long, blond hair parted in the middle. He explained this was Blaine Cook, Twitter's first engineer; the reply functionality, and the word "tweet"—that was him. He'd heard about #BuyTwitter, and he loved the idea. He said, actually, that early on he'd written code to make Twitter an open, federated network. But his prototype didn't stick.

"I suspect it was avoided out of a generalized fear of the unknown," Cook told me, "a concern about how it might make the business model even more complex and difficult, at a time when *any* business model was still imaginary." The company clung to a more familiar strategy in tech, which was what most investors expected: a well-fenced enclosure and the chance of seizing an entire new market.

One fan of the federation idea, at least, was Fred Wilson, an-other partner at Union Square Ventures—a longtime VC who has since written that, more than people tend to realize, "business model innovation is more disruptive than technological innova-tion."[34] And in this case he was right. The technology wasn't what kept Twitter from being the open utility it could have been from the start; the trouble was the business model. Federation seemed at odds with the usual habits of investor ownership. Cooperatives, on the other hand, have been federating for ages. It's in their na-ture. A spree of modest-sized, trustworthy co-op nodes, sharing open-source code, could build another kind of social network. It wouldn't be just a co-op version of the same thing. It could work with forms of connection and value that investor-owned compa-nies won't allow themselves to notice.

There is a hidden internet, a kind of dark web, that lurks among stray tools, habits, and unmet needs that could be mar-shaled into economies of cooperation. There is no special browser plug-in that allows us to see it, but ingesting the patterns of co-op history can help. Those of us who have come to be involved be-lieve, or at least hope, that a more cooperative internet would be a better one—fairer, more just, more free. We can't know what would happen there, but we would have more of a say in making it. Our internet would be more fully ours to lurk and troll, to con-tribute and debug, to explore and share.

6

Free the Land

Power

Candidate Donald Trump made a campaign stop in February 2016 hosted by South Carolina's Broad River Electric Cooperative. After taking the auditorium stage, observing that "it's a lot of people" and joining the audience in a chant of his surname, Trump began by asking, "Do we love electricity, by the way, all you electricity people?" He went on, "How about life without electricity? Not so good, right, not so good." Then he changed the subject.[1]

His remarks suggest that Trump had just been briefed on the US electric co-ops' cherished origin story. It goes something like this: By the onset of the Great Depression, as little as 10 percent of people in the rural United States had electricity at home. The companies that had lit up the cities simply didn't see enough profit in serving far-flung farmers. But gradually some of those farmers started forming electric cooperatives—utility companies owned and governed by their rate-payers—and strung up their own lines. Many bought cheap power from dams on federal land. Their ingenuity inspired a New Deal program, which Franklin Roosevelt initiated in 1935 and Congress funded the following year. The Department of Agriculture began dispensing low-interest-rate loans across the country. The farmers used them to organize co-ops, even as corporate competitors tried to undermine them, building stray "spite lines" through their prospective territories. But the cooperators prevailed. Together with the policy nudge from Washington, they brought electricity to most of the unserved areas within a decade. They switched on the lights.

Cooperators tend not to like counting on politics from on high. They like their co-ops to be really theirs to build and shape. Co-ops are autonomous, the International Cooperative Alliance insists. Governments have tried to control them in various times and places, such as in the Soviet bloc and Peronist Argentina; it rarely does much good. Yet, like any other kind of business, co-ops depend on the laws and benefits that governments do or don't set out. They have to confront the political perks that investor-owned competitors are already getting. To level the field, they have to enter the same untidy business.

The right and capacity to cooperate have come through amassing political power—as have the contradictions that come with holding it. That's certainly the story of rural electric power in the United States.

People who are used to paying their utility bills in cities tend not to know that 75 percent of the US landmass gets its electricity from cooperatives. That adds up to about 42 million member-owners, 11 percent of the total electricity sold, and $164 billion in assets, amounting to a vehicle for wealth creation in 93 percent of persistent-poverty counties in the country.[2] Local co-ops band together in larger co-ops of co-ops—power suppliers that run power plants, shared mining operations, co-op banks, and co-owned tech firms. Population growth and sprawl have brought wealthy suburbs to many of their once-rural territories. It's a scale of cooperative enterprise unheard-of for those who associate *co-op* with grocery stores or apartment buildings. It's also a neglected democracy—neglected by member-owners of the co-ops, who often don't know that they're anything more than customers, and by a society that forgets how much the combination of government power and cooperative enterprise once enabled it to achieve. We neglect what we might achieve next.

Republican Presidents Eisenhower and Nixon regarded electric cooperatives as creeping communism, whereas Democratic presidents tended to benefit from the sector's support in elections; Lyndon Johnson helped set up the co-op that served his ranch, and Jimmy Carter's father had been on the board of theirs. But the progressive base retreated to urban centers, and Bill Clinton singled out the co-ops for cuts. More recently, between 2010 and 2016, the political giving of the National Rural Electric Cooperative Association, or NRECA, flipped from 50-50 between the parties to 72 percent Republican. Vice President Mike Pence has had long-standing ties with Indiana electric co-ops. And the co-ops, this remnant of rural progressivism, helped deliver the Electoral College and Congress to him and President Trump.[3]

Among those celebrating after the 2016 election was Jim Matheson, a former Democratic congressman from Utah who had come to serve as CEO of the NRECA. "Rural America's voice was heard in this election and it will be a powerful voice moving forward," he was quoted in a press release as having said.[4] A spike in rural, right-leaning voter turnout coincided with his organization's Co-ops Vote campaign, which mobilized member-owners in a subset of the country's 838 local electric cooperatives. What's more, the next president would be the candidate who had promised to scrap his predecessor's Clean Power Plan, which the NRECA under Matheson regarded as too onerous for its membership. Subsequent press releases praised Trump's climate-denialist, regulation-smashing cabinet appointees.

The administration's initial "America First" budget draft proposed slashing a batch of rural programs, however, including the Department of Agriculture's Rural Cooperative Development Grants. When the draft came out in March of 2017, Matheson attempted to reassure his members. "This is only the first step in the budget process," he said in a statement. Days later, Matheson had the opportunity to celebrate an executive order meant to doom the Clean Power Plan.[5]

Electric cooperatives have become conservative institutions, carrying out the business of reliability while balancing their members' interests with formidable inertia. But they're also poised to lead a shift to a more renewable, distributed energy grid. They can harbor long-entrenched establishments, but they're also bastions of bottom-up, local self-governance. They tend to be far less regulated by states than investor-owned utilities, on the rationale that their member-owners do their own regulation. This is a chunk of the US energy system that depends not just on the whims of investors, or on the promises of a president, but on the readiness of the people who use it to organize.

Some local co-ops have been bucking the inertia. One of them is Delta-Montrose Electric Association, on the western end of Colorado. Jim Heneghan, DMEA's renewable energy engineer, drove me around DMEA's territory in the fall of 2016. We checked out a company pickup from DMEA's headquarters, a complex that includes one of the cooperative's two ten-kilowatt solar farms. From there, we drove to the hydroelectric plants by which DMEA draws power from the South Canal, a narrow waterway that winds through dusty hills and sagebrush out from the Gunnison Tunnel, which President William Howard Taft inaugurated in 1909.

Jim Heneghan at the controls of a DMEA hydro plant.

Heneghan was project manager for the construction of the first two plants. They opened in 2013 and operate mostly without human intervention, but he tends to them when he can. "I like to start the plant manually," he told me in one of the control rooms. His talk was as precise as the shape of his mustache. A small man of terrific posture, he made his way among the towering, whirring machines like a librarian among shelves of rare books.

The first two plants proved the business model. Soon, other developers wanted to build plants along South Canal and sell the power to the local co-op. By 2015, the model was the subject of a federal regulatory dispute.

Like most electric "distribution" co-ops, DMEA is a member-owner of a larger "generation and transmission" co-op, or G&T. The contract DMEA has with its G&T, Tri-State, specifies that Tri-State must provide at least 95 percent of the energy DMEA sells. This has long been a sensible arrangement; distribution co-ops don't have the resources to run big power plants, and a near-monopoly helps the G&T, and thus its forty-three member co-ops, obtain affordable financing from the government, the cooperative banks, and private markets. Federal policy dating to the 1970s required that much of this investment went into coal plants, which account for 71 percent of all G&T power production, compared to 33 percent for the national grid.[6] But DMEA was finding opportunities to generate more of its power locally—from ever-cheaper solar panels and hydro plants to the methane leaking from the area's retired mines. The member-elected board liked these opportunities, for reasons of cost, conservation, and development.

"Part of the culture here in this area is the desire to keep things local," says Virginia Harman, manager of member relations and human resources. DMEA is also one of the co-ops across the country that has begun bringing fiber-borne, affordable, broadband internet to its underserved rural membership—a development that parallels the circumstances that gave rise to electric co-ops in the first place.

When DMEA hired Jasen Bronec as CEO from a Montana co-op in 2014, he brought with him a new strategy; half a smile sneaks into his all-business demeanor when he talks about it. The co-op filed a request with the Federal Energy Regulatory Commission, inquiring about whether a Carter-era law enabled DMEA to exceed the allowance for local power in the Tri-State contract if a more affordable, renewable option were to appear. In June 2015, FERC ruled that DMEA was in fact required to do so. Tri-State objected, but the ruling held.

Heneghan lives on a farm so out of the way that it's off even the DMEA grid. He produces his own power there. "I'm confident that we won't keep the central generation model," he said as we drove on the narrow dirt roads between plants. "There are so many things that point to a structural change in the electrical industry." He compared the change to what cellular did to telephones. He daydreamed about testing one of the new Tesla Powerwall batteries and reveled in the ongoing convergence of moral, environmental, technological, and economic imperatives—if only we give up the self-imposed constraints to embracing them.

Heneghan believes co-ops are uniquely poised to benefit. Their lean, local, customer-centered kind of business has already made them pioneers in providing new members with easy financing for energy-efficiency improvements and renewables. Like city-owned power companies, they're accountable to a more flexible bottom-line than investor profits. In 2016, about one-fourth of the power delivered to Tri-State's members came from renewables, and the G&T announced the closure of two coal stations that were no longer economical. According to the NRECA, the co-op sector's solar capacity more than doubled over the course of 2017.[7] Co-ops without G&T contracts have been especially ambitious in switching to renewables. DMEA's southern neighbor, Kit Carson Electric Cooperative, ended its Tri-State contract altogether and now aims to meet its entire daytime demand with solar by 2022. Hawaii's Kauai Island Utility Cooperative, formed in a 2002 resident buyout of the island's electric monopoly, is on track to reach 50 percent renewable by 2023. It generates so much solar that it encourages consumers to install storage batteries in their homes.

"We are experiencing a phenomenally exciting technological revolution," says Christopher McLean, who oversees electric programs at the Department of Agriculture's Rural Utilities Service, the federal agency that still provides low-interest loans to co-ops—today, a nearly $4 billion, revenue-positive fund. "Used to be the electric program was kind of like the boring program, but now we get all the exciting stuff."

McLean's enthusiasm obscures the fact that electric co-ops lag behind the national average in their use of renewables. The local co-ops are bound to their decades-long G&T contracts, and the G&Ts can't afford to walk away from their past investments in coal anytime soon. They owe it to their members, the co-ops say. On the record and off, executives talk a lot about their commitment to the seven principles that hang on their boardroom walls, and Heneghan was careful to justify every project in terms of a cost-benefit calculus for members. But this democracy is in some respects nominal—a right on paper, though by no means a guarantee in practice. Other forces govern their behavior, too. After the FERC ruling, for instance, Tri-State and fellow G&Ts started encouraging member co-ops to submit waivers, ensuring their boards won't follow in DMEA's footsteps. Economic constraints that date back decades are still constraining the pace of change.

"There are some cracks in the chains," says John Farrell, who directs the program on energy democracy at the Institute for Local Self-Reliance, a careful observer of electric co-ops. If so, it has been a long time coming. By the late 1970s, the author of a study on electric co-ops, *Lines Across the Land*, described a situation that is precisely the case today: "Rural electric interests have turned their political muscle to undoing environmental laws rather than leading the fight for their compliance." Yet even then it seemed clear that "rural electric cooperatives are in a unique position to pursue a range of localized energy alternatives."[8] Then, as now, the co-ops' future depended on whether members bothered to raise their voices louder than market forces and the old inertia.

As I concluded my visit to DMEA's headquarters, I met a woman on the way out the door who had come to pay her bill. Photos of board members hung on the wall next to us. I asked if she liked being a member of the co-op, and she looked at me like I was speaking the wrong language. I asked the question again but said "customer" instead. She smiled and said she'd been getting power from DMEA for twenty years and loved it—great service, super reliable. She'd grown up in Hawaii with no electricity, so she appreciated being able to turn the lights on when she came home.

———

In the early years of the federal co-op program, the Rural Electrification Administration (now the Rural Utilities Service) produced booklets to explain co-op principles and practice to future member-owners. The bureaucrats also saw the need to explain electricity itself. Throughout, they included artful prints depicting the uses of electrical power ("There are over 200 of them") and enticements to exploit its full potential ("The more you use electricity the cheaper it gets").

Those were years when the US government backed co-ops not just with loan funds but with propaganda. Films depicted the

Pages from the 1939 edition of A Guide for Members of REA Cooperatives.

democratic promise of an interlocking cooperative economy, enjoining citizens to sign up as co-op members; membership would become the next extension of citizenship. In a preface to one of the electric co-op booklets, Secretary of Agriculture Henry A. Wallace wrote, "Do not let anyone tell you that your cooperative will fail. Or that the Government will have to take it over in a short time and will be forced to sell it to the nearest private utility for a song. Such a disaster can happen only if you and your fellow cooperators fall asleep on the job."[9]

———

Five times during the fall of 2016, Della Brown-Davis and her twelve-year-old daughter made the five-hour round-trip drive from their home in Tylertown, Mississippi, to Jackson and back. Their purpose was to learn about electric cooperatives. Brown-Davis was a schoolteacher and therapist, as well as a member-owner of Magnolia Electric Power Association, one of the nine co-ops that fell under a new campaign orchestrated by One Voice, a mobilization affiliate of the state's NAACP.

In the sessions One Voice held in Jackson, Brown-Davis and her daughter became acquainted with the lofty cooperative principles shared by co-ops around the world. They learned how to read the tax forms that the electric co-ops' nonprofit status requires they make public. And they saw evidence that fellow African American co-op members across Mississippi were not getting their due—exorbitant bills, all-white boards in black-majority districts, opaque governance procedures that prevent participation. Brown-Davis noticed a picture of white high-school students representing her co-op on a trip to Washington, DC. On the drives home, she and her daughter would discuss what they learned.

"It's disappointing to find that, in this day and age so many things are occurring the way it did back in the fifties and the sixties," Brown-Davis told me.

In 2014, Benita Wells, One Voice's chief financial officer, helped out on a review of co-ops by the state Public Service Commission. It was her first exposure to the distinct mechanics of cooperative accounting, but she knew enough to notice incongruities. Executives were getting inflated salaries, together with board members who had been on the payroll for decades. Co-ops weren't returning millions of dollars in accumulated equity to members, to the point of risking their privileges as nonprofits. "None of the numbers added up," she says. Making her task harder, co-ops have few disclosure requirements, and they frequently resist sharing financials even with members.

One Voice invited down researchers from MIT and Cornell to better understand the problem. They conducted listening tours, scrutinized utility bills across the state's Black Belt, and used what they learned to help develop the Electric Cooperative Leadership Institute—with Brown-Davis and her daughter in the first cohort, along with other co-op ratepayers ready to organize their neighbors. But the first day, many weren't yet aware of their status as co-owners with voting power over their co-ops' boards.

Mississippi is unusually dense with electric cooperatives. Nearly half of residents get their power from one. And although 37 percent of Mississippians are African American, One Voice found at the outset of its effort that they held only 6.6 percent of co-op board seats. Women held only 4 percent. In the largely poor districts the campaign identified, residents might spend upward of 40 percent or more of their incomes on electricity.

Basic co-op education was the first step of a larger plan. According to Derrick Johnson, president of both the state NAACP and One Voice, "Our ultimate goal is to help them understand how to develop a strategy to maximize member participation." Then, he also hoped, "they can begin to think about renewable energy differently."

There does appear to be some correlation between member participation and energy innovation. Roanoke Electric Cooperative in North Carolina, for instance, underwent a black-led member-organizing campaign in the 1960s; that set a process in motion that is still at work today. Its current CEO, Curtis Wynn, is vice president of the NRECA board and the board's sole African American member. Roanoke has meanwhile become the first co-op in the state to adopt financing for members to make energy-efficiency improvements. It also allows members to buy in on a community solar array and is developing a broadband internet program.

"When the make-up of your management staff or your board of directors isn't fully reflecting the make-up of your communities," Wynn told me, "there could easily be a disconnect between what the constituents want and need, and what decisions the board and the management team will make." Without member pressure, for instance, managers may default to simply trying to sell more power, rather than helping members reduce their consumption, their costs, and their carbon footprints.[10]

The successful organizing at Roanoke was more an exception than the rule. During the 1980s and 1990s, the Southern Regional Council mounted the Co-op Democracy and Development Project, a series of campaigns in co-op districts across the South, including some of the same ones that One Voice has been targeting more recently. The campaigns won only a single Louisiana board seat. It was too easy for incumbent boards to adjust the bylaws and election procedures to protect themselves. In some cases, these co-ops were carrying on habits that went back to their origins in the 1930s and 1940s, when white residents could expect to see power lines earlier than their black neighbors and to pay less for them.[11] But One Voice may fare better than its predecessors. Before the first set of trainings was over, Johnson told me, at least two Mississippi co-ops appointed their first African American directors.

The co-op associations tend to remain aloof to the kind of organizing efforts One Voice has undertaken. A spokesman for the state association, Electric Cooperatives of Mississippi, told me he'd never heard of the campaign. His counterpart at NRECA merely alluded to the organization's general support for fair elections. Nor have concerns about racial justice unsettled the Rural Utilities Service, whose lending comes with a requirement of nondiscrimination. "We have a very low level of complaint to the Office of Civil Rights on issues like this," says Christopher McLean. Even so, the concerns motivating co-op members like Della Brown-Davis are limited to neither Mississippi nor African Americans. They're symptoms of more widespread neglect.

Jim Cooper, a Democratic congressman from the Tennessee district that includes Nashville, was raised by a father who helped start an electric co-op where they lived. When Cooper later visited co-ops as a politician, he'd make a point of browsing their tax forms, and he noticed some of the same things that Benita Wells did. "I'd congratulate them for being so wealthy, and they'd look at me like I was crazy," Cooper told me. This led him into an investigation into what he calls "a massive, nationwide cover-up." He published his findings in a scathing 2008 essay for the *Harvard Journal on Legislation*. In particular, he pointed out the billions of dollars in "capital credits" that co-ops collectively hold—surplus revenues technically owned by members, but which often go unclaimed, serving as a pool of interest-free financing. Policies vary, but some co-ops even prevent members or their families from recouping equity. This can go on for generations. "Local co-ops are primarily owned by dead people," Cooper says.

Cooper's article proposed a series of reforms, including mergers to unlock efficiencies and more mandatory disclosures to members and the public. He suggested that unless co-ops take on a new New Deal of economic development and environmental conservation, they should not be entitled to never-ending federal support. His essay entered the congressional record the year it was published, but the co-op lobby fought back hard, and his proposals didn't get any further than that.[12] "When I talk with my colleagues about this, they shut their eyes and close their ears," he says. "The NRECA pretty much gets what it wants."

The see-no-evil stance of the associations has helped inspire a new wave of agitation, of which One Voice is only part. We Own It, for instance, is a network started by young but seasoned cooperators determined to support organizing among co-op members—rather than the executives and directors who steer the associations. They're connecting activist members at electric co-ops around the country, helping them learn from one another about policies to seek and strategies for winning them. In an online forum, they pass around news about co-op corruption alongside tricks for financing solar power and efficiency improvements. "Our goal is to build a social movement," says founder Jake Schlachter.

A movement will take some doing. According to a study by the Institute for Local Self-Reliance, nearly three-fourths of co-ops see voter turnout of less than 10 percent in board elections.[13] When I attended a board-candidate forum for an electric co-op near where I live, there were more candidates and staff present than anyone else. Only one of the four seats on the ballot was contested. (Hundreds of members nevertheless come to the annual meetings, where the final vote is held, which include door prizes, a hearty dinner, live entertainment, and Tri-State's robot mascot.) By way of explanation, a staff member repeated what I've been told by leaders of other big co-ops: low turnout means members are satisfied.

The movement-makers don't accept that. "The most important lesson I've learned over the years is that the cooperative system is really dependent on member involvement," says Mark Hackett, a We Own It participant who was part of a successful organizing effort after a corruption debacle at his co-op in Georgia, Cobb EMC. "If the members are not involved in any significant way, the directors become very insular, and they can basically do with the co-op as they please."

The conditions of managerial capture are not so arbitrary. The best and worst co-op managers alike carry on their books and in their habits the weight of decades-long contracts, of old loan conditions, of billion-dollar coal plants. There have been astonishing cases of self-dealing by boards and staff. But co-ops can still serve as vehicles of participatory economics at vast scale, just as when farmers suspicious of banks and abandoned by capitalists built utilities for themselves—so well that Washington saw fit to give them almost bank-rate loans. The Colorado Rural Electric Association still holds summer camps where kids learn to organize and run a co-op of their own. These co-ops came from a rare bit of development policy designed to actually, directly empower the intended recipients.

Murray Lincoln, who later led the Cooperative League and Nationwide Mutual Insurance Company, was an early architect of the electric co-op system in Ohio. He recalls in his memoir the nature of the enterprise. "Farmers were just itching to have electricity, and to have it from their own cooperative was a dream come true," he wrote. "We rushed into the business half-blind, not knowing what it was going to cost us, but knowing that it was something that ought to be done and something that we ought to be doing for ourselves."[14] That was the spirit these co-ops were born in, and their vitality depends on it somehow recurring.

————

Congressman Cooper raised another uncomfortable question about the electric co-ops: What if they're not really co-ops? "Part government agency, part agricultural cooperative, and part not-for-profit company," he wrote in the 2008 article, "this curious hybrid was named for the most innocent-sounding of its three components."[15] The first International Cooperative Alliance principle, "voluntary and open membership," doesn't fare well when the co-op has a monopoly over an essential service in its state-designated territory. The electric co-ops like to talk about the "open" part, but "voluntary" is a problem. In a sector dependent on government loans, the principle of autonomy suffers as well.

The US Department of Agriculture uses *cooperative* as a technical term for determining program eligibility, and it has concocted its own set of cooperative principles in which the matter of voluntarism is conveniently absent:

1. *User-Owner Principle*: Those who own and finance the cooperative are those who use the cooperative.
2. *User-Control Principle*: Those who control the cooperative are those who use the cooperative.
3. *User-Benefits Principle*: The cooperative's sole purpose is to provide and distribute benefits to its users on the basis of their use.[16]

It's not a bad list. But when a set of cooperative principles hangs in the office of an electric co-op, it's typically not the concise formulation of the US Department of Agriculture; it's the lovelier International Cooperative Alliance principles, whose very first word these co-ops seem to systematically violate. Scratch any co-op, really, and there are likely to be vices against the principles. There will be compromises with and for power.

––––––––

At the time of Roosevelt's Rural Electrification Act, the national Cooperative League's founder and president, James Peter Warbasse, was ambivalent. Once a member of the anarchist-leaning Industrial Workers of the World, Warbasse professed "constructive radicalism," a version of revolution that required no barricades, no general strikes, no dictatorship of the proletariat. But the transformation he envisioned was no less radical.

"In the cooperative movement," Warbasse contended, "the ultimate tendency is toward the creation of a social structure capable of supplanting both profit-making industry and the compulsory political state."[17] Corporations and governments would recede before the co-op tide, in other words, withering away until they finally disappear. Corporate profits wouldn't be able to withstand the onrush of cooperative savings, and government coercion would crumble in the face of cooperative free association. Gone with them would be courts and jails, replaced by co-op arbitration committees. The cooperatives' endemic educational activities would replace state schools. Rather than being citizens of a single government, people would hold membership in some overlapping combination of co-ops; certain functions of a federal government would become the purview of the federations and associations—organizations like the one Warbasse founded.

His belief that co-ops' self-reproducing acid would dissolve the state—along with investor-owned corporations—has not weathered evidence well. The insurance industry that began with cooperative-like mutuals tended to reorganize, by the second half of the twentieth century, under government control in Europe and corporate control in the United States. From Benjamin Franklin's cooperative fire station and library came additional expectations of government; from grocery co-ops came Whole Foods Market. Socialist regimes, from Yugoslavia to Venezuela, have used state-controlled co-ops as a vehicle of economic policy. In a manner only somewhat more subtle, US electric co-ops have held on to their cooperation partly thanks to a privileged relationship with the Department of Agriculture.

This relationship was the result of a deliberate political strategy, combined with institutional inventiveness. And as political deadlocks and private shortsightedness stymie necessary infrastructure, we might turn to this strategy again. We might, as Warbasse hoped, govern through cooperation. In the 1930s, farmers who needed electricity bypassed corporate providers to do it for themselves; today, the health-care impasse might require similar treatment.

When Aleta Kazadi took to the streets of Denver to collect petition signatures throughout the summer of 2015, the most common response she got was, "I'm okay." This normally meaningless idiom seemed more telling than usual under the circumstances. She was, after all, asking people whether they'd like to support a state ballot initiative for universal health care. Maybe they were okay, but what about the more than three hundred thousand Coloradans without medical coverage?

"The concept that we are our brother's keeper obviously never entered their minds," Kazadi told me. "If we don't see our neighbor in need, what kind of society are we living in?" She was okay herself, as a retired teacher with insurance for life. But a decade living in the Democratic Republic of the Congo taught the Illinois native and grandmother something about neighbors in need. She remembered her whole village waking up to the wailing of families who had lost a child to malaria.

Kazadi figured that she could claim at least seven hundred signatures of the 158,831 collected by more than five hundred fellow volunteers, along with paid help, between April and October that year. Bernie Sanders rallies at the beginning and end of the process provided especially sympathetic crowds, as did Pride and Juneteenth. The campaign needed 98,492 signatures to get the issue on the ballot; the secretary of state's office deemed 109,134 valid in the end. Thanks to people like Kazadi, medical coverage for all was a choice before Colorado voters in November

2016. And it would take the form of a cooperative—one with an ambiguous relationship to government.

ColoradoCare would opt the state out of the Affordable Care Act and provide comprehensive coverage for every resident. This would be paid for by a 3.33 percent income tax and a 6.67 percent payroll tax for employers—or up to 10 percent for the self-employed. These were steep hikes, but for most Coloradans it would mean paying less than they previously paid for insurance premiums. (Penalizing contract workers, however, was no way to win friends among the state's many young and entrepreneurial newcomers.) Supporters believed the system would cost a total of $6 billion less than the status quo in a given year.

ColoradoCare's original name was the Colorado Health Care Cooperative, until co-op people complained that membership wouldn't be voluntary, because Coloradans couldn't opt out of the tax. But the quasi-cooperative design was a necessary trick. It was an attempt to bypass a constitutional provision that prevents the state legislature from levying new taxes. The legislature wouldn't be able to touch ColoradoCare's revenues; they would

Colorado state senator Irene Aguilar, a physician and the architect of ColoradoCare.

go straight to a fund overseen by trustees whom residents would elect directly. It was a half-socialist, half-libertarian experiment in co-ownership and co-governance on the scale of more than five million people.

ColoradoCare was the design of state senator Irene Aguilar, a family doctor who entered politics several years earlier to fix a system that she'd watched harm her underinsured patients for decades. She made a few earnest attempts to pass health care reform in the state capitol, but to no avail. Eventually, Aguilar and a core band of allies—disproportionately psychologists, as it happens—decided to go for a ballot initiative, putting tens of thousands of their own dollars into the effort.

Using this same referendum process in 2012, Colorado voters made their state, along with Washington, the first to legalize recreational marijuana. Other states followed. ColoradoCare's backers hoped to set off a similar chain reaction in health care. Bernie Sanders said the state could "lead the nation" if it passed ColoradoCare, and he stumped for the proposal before the final vote.[18]

It would be hard to cast a better antagonist for this undertaking than Jonathan Lockwood—executive director of Advancing Colorado, an outfit formed in 2014 to serve, says Lockwood, "as a voice for free-market believers and advocates." He was a slick dresser and a fast talker, slight in build and vociferous with opinions. A veteran of the Koch brothers' millennial-outreach operation, Generation Opportunity, he also looked young enough that, he told me, people sometimes wouldn't believe that he was his own boss. On the morning of October 23, Lockwood counted among the handful of those who came to witness the delivery of petitions to the back entrance of the Colorado secretary of state's office. He stuck close to a young woman from America Rising PAC—"a new generation of Republican research and rapid response"—who was recording the proceedings with a camcorder.

The petitions arrived, for effect, on a gurney in a rented ambulance. (The driver confessed to me, "I've done crazier things before for enough money.") Aguilar, in her white lab coat, helped guide the gurney toward a service entrance. Afterward, she and several dozen supporters gathered at the Greek Theater, an outdoor colonnade in Denver's political district, for a press conference. Discerning that I was one of the few reporters present, Lockwood introduced himself and suggested that I interview him. I knew him by reputation already; together with the Kochs' Americans for Prosperity, Advancing Colorado was so far one of the few public opponents that had bothered to confront ColoradoCare head on.

Lockwood made several attempts to convince me of ColoradoCare's follies, each based on an inaccurate claim about the contents of the proposal. But there was an especially radical, factual feature of it that he didn't bring up, one which I never saw discussed during the campaign: ColoradoCare would cast a model for politics detached from the budget and decision-making for the rest of the state. Many jurisdictions already have issue-specific elections for school boards and other seats, but this would go further. Beyond medical coverage, ColoradoCare could lead a shift of other ill-managed services from government or corporations to cooperative mechanisms.

The campaigners tried to appeal to the state's go-it-alone political culture. "This is not government health care," Aguilar said from the steps of the Greek Theater. "I've been in government, and we can't get health care done."

ColoradoCare followed in the footsteps of Michael Shadid, an immigrant from what is now Lebanon. Starting in 1929, he formed the first patient-owned cooperative hospital in Elk City, Oklahoma, an arrangement that the doctors of the American Medical Association set out to suppress as a threat to their guild's authority, rendering the model illegal in states across the country. Something similar happened to the more recent CO-OPs, or "consumer operated and oriented plans," that the Affordable Care Act enabled, which soon suffered crippling restrictions and a two-thirds cut in their promised loan budget from Congress while still in their startup phase.[19] ColoradoCare threatened even more constituencies, and they stopped it before it began. Opposed by prominent Democrats and Republicans alike, and with a daunting reference to the tax hike at the start of the ballot text, the proposal won just over 20 percent of the vote.

During the campaign, Aguilar liked to recite the Margaret Mead line about "a small group of thoughtful, committed citizens" changing the world. But not this time. The state missed a chance for universal coverage; the cooperative commonwealth missed a chance to spread again, and to meet an essential need for millions of people with a political coup.

————

In fits of sense at various times and places, politicians have adopted policies that support the development of cooperative enterprise. They have seen value, for instance, in the capacity of co-ops to keep profits recirculating in their communities—which is to say, their tax base—and to compensate for the failures of markets to meet the needs of vulnerable constituents. These policies have included, for instance:

- *Financing aids*, such as low-interest loans, loan guarantees, and tax exemptions, enabling co-ops to compete with the low costs of capital for investor-owned firms

- *Development assistance*, by funding organizations that offer advice and advocacy for the local cooperative economy

- *Mandates*, requiring sensitive sectors of the economy to operate through cooperative models, or requiring that government purchasing agents give preference to co-ops

- *Enablers*, including appropriate incorporation statutes and incentives for co-ops to cooperate with each other[20]

Italy has some of the world's most developed co-op laws. The national constitution itself has a provision, Article 45, that enshrines free, cooperative enterprise as a right—much needed in the wake of Benito Mussolini, who regarded independent co-ops as a threat to his regime. He dissolved both the socialist and Catholic federations, attempting to replace them with a federation of his own, but after his demise they promptly reorganized

and gained the political might to write their own rules. Cooperators from around the world now come to Italy to study these
arrangements.

A law dating to the early 1970s, for instance, lets co-ops hold
tax-free "indivisible reserves," making it easier to raise capital
from members. The following decade, co-ops gained the ability
to own and manage noncooperative subsidiary firms. A 1991 law
created a corporate container and tax benefits for social cooperatives, which serve as an extension of the public welfare system.
A law passed the following year requires co-ops to contribute
3 percent of their surpluses—profits, in capitalist-speak—to
their federations, for the sake of financing new co-ops and the
growth of existing ones.[21] The result has been an ever more self-
perpetuating sector, a network of cooperating co-ops that aid each
other's flourishing.

Until recently, the United States has mostly forgone co-op
policymaking and has relied on the remnants of pre–World War II
laws. But that is changing, especially among cities looking to spur
worker-owned business, led by entrepreneurs who have learned
firsthand how fully the economy is organized in favor of investor
ownership. The law can be a mighty lever. Policies like these have
been borrowed and adapted, forgotten, and then revived. But
there is no single formula.

Policies don't stand in isolation from the habits and history
that precede them, that inform what they might mean for those
carrying them out. Policies are politics. And for those who need
equitable policies most, politics means struggle.

———

On February 21, 2014, forty-nine years to the day after Malcolm
X's earthly form fell to assassins' bullets in Harlem, Chokwe Lumumba, the mayor of Jackson, Mississippi, came home to find the
power out. The outage affected only his house, not any others on
the block. He phoned friends for help, including an electrician,
an electrical engineer, and his longtime bodyguard—each in some
way associated with his administration. They couldn't figure out

the problem at first. They called the power company, and waited, and as they did they talked about the strange notions that had been circulating. At the grand opening of Jackson's first Whole Foods a few weeks earlier, for instance, a white woman said she'd been told at her neighborhood-association meeting that the mayor was dead. He'd been coughing more than he should have, and his blood pressure was running high, but he was very much alive. That day at the grocery store, he made a speech.

Lumumba's friends found it hard not to be on edge. He had come to office in a Southern capital on a platform of black power and human rights. He built a nationwide network of supporters and a local political base after decades as one of the most outspoken lawyers in the black nationalist movement. At the time, Black Lives Matter was still nascent, more a hashtag than an on-the-ground movement. DeRay Mckesson was still working for the Minneapolis Public Schools between sending off tweets. But those paying attention were coming to see Jackson as a model, the capital of a new African American politics and economics, a form of resistance more durable than protest.

Earlier that February, Lumumba gave a video interview to progressive journalist Laura Flanders. Flanders pressed him on his goals on camera, and the mayor was more forthcoming than he'd been since taking office the previous July.[22] He discussed the principle of cooperative economics in Kwanzaa, *ujamaa*, which guided his plans for upending how the city awarded its lucrative infrastructure contracts; he wanted to redirect that money from outside firms toward creating local worker-owned co-ops. He also spoke about something called the Kush District, starting with eighteen contiguous counties with large black populations, which he and his closest allies wanted to establish as a safe homeland for African American self-determination. Jackson was to be its capital. Implied in this kind of talk was a very tangible transfer of power from the white suburbs to the region's black majority.

Four days after the outage at Lumumba's home, he phoned his thirty-year-old son, Chokwe Antar Lumumba. He felt tightness in his chest. Chokwe Antar, an attorney like his father, was in court, but he rushed over to the house, eased his father into the car, and drove him over Jackson's cracked and cratered roads to St. Dominic Hospital. There were tests, and then they waited. Nurses brought Lumumba into a room for a transfusion around four o'clock that afternoon. They weighed him. After they finished, he leaned back on the bed, cried out about his heart, shook, trembled, and lost consciousness. Less than eight months after he had taken office, Lumumba was dead.

As word of what had happened began to spread through city hall, Kali Akuno made calls. Akuno had been one of the mayor's top deputies. He set in motion the local and national security protocol of the Malcolm X Grassroots Movement, the organization to which he, Lumumba, and many of the others in the administration belonged. He saw clerks rummaging through the mayor's office, and downstairs, the city council was already jockeying to fill the power vacuum. The administration, together with Akuno's job, was already all but over.

That evening, Akuno himself started feeling something strange in his chest. He'd been having heart problems, too, a clotting issue. He checked himself into St. Dominic at about ten o'clock and was taken near where the mayor's body lay. As Akuno waited to be seen for whatever was happening to him, he heard voices down the hall.

"I'm glad he's dead," Akuno remembers hearing. "I don't know what the hell he thought he was doing. He was trying to turn this place into Cuba."

There is a way of doing things in Mississippi, and Lumumba had his own way. There are lines you don't cross, and he had crossed some. One county supervisor wondered aloud on TV what a lot of black people in Jackson were thinking: "Who killed the mayor?"

Louis Farrakhan helped pay for an autopsy by Michael Baden, who had also examined the exhumed remains of Jackson's most famous civil-rights martyr, Medgar Evers, and who performed an autopsy on Ferguson martyr Michael Brown. Baden judged the cause of death to be an aortic aneurysm, likely enough a consequence of the mayor's tendencies for overwork and undernourishment. He had been trying harder than was healthy to make the most of the opportunity, to do as much as he could with the time he had left.

As Akuno, off camera, watched Lumumba give his interview with Flanders that February, he felt that his boss was finally ready to stop playing nice with the establishment, as he had been so far. The honeymoon was over; the gloves were coming off.

"Mayors typically don't do the things we're trying to do," Lumumba said. "On the other hand, revolutionaries don't typically find themselves as mayor."

At the center of Jackson's civic district, Mississippi's former capitol building looms over Capitol Street, which has been subject to a variably successful renovation effort seeking to replicate the urban revival sweeping hollowed-out cities across the country. Intersecting Capitol Street to the north, the segregation-era black business district, Farish Street stands nearly empty. Historical signs are more plentiful than pedestrians. The Old Capitol Museum presents slavery and Indian removal—the city was named after President Andrew Jackson, in gratitude for his role in the latter—as quandaries to be pondered rather than obvious moral disasters. After all, these were law; there were treaties and contracts. The same could also be said of the predatory mortgages that, in the Great Recession, wiped away what gains civil rights had brought to African American wealth, especially in places like Jackson.

Capitol Street changes abruptly after crossing the railroad tracks on the west end of downtown as it heads toward the city zoo. Lots are empty and overgrown, right in the shadow of the refurbished King Edward Hotel. Poverty lurks; opportunity for renewal beckons. And right there, at the gateway of this boarded-up frontier, is a one-story former day-care building painted red, green, and black: the Chokwe Lumumba Center for Economic Democracy and Development. Standing guard against the gentrification en route, this became the most visible remnant of the late mayor's four-decade legacy in the city.

Lumumba first arrived in Mississippi when he was twenty-three years old, in 1971. He had been born Edwin Finley Taliaferro in Detroit, but like many who entered black nationalist movements in the 1960s, he relinquished his European names and took African ones—each, in his case, with connotations of anticolonial resistance. While at Kalamazoo College, in southwest Michigan, he joined an organization called the Republic of New Afrika, or RNA. Its purpose was not to achieve mere integration or voting rights, but to establish a new nation in the heartland of US slavery, one where black people could rule themselves, mounting their own secession from both Northern and Southern styles of racism. This quest was, to its adherents, a natural extension of the independence movements then spreading across Africa.

The authorities in Jackson did not prove welcoming. That August, police officers and FBI agents, armed with heavy weapons and a small tank, raided a house RNA members were living in; the resulting confrontation left an officer dead. Lumumba wasn't there that day, but the fallout kept him in Jackson a few years longer. A 1973 RNA document in the archives of the Mississippi Sovereignty Commission—the state's segregationist Gestapo—records him as the RNA's minister of justice. The document calls for reparations, in cooperative form: "We are urging Congress to provide 200 million dollars to blacks in Mississippi for a pilot co-op project to make New Communities, jobs, training, fine free housing, and adequate food and health for thousands."[23]

Lumumba soon returned to Detroit, where he graduated from law school at Wayne State University in 1975. Malcolm X wished he could become a lawyer; Lumumba's aspiration, he'd later tell his son, was to be the kind of lawyer Malcolm would have been. He defended Black Panthers and prison rioters. He unsuccessfully argued that Mutulu Shakur—who was facing charges of bank robbery, murder, and aiding the jailbreak of Assata Shakur—deserved the protections of the 1949 Geneva Convention as a captured freedom fighter. (He would later also defend Mutulu's stepson, the rapper Tupac Shakur.) He became renowned to some and notorious to others. A federal court in New York held him in contempt for referring to the judge as "a racist dog."[24] Then, in 1988, he persuaded his wife, Nubia, a flight attendant, to move with their two children back to Mississippi. He wanted to continue what he and the RNA had started years before.

The change that came over Jackson after the early 1970s was a cataclysmic but also entirely familiar story of American urban life. ("As far as I am concerned, Mississippi is anywhere south of the Canadian border," Malcolm X once said.) The end of segregation inclined most of the city's white residents to flee for the suburbs, while maintaining their hold on political power and the economic benefits of city contracts. They regarded the city's subsequent decline as a case in point. To Hollis Watkins, a local civil rights hero, the story of the city's transformation after white flight was simple: "intentional sabotage."

Lumumba helped found the New Afrikan People's Organization in 1984, and the Malcolm X Grassroots Movement formed as an offshoot by 1990. MXGM, whose first chapter was in Jackson, set out to bring black nationalism to a new generation of activists. Adults organized and strategized; kids joined the New Afrikan Scouts and attended their own summer camp.

Safiya Omari, Lumumba's future chief of staff, came to Jackson in 1989. At rallies, they chanted the old RNA slogan, "Free the land!"—three times, in quick triplets with call-and-response—followed by, in dead-serious unison, its Malcolmian addendum, "By any means necessary."[25] Their names and message were foreign to local black folks, and scary to many whites, but with time they became part of the landscape.

———

Holding court at his makeshift desk in the Lumumba Center's multipurpose room, Kali Akuno described his world to me as a confluence of "forces." For a generation whose radicals tend toward impossible demands and reactive rage, he is the rare strategist. He thinks in bullet points, enumerating and analyzing past mistakes as readily as future plans, stroking the goatee under his chin as his wide and wandering eyes look out for forces swirling around him. After Lumumba's passing, Akuno became the spokesman for what remained of their movement.

Akuno came of age in California—Watts of the 1970s and 1980s—immersed in the culture of black pride and power, descended from followers of Marcus Garvey and New Afrikans. His use of *Akuno* came later in life, but his first name was Kali from birth. People he grew up around talked about cooperative economics, about Mondragon, about businesses controlled democratically by the people they serve. In college at UC–Davis and after, Akuno drifted among experiments in cooperative living and organizing. After Lumumba and his comrades founded MXGM, Akuno gravitated to its Oakland chapter. He would become one of the organization's guiding theorists.

Hurricane Katrina brought him south. When it became evident how the storm had devastated black neighborhoods of New Orleans, and the government response only made matters worse, MXGM mobilized. Lumumba's daughter Rukia, then in law school at Howard University, began flying down every chance she could to organize volunteers. Akuno moved from Oakland and took a position with the People's Hurricane Relief Fund.

"We were trying to push a people's reconstruction platform," said Akuno, "a Marshall Plan for the Gulf Coast, where the resources would be democratically distributed." But mostly they had to watch as the reconstruction became an excuse for tearing down public housing and dismembering the public schools. It was not rebuilding; it seemed more like expulsion.

"Katrina taught us a lot of lessons," Rukia Lumumba said. The group started to think about the need to control the seats of government, and to control land. "Without land, you really don't have freedom."

Akuno and MXGM's theorists around the country got to work. What they developed would become public in 2012 as *The Jackson-Kush Plan: The Struggle for Black Self-Determination and Economic Democracy*, a full-color, twenty-four-page pamphlet Akuno authored, with maps, charts, photographs, and extended quotations from black nationalist heroes. It calls for "a critical break with capitalism and the dismantling of the American settler colonial project," starting in Jackson and Mississippi's Black Belt, by way of three concurrent strategies: assemblies to elevate ordinary people's voices, an independent political party accountable to the assemblies, and publicly financed economic development through local cooperatives.[26] Each would inform and reinforce the others.

By 2008, the scheming led to talk of running a candidate. MXGM had been organizing in Jackson for almost two decades, and it had a robust base there. Akuno suggested that MXGM should run the elder Lumumba and begin training Chokwe Antar—who was then finishing law school in Texas—to run for office in the future. The Jackson-Kush revolution would start with mere elections.

In 2009, Lumumba ran for a city council seat in Jackson; with the help of MXGM's cadres and his name recognition as an attorney of the people, he won. On the council he cast votes to protect funding for public transit and expand police accountability. But in Jackson, the real power—in particular, power over infrastructure contracts—lay with the mayor's office. Those contracts were still going largely to suburban, white-owned firms. Black people had long been the majority of Jackson's population, but MXGM's strategists held that the city's land wasn't really free until the majority benefited economically.

Few among Jackson's small, collegial elite bothered to notice the Jackson-Kush Plan when Lumumba announced his run for mayor in 2013. He was just one in a crowded pool of candidates. And the plan was still little more than a set of ideas. The co-ops didn't exist; the assemblies, when they actually took place, were small and populated mostly by true believers. Yet Lumumba understood his role as an expression of the popular will, which the co-ops and assemblies would someday articulate. At important junctures he would say, "The people must decide."

The mayoral campaign was a testament to what Lumumba had built in Jackson and the support MXGM members nationally could muster. He soundly defeated the incumbent in the primary, together with Jonathan Lee, a young black businessman who was little known in town, except to his friends on the state chamber of commerce. The $334,560 that Lee raised in 2013 was much more than the $68,753 Lumumba's campaign raised the same year. But MXGM's organizing efforts, combined with Lumumba's reputation, resulted in a landslide. On May 21, he won 86 percent of the Democratic primary vote, guaranteeing him the mayoralty. The Lumumba campaign's slogan, "One city, one aim, one destiny"—an homage to an old Garveyite saying—seemed to be coming true.

Not everyone was on board, however. "I remember getting all these calls when he was elected mayor from white business owners—they were terrified," City Councilman Melvin Priester Jr. told me. "They were afraid that he was going to treat them like they had treated a lot of black people, like a Rhodesia situation."

For Lumumba and his new administration—full of MXGM partisans—the first order of business was damage control. The city's roads and pipes had been allowed to deteriorate to the point of dysfunction. A federal Environmental Protection Agency consent decree required action on the crumbling wastewater system. Funds needed to be raised for repairs; perhaps afterward, the money could be used to seed cooperative businesses for doing the necessary work. Lumumba used the political capital he'd won in the election to pass, by referendum, a 1 percent sales tax increase. He raised water rates. Practical exigencies won the day.

"We didn't win power in Jackson," Akuno later said. "We won an election. It's two different things."

To pass the 1 percent tax, Lumumba had to accept oversight for the funds from a commission partly controlled by the state legislature—a concession that not even his more conservative predecessor would accept. He hoped that, later on, he could mobilize people in Jackson to demand full control over their own tax revenues, but the city was in an emergency, so for the moment the commission would have to do.

From his new position as director of special projects and external funding, Akuno tried to keep the Jackson-Kush Plan on track. However long the administration would last, he wanted to set up structures that would outlive it. He drew up plans for a $15 million development fund for cooperatives, using money from the city, credit unions, and outside donors. He wanted to create worker-owned co-ops corresponding to the city's major expenses—for collecting garbage, for growing the food served at schools, for taking on the plentiful infrastructure challenges. The city would put co-op education in schools, provide co-op training, and help co-ops obtain financing and real estate.[27] And there were plans to roll out a participatory budgeting process, based on models in Brazil and New York, through which Jacksonians could decide how to allocate public funds. Lumumba, meanwhile, moved more cautiously.

Jackson's troubles, by 2013, were more than black and white. An investment firm in Santa Monica had bought up more than half of the private buildings downtown. Investors from Israel and China were getting in on the action, too. Far from the RNA's old secessionist strategy of the 1970s, Lumumba was forming coalitions where he could, with whomever would work with him. Co-ops and assemblies took a backseat to balancing the budget, at least as far as official business went.

Ben Allen, president of the city's development corporation, started getting to know the new mayor, and he was pleasantly surprised. When he invited Lumumba to a garden party at his country club, the mayor made an appearance. "Our fears were gone," remembered Allen, who is white. "He wanted to work with us."

Two miles from downtown along Capitol Street, just blocks from the entrance to the zoo, another germ of the cooperative vision was beginning to sprout. In early 2013, MXGM members Nia and Takuma Umoja moved with their children from Fort Worth, Texas, into a small wooden house next to a local dumping ground. As they befriended their new neighbors, they started clearing the garbage away and replacing it with raised soil beds. Their neighbors, many of whom grew up as sharecroppers, formed a construction crew and started growing food. Together, they designated an eight-block district the Cooperative Community of New West Jackson and began buying lots there, intending to transfer them to a community land trust. The construction crew renovated abandoned houses and painted them with bright colors. The Umojas and their neighbors were making on-the-ground progress while Akuno remained focused on fund-raising and elections.

It was all part of the struggle. But every success still felt tenuous. Back in Fort Worth, the Umojas' community center had fallen victim to the threat of eminent domain. The danger was just as real in Jackson. According to Ben Allen's email signature at the time, "downtown redevelopment is like war."[28]

———

The forces that kept #BlackLivesMatter trending after the hashtag first appeared in 2013 were not exactly what one might expect from the headlines of black men killed by police. In reality, it was frequently a queer- and women-led uprising. The leaders were not afraid to use the word *capitalism*, and they did so derisively. (The "Black Lives Matter" slogan originated with Alicia Garza, a labor organizer with the National Domestic Workers Alliance.) They believed that black lives will not matter without a different system for determining what and who matters, and cooperative economics figured prominently in the movement's policy proposals. Yet, as in so many social movements of the past, only a tiny sliver of its variform lifeblood got into the news.

The civil rights struggle of the 1960s was no exception, for it was never about civil rights alone. Malcolm X preferred to speak of "human rights," and it was in those terms that he wanted to bring a case against the United States before the United Nations. Martin Luther King Jr. marched for "justice and jobs"; he died supporting sanitation workers. "Black power," "black liberation," "black lives"—these betray demands more comprehensive than either headlines or mythic hindsight allow. And they always had to do with economics.

In the mid 1960s, *black power* entered the movement lexicon while Stokely Carmichael was living among landowning co-op members in Lowndes County, Alabama. Wendell Paris, a civil rights activist and cooperative developer at the time, explained this to me when I visited his office at a Jackson-area church. "The black power concept came into being," he said, "because of those farmers who were independent in and of themselves and understood the value of collective organizing and collective ownership." In cities, black power would conjure images of the Black Panthers' rifle-toting demonstrations, but it was also at work in their less-visible programs for providing food, housing, and health care.

For years, Paris traveled around the South helping black farmers hold on to their land and build wealth cooperatively. It was a strategy for survival as well as resistance. Black farmers in Louisiana weren't getting paid fairly for their sweet potatoes, so they started a sweet potato cooperative and found their own markets—in many cases way up in the North. In Alabama, farmers who were getting a raw deal on local fertilizer formed a co-op to buy it in bulk elsewhere. Paris assisted in the formation of the Federation of Southern Cooperatives in 1967. Black activists during that period visited co-ops in Africa and Israel. Martin Luther King Jr. tried to set up credit unions during the Montgomery Bus Boycott and at his church in Atlanta—efforts that faced resistance from federal regulators. After years of agitating for voting rights, Fannie Lou Hamer organized the Freedom Farm, a cooperative meant to secure the gains of civil rights with food sovereignty. When Student Nonviolent Coordinating Committee members agitated for voting rights in Jackson, they also helped create cooperatives; later, black churches kept up the work by building bulwark institutions such as the Hope Credit Union.[29] Cooperation has bound survival and resistance together.

The generation of farmers that organized under the Federation of Southern Cooperatives in the 1960s and 1970s is aging out of existence, and the next generation of black-led cooperation is still just beginning to emerge. Individual co-ops are getting started in many cities, and the new Southern Reparations Loan Fund has been making its first loans. The story continues. But this story of black cooperatives, as much as it is one of tenacity and enterprise, is a story of loss. The loss once came in the form of Governor George Wallace's Alabama state troopers pulling over a truck full of cucumbers and keeping it there until the crop turned to mush in the summer sun, then it was a police raid with a tank, then an aortic aneurysm.

———

When Chokwe Antar first looked upon his father's body in the hospital room, he made the decision to finish what had been begun. He didn't say anything at first; there still had to be discussions in MXGM about the next move. His wife was pregnant. Some felt he wasn't experienced enough. But eventually the movement's decision echoed his own, and he ran for mayor in the special election to succeed his father. Throughout the country, MXGM members mobilized again. But by the time of Lumumba's death, the Jackson-Kush Plan was secret no more, and the city's business class was better prepared to oppose it.

Socrates Garrett is Jackson's most prominent black entrepreneur. He went into business for himself in 1980, selling cleaning products to the government; now, he and about one hundred employees specialize in heavy-duty environmental services. The story of his success is one of breaking through Mississippi's white old-boy network, and to do that his politics have become mainly reducible to his business interests. He is a former chairman of the chamber of commerce and serves on the boards of charities. He is a self-described progressive who supported the Republican governor Haley Barbour. He became a political operator—one with less ideological freight than the partisans of MXGM.

"I had to have relationships with politicians," Garrett told me. "If you're not doing business with the government, you're not in mainstream America."

Garrett became a Lumumba supporter only when it became clear who was going to win the election, and he grew disillusioned quickly. The MXGM-led administration didn't play his kind of politics. "They started putting people in from different walks of life," he recalled. "They had a lot of funny names, like Muslim names." Garrett was informed that he should not expect special treatment. Safiya Omari, Lumumba's chief of staff, insisted that he was being treated like any other contractor, but Garrett perceived it as a snub—right when the militant black mayor seemed to be bending over backward to assuage the white establishment. Garrett couldn't wrap his head around how cooperatives were going to take on big-city contracts, with all the financing and hardware such work requires. Mississippi law doesn't even have a provision for worker or consumer cooperatives; those that do exist must incorporate out of state.

"Here you are, a black man—you start from scratch and work your way up, thirty years out here struggling—and there's something wrong with my business model?" Garrett said. "In my opinion, it was going to produce chaos."

Garrett set about looking for a new mayor to raise up and before long came upon Tony Yarber, a young, bow-tied city council member and pastor from a poor neighborhood. What he lacked in age and experience was more than made up for in his willingness to collaborate. Garrett and Yarber quietly set out to organize a run against Lumumba in 2017, but when the mayor died, their chance came sooner than expected. The establishment that had tolerated and even come to like Mayor Lumumba wasn't ready to risk his little-known son. *Jackson Jambalaya*, a straight-talking conservative blog, ridiculed him as "Octavian." Chokwe Antar's posters, between plentiful exclamation points, made promises of "continuing the vision"; Yarber, for his part, told the *Jackson Free Press*, "I don't make promises to people other than to provide good government."[30] Garrett was his top individual donor.

The result was a reversal from the election a year earlier. Jackson's population is 80 percent black, and Chokwe Antar won a solid majority of the vote in black neighborhoods. But the white minority turned out in droves, urged by last-minute canvassing in more-affluent areas, which voted 90 percent for Yarber. Narrowly, on April 22, Yarber won.

Yarber removed almost all the members of the previous administration. Even Wendell Paris, who'd been working part-time to develop community gardens on city land since before Lumumba took office, was dismissed. When I visited city hall a year later, Yarber's sister, a police officer, was sitting by the metal detector at the entrance, pecking on the same iPhone that was once issued to Lumumba.

"The whole sense that we were going to do something great sort of dissipated," Safiya Omari told me.

Sitting on his front porch, wearing a faded T-shirt from the first mayoral campaign and a black cap with Che Guevara inside a small red star, Akuno tried to explain to me the experience as he slathered his two small children in natural bug repellent. With

*Chokwe Antar Lumumba in his law office in 2015, behind a photograph
of himself as a child with his father.*

the 1 percent tax and the water-rate hikes, they'd alienated part of
their base. But capitalism didn't leave them a choice. He was following the news of Syriza, the leftist party in Greece, as it tangoed
with the Troika. "I feel like I know exactly the conversations they
are having behind the scenes," he said. "I've been there."

Across town, Garrett was feeling blessed. Mayor Yarber put
things back to what he was used to. "Every time, God sends an
answer," he told me. "But I can assure you that that movement
is alive and well. And I can assure you that unless Yarber is razor
sharp, they'll be back."

So they were. In May 2014, just months after Lumumba's
death, hundreds of people came to Jackson State University from
around the country and the world for a conference called "Jackson Rising." They heard the history of black-led cooperatives from
Jessica Gordon Nembhard, who had just published her book
on the subject, and they took stock of what might have been in
Jackson—and what might be. Lumumba's image appeared on the
cover of the program, and on the first page, he spoke from the
grave with a signed-and-sealed resolution from the mayor's desk.
"Our city is enthused about the Jackson Rising Conference and
the prospects of cooperative development," it said, as if nothing
had changed.

MXGM was meanwhile hatching a new organization, Cooperation Jackson, to carry on the work that had been started. Akuno enumerated a four-part agenda: a co-op incubator, an education center, a financial institution, and an association of cooperatives. Plans were soon underway to seed, first, three interlocking co-ops: an urban farm; a catering company named in honor of Lumumba's wife, Nubia, who died in 2003; and a composting company to recycle the caterers' waste back into the farm. Akuno raised money from foundations, entertainers, and small donors, and the Southern Reparations Loan Fund pitched in as well. Cooperation Jackson started buying up land for its own community land trust. Its members restored and painted what would become the Lumumba Center.

Jackson's summer heat felt especially apocalyptic in 2015. In South Carolina, Dylann Roof murdered nine African American worshipers in a Charleston church; day after day, there was news of black churches across the South burning. Calls were mounting to take down the Confederate battle flag flying over the South Carolina capitol, but comparatively few were talking about the stars-and-bars that still covered a substantial portion of the Mississippi state flag everywhere it appears. The Supreme Court declared same-sex marriage the law of the land, overturning the Mississippi constitution's marriage amendment, and the preachers who heavily populate the radio spectrum in Jackson declared the United States of America now, at last, definitively captive to the devil's grip.

In the Lumumba Center's backyard, Cooperation Jackson's Freedom Farm consisted of a few rows of tilled earth, and in the kitchen, Nubia's Place Cafe and Catering Co-op was having its first test run. Akuno and others were planning a trip to Paris for the UN climate summit. Down the road at the Cooperative Community of New West Jackson, Nia Umoja and her neighbors had bought fifty-six properties for their land trust. "We've taken almost all the abandoned property off the speculative market," Umoja said.

In the wake of Roof's shooting spree, Chokwe Antar helped organize a rally at the state capitol to demand changing Mississippi's flag, alongside local politicians, personalities, and hopefuls.

The actress Aunjanue Ellis, flanked on either side by guards in black MXGM T-shirts, called for "rebranding our state" and "a different way of doing business." Chokwe Antar led a chant: "Stand up, take it down!" "Free the land!" followed. Then, of course, "By any means necessary."

Chokwe Antar's name was in the national news a week later. In Clarke County, a police officer stopped Jonathan Sanders, a black man on a horse-drawn buggy, who wound up dead after the officer put him in a chokehold. Chokwe Antar took the case. The incident became a potential flash point for the Black Lives Matter movement's roving attention, but the story didn't long hold the national gaze, and the following January, a grand jury declined to indict the officer. The rebel flag still flies over Mississippi.

Chokwe Antar told me a few days before the flag rally that he'd decided to run for the mayor's office again. As the 2017 Democratic primary approached, in the wake of Donald Trump's election, he ran with support from emboldened progressives across the country. He didn't disavow the Jackson-Kush Plan, nor did he advertise it. But he did talk about shared ownership—about the Green Bay Packers and Land O'Lakes and Ace Hardware. "My vision is that the city use its bully pulpit to encourage the development of cooperative businesses," he told a reporter.[31] Yarber had succumbed to a series of scandals and mishaps; Garrett withdrew support. Chokwe Antar won by a landslide. But winning an election was still just winning an election.

Back in late June of 2015, the flag campaign was the subject of conversation while cooking vegetables and chicken for dinner in the Lumumba Center's backyard. Akuno, pacing back and forth over the grill, led the discussion. "I think with some of this Confederate stuff—that's a distraction," he said. "Is that really our agenda? Did we define it, or did the media define it, saying that this is within the limits?" He'd been saying as much to Chokwe Antar. Akuno wanted to keep the focus on the co-ops and assemblies and elections—real counterpower, backed by self-sufficiency.

"Nothing don't change, whether the flag comes down or not," said New Orleans housing activist Stephanie Mingo, from the other side of a picnic table. "There's still going to be red, white, and blue."

"I'm not a fan of the Black Lives Matter thing—because, to be honest with you, they don't," Akuno went on. "Your life did matter, when you were valuable property. You were very valuable at one point in time. We're not valuable property anymore." His pacing took him and his gaze back to the grill, where he flipped over a piece of chicken.

"My argument is to tell other black folk, let's start with the reality."

———

It can be hard to sort out reality sometimes, especially in the midst of brave, big dreams. Cooperation Jackson's enterprises, when I visited, paled in comparison to how Akuno could talk about them. I've lived among great cooperative achievements and barely noticed; others I've heard much about but never seen. I confess: I've never made the pilgrimage to see mighty Mondragon for myself.

I don't know if a cooperative commonwealth can really take power and hold it, if it can dissolve the state and the corporations as Warbasse imagined, if its democracy can be durable enough to last beyond the founding generation. But flashes of the commonwealth keep appearing, if you know where to look—each time a new evolution for the old cooperative movement, the next equitable pioneers expanding the territory of democracy.

I can think of one place, at least, where Warbasse's stateless commonwealth might be closest to happening. Ever since I first learned about Rojava—at a fund-raiser in a New York City anarchist storefront, carefully skirting laws on financing foreign militants—I've been trying to understand what is real there. People I know have gone to visit, including a nemesis, a freelance diplomat, and a magazine editor, but there is a certain untrustworthy self-selection in who ships out to join a revolution. Pablo Prieto, a friendly biologist who showed me around the Catalan Integral Cooperative's Calafou colony, made his way to Rojava with the Bitcoin hacker Amir Taaki.[32] We corresponded for months by encrypted email, but he could never quite arrange the interviews with local leaders I asked for. It was a war zone, after all.

Rojava is an idea shared across three Kurdish-majority regions in northern Syria, along the Turkish border. These regions furnished the Kurdish fighters, including women and foreign recruits, that US forces came to rely on in the fight against ISIS. (This was a troubling arrangement for Turkey, whose rulers have spent decades suppressing Kurdish insurgencies inside their borders.) The Kurds, at last out of Damascus's reach, declared their new regime in 2012, among the ruins left from the ISIS occupation and subsequent liberation. They professed a doctrine of "democratic confederalism," derived from the ideas of US philosopher Murray Bookchin, as synthesized by Kurdish leader Abdullah Öcalan from his jail cell in Turkey. It's a system meant to render the nation-state obsolete through overlapping networks of local "communes." Gender equality, environmentalism, and ethnic pluralism are celebrated, and the police—while perhaps necessary for a time as the war goes on—are designed for eventual abolition.

The confederalist economy is made of co-ops. First, after the 2012 liberation, this started with agricultural co-ops; land that the Syrian government had owned was parceled out to locals, especially the families of fighters. But soon there were co-ops for bread baking, for textiles, for producing cleaning materials. Networks of co-ops formed—including ones for creating and supporting co-ops of women. But the co-ops were designed to resist outside control. They were to be accountable to local communes, the basic unit of the confederalist system. A person's commune, for instance, could revoke her co-op membership.[33]

The global powers attempting to steer the Syrian conflict have mostly ignored the revolution at hand or wished it didn't exist, even while benefiting from the resolve of its fighters. It's an economy inscrutable to those not willing to cooperate. An analyst from The Washington Institute, a DC-based think tank tied to the hawkish Israel lobby, once complained of Rojava that "attracting investors into such an anti-capitalist system would be difficult. Entrepreneurship is encouraged in Rojava, but only within the framework of cooperatives."[34] It was a rare bit of outside confirmation that the commonwealth so celebrated in anarchist infoshops around the world was really happening.

In October 2015, Prieto invited me to come join him. I wish I could have—I think. He wrote, "It's just like the Spanish revolution all over. There are so many similarities." He was referring to the period when anarchist collectives controlled much of Barcelona and the countryside, a passing utopia in the vacuum of war. "We have access to as much land as we want, and lots of resources. The possibilities here are endless, but we need people to come. We are going to build our open-source city here. It will be like an anarchist village, sort of like Calafou, but much bigger and better."

He wrote in another message, "This is THE goddamn real revolution! Or at least the closest we can get."

7

Phase Transition

Commonwealth

The first time I saw it, I took the metaphor literally. "We will all meet in Quito for a 'crater-like summit,'" the website said. "We will ascend the sides of the volcano together in order to go down to the crater and work." Alongside those words was a picture of Quilotoa, a caldera in the Ecuadorian Andes where a blue-green lake has accumulated in the hole left by a cataclysmic eruption seven hundred years ago, enclosed by the volcano's two-mile-wide rim.[1]

What the website beckoned visitors to was something less geologically spectacular than Quilotoa, but possibly earth-shaking in its own right. The government of Ecuador had sponsored a project to develop policies for a new kind of economy, one based on concepts more familiar in hackerspaces and startups than in legislatures. The project was called FLOK Society—*free*, *libre*, *open* *knowledge*. Its climactic event, which took place in May 2014, was called a summit, but the nod to Quilotoa's crater was a way of saying this wasn't the usual top-down policy meeting. Nor were the people behind it the usual policymakers.

Michel Bauwens, the fifty-six-year-old leader of the FLOK Society research team, held no PhD, nor experience in government, nor steady job, nor health insurance. A native of Belgium, he lived in Chiang Mai, Thailand, with his wife and their two children, except when he left on long speaking tours. He dressed simply—a T-shirt to the first day of the summit, then a striped tie the day of his big address. His graying hair was cropped close around his bald crown like a monk's. He spoke softly; people around him tended to listen closely. The Spanish hacktivists and Ecuadorian bureaucrats who dreamed up FLOK chose for their policy adviser an unemployed commoner.

If Ecuador was to leapfrog ahead of the global hegemons, it would need a subversive strategy. "It's precisely because the rest of the world is tending toward greater restrictions around knowledge that we have to figure out ways of producing that don't fall within the confines of these predominant models," Ecuador's minister of education, science, technology, and innovation, René Ramírez, told me. He and other government officials were talking about dispensing with such strictures as copyright, patents, and corporate hierarchies. "We are essentially pioneers in this endeavor. We're breaking new ground."

At first this was a subversion mutually beneficial to guests and hosts alike. Several months before the summit, Bauwens said that FLOK was a "sideways hack"—of the country, maybe even of the global economy. "It's taking advantage of a historic opportunity to do something innovative and transformative in Ecuador." He saw a chance to set the conditions for a commonwealth.

FLOK bore the style and contradictions of Ecuador's brand at the time. The president, Rafael Correa, sometimes spoke in favor of open-source software; WikiLeaks founder Julian Assange had been living in Ecuador's London embassy since 2012. Even while exploiting rain-forest oil resources and silencing dissenters, Correa's administration called for changing the country's "productive matrix" from reliance on finite resources in the ground to the infinite possibilities of unfettered information. Yet most of the North Americans I met in Quito were out of a job because Correa had recently outlawed foreign organizations, likely for circulating inconvenient information about human rights.

Michel Bauwens at the convention center in Quito.

As the summit approached, local politicians seemed to evade Bauwens and the team of researchers he'd brought there. Team members weren't paid on time. Two dozen workshops about open knowledge took place across the country, with mixed response. By the time I met Bauwens in the gaudy apartment he was renting in Quito, a few days before the summit began, he looked exhausted from infighting with the Spaniards and wresting his staff's salaries from the government. "It's going to be a much harder fight than I anticipated," he said.

Bauwens had a knack for seeking out potent knowledge. He grew up in Belgium as the only child of two orphan parents. His curiosities drifted from Marxism as a teenager to, as an adult, various Californian spiritualities, which led him to Asian ones, then esoteric sects like Rosicrucianism and Freemasonry. Meanwhile, Bauwens put his cravings to work in business. He worked as an analyst for British Petroleum and then, in the early 1990s, started a magazine that helped introduce Flemish readers to the promise of the internet. As an executive at Belgacom, Belgium's largest telecommunications company, he guided its entry into the online world by acquiring startups. And then, in 2002, he'd had enough. He quit, then moved with his second wife to her family's home in Chiang Mai.

"Capitalism is a paradoxical system, where even the ruling class has a crappy life," he says. He started to believe his unhappiness had cataclysmic causes.

For two years in Thailand, Bauwens read history. He studied the fall of Rome and the rise of feudalism—a "phase transition," as he puts it. It was an age when the previous civilization was in crisis, and he concluded that what led the way forward was a shift in the primary modes of production. The Roman slave system collapsed, and then networks of monasteries spread innovations across Europe, helping to sow the seeds of the new order. What emerged was an interplay of craft guilds organizing free cities, warlords ruling from behind castle walls, and peasants living off common land. As the feudal system grew top-heavy, networks of merchants prepared the way for the commercial, industrial reordering that followed.

With the internet's networks, he came to believe that industrial civilization faced a crisis of comparable import, as well as the germ of what could come next. He zeroed in on the notion of commons-based peer production—the modes by which online networks enable people to create and share horizontally, not as bosses and employees but as equals. It was a new rendition of the old medieval commons, but poised to become the dominant paradigm, not just a means of survival at the peripheries. He set out to find examples of where this world-transformation was already taking place. By seeking, he found.

The bulk of Bauwens' oeuvre lives on the collaborative wiki that long served as the website of his Foundation for Peer-to-Peer Alternatives—the P2P Foundation, for short.[2] Its more than thirty thousand pages, which he has compiled with more than two thousand online coauthors, include material on topics from crowdsourcing to distributed energy to virtual currencies. His life's work takes the form of a commons.

Bauwens tends to talk about his vision in the communal "we," speaking not just for himself but for a movement in formation. He borrows a lot of the terms he relies on from others, then slyly fits them into a grander scheme than the originators envisioned. Put another way: "I steal from everyone." Nevertheless, one is hard-pressed to locate any enemies; rather than denouncing others, he tends to figure out a place for them somewhere in his system.

It was in and for Ecuador, together with his team, that Bauwens mapped out the next world-historical phase transition for the first time. He believes that cooperatives are the event horizon. They're bubbles of peer-to-peer potential that can persist within capitalism, and they can help the coming transition proceed. They can decentralize production through local makerspaces while continually improving a common stock of open-source designs. They can practice open-book accounting to harmonize their supply chains and reduce carbon emissions.[3] Open intellectual-property licenses can help them share their resources for mutual benefit. As these networks grow, so will the commons they build, which will take over roles now played by government and private markets. Soon all the free-flowing information, combined with co-op businesses, will turn the economy into a great big Wikipedia or Linux—by anyone, for anyone. The industrial firm, whether capitalist or cooperative, will dissolve into collaborations among peers. Bauwens calls this process "cooperative accumulation."

Co-ops are not an end in themselves. They're not the destination. But they're the passageway to a peer-to-peer commons. "We see it as *the* strategic sector," he told me. New cooperative experiments were spreading from Mississippi to Syria, and here was a chance to show how they could grow to the scale of an entire country.

The Quito convention center is a two-story complex with stately white columns and hallways enclosed in walls of glass. Visible just a few blocks away is the National Congress building, the supposed destination of FLOK Society's proposals. Volcanoes stand in the distance behind it, the city rising up as high on their slopes as it can manage. During the four days of the "Good Knowledge Summit," as the event was called, bureaucrats in business casual worked alongside hackers in T-shirts to develop and distill the discussions into policy.

The opening night included bold pronouncements. "This is not just an abstract dream," said Guillaume Long, Ecuador's

minister of knowledge and human talent. "Many of the things
we talk about these days will become a reality." Rather than tax
havens, added the subsecretary of science, technology, and innovation, Rina Pazos, "we need to establish havens of open and
common knowledge."

Bauwens spent most of his time in the sessions on policies for
cooperatives. In Ecuador, as in many places, it is harder to start
a co-op than a private company. The Canadian co-op expert John
Restakis, a member of Bauwens's research team, called on Ecuadorian officials to loosen the regulations and reporting requirements on co-ops, and to enable more flexible, multi-stakeholder
structures. The officials pushed back; the regulations were there
for a reason, after waves of co-op failures and abuses. Restakis
and Bauwens pressed on. They wanted Ecuador's government to
serve as what they called a "partner state," nurturing commons-
oriented activities without seeking to direct or control them.[4]

By the summit's end, the working groups had amassed a set of
proposals, some more developed than others: wiki textbooks and
free software in schools, open government data, new licenses for
indigenous knowledge, community seed banks, a decentralized
university. Mario Andino, the newly elected governor of Sigchos,
one of Ecuador's poorer regions, wanted to develop open-source
farm tools for difficult hillside terrain. Before the summit, Bauwens visited Sigchos and received a standing ovation for his presentation. "We could be a model community," Andino said. But
there were no promises.

Over the course of his life, Plato made several journeys from
Athens to Syracuse, in Sicily, with the hope of making it a model
of the kind of society he described in his *Republic*. The rulers
there, however, fell far short of being the philosopher-kings he
needed; he returned home to retire and compose a more cyni-
cal kind of political theory. If not quite so discouraged, Bauwens
seemed adrift after the summit ended. The work of FLOK Society
was now in the hands of the Ecuadorians, and by that time, there
was little indication the government would take more from the
whole effort than a publicity stunt. Bauwens was already starting
to look toward the next iteration; thanks in part to the process

in Ecuador, there were signs of interest from people in Spain, Greece, Brazil, Italy, and Seattle. The same month as the summit, Cooperation Jackson held its Jackson Rising conference.

"Recognition by a nation-state brings the whole idea of the commons to a new level," Bauwens said. "We have to abandon the idea, though, that we can hack a country. A country and its people are not an executable program."

———

The fourteenth-century Tunisian polymath Ibn Khaldun described world history as an interplay between two groups of people: the sedentary and the nomadic.[5] There are those attached to a place, who build power through buildings and property and civilization, and then there are those who swirl at their world's edges. Ibn Khaldun was a dedicated skeptic, and he would be the first to point out that no single distinction explains everything. But today his distinction strikes me as especially useful again. It helps describe the "phase transition" that so concerned Bauwens. It's a distinction about how we own and what we need.

In Ibn Khaldun's time, sedentary civilization was ascendant, as feudalism began consolidating into mercantilism. Today, nomadism appears to be on the rise. When I was a toddler my son's age, I'd lived in two homes that my parents owned; they owned two cars between them. My father was a partner in a small, busy real-estate brokerage. He poured his energy into shepherding families through the process of purchasing their home, usually their most important asset. My son, in contrast, was born into a rental apartment with rental furniture; his parents have between them one car and a car-sharing membership. We partake in a generational trend, partly thanks to the concurrent rise in education debt and real-estate prices, together with a post-recession job slowdown.[6] But it's also a choice and an investment. My wife and I see value in owning less so we can move around more easily, following opportunities as they appear. We don't have a backyard, but we have a community garden plot and our choice of common, public parks. We know there are benefits to staying as nomadic as we can manage.

This is a sort-of-chosen kind of nomadism. Others come by their nomadism less voluntarily. Following the 2008 financial crisis, giant holding companies started buying homes once owned by resident families, turning more residents into tenants. We live in a time, meanwhile, of mass migrations due to the linked causes of war, climate change, and famine. Stateless insurgents sow terror through spectacle. Spells of automation and other disruptions keep workers on the run, changing occupations more during their lifetimes than in times past. We're living through a shift of population from rural areas to cities, a shift far more drastic and sudden than anything in Ibn Khaldun's historical data set. But our cities are different; they're not so sedentary. Transnational corporations have turned disparate cities into franchisees. Business travelers can jet around the world, stay in the same hotel chains everywhere they go, and buy citizenship wherever it's most convenient. Hovering over all this are the clouds—the physical, technological, and metaphorical objects that offer the allure of constancy. Wherever you go, Google's cloud is there to collect your search data in exchange for whatever information you could possibly want. Uber and Airbnb will introduce you to useful locals without the trouble of cultural competency or haggling over a price.[7]

Surely Bauwens is right that something world-historical is going on here. But the outcome may not be an egalitarian commons of borderless, permissionless, peer-to-peer productivity. Alongside the new nomads, there remains an enormous sedentary class—those of us not swept up in either jet-setting or sudden migration, whose fortunes have been constant or declining. On the whole, in the United States, geographic mobility is on the decline; the new nomadism is too expensive.[8] The sedentary peoples denounce both the involuntary migrants and the privileged "globalists." This mass of us is voting for firmer borders, for ethnic retrenchment, for brakes on democracy until the world stops changing so quickly. The postindustrial identity crisis for some is built from the trauma of an industrial revolution happening all over again for billions more.

Part of the sedentary peoples' complaint is that ownership has become nomadic, too. In the old feudalism, the lord was lord of a place; power had to do with land. Now wealth roams freely around the world, more freely than people, like the far-flung ownership of buildings in downtown Jackson or the California apps squeezing Denver's taxi drivers. From crisis zones to absentee investments to tax shelters, capital alights for a while where it can accumulate, then flits elsewhere to accumulate more. The domains of the new lords are virtual, and through the virtual clouds they own and control, their reach is far beyond what feudalisms of the past could have imagined. Their kind of nomadism is everywhere and nowhere at once, or at least it's meant to be perceived that way. At bottom, as with lords past, these lords depend on everyone else's respect for their ownership claims—over warehouses full of whirring servers, over proprietary algorithms, over rights backed by the force of governments and treaties.

The tech industry has long sought to claim otherwise. John Perry Barlow's 1996 "Declaration of the Independence of Cyberspace" asserted on behalf of the internet that the industrial world's notions of property and control no longer apply. "They are all based on matter," he wrote, "and there is no matter here." The Silicon Valley culture for which Barlow served as a prophet enacts this claim in the user experiences its companies design. There's no need to own a car; Uber can find someone willing to drive you. Don't bother managing the data of your life; share it with your friends on Facebook. Replace old-fashioned institutions and bureaucracies with free-form projects among freely associating commoners. Such invitations even seem to edge us closer to that old universal destination of goods, by which all things are truly common. The ownership-oriented cooperative tradition that has been the subject of this book might be verging on obsolescence.

Part of me wishes we could dispense with the freight of property as easily as Barlow imagines. The early anarchists were onto something when they declared that property is theft. But as commoners relinquish ownership today, the lords of the cloud do not. They keep on claiming their ownership rights. If there is to be a new era of sharing, they want it to be on their terms, by their rules, for their benefit.

Lawyers talk about ownership as a bundle of rights. The bundle can be untied, picked apart, and rearranged. This is what has happened on the clouds, where users allegedly own their data even after, knowingly or not, they've granted the cloud-owners nearly limitless rights to hoard and profit from it. But this is also how coders hack copyright law to create free, open-source software and how Guatemalan weavers secure collective ownership of traditional patterns against corporate copycats.[9] They know they can't afford to skip straight to some perfect, ready-made commons; they're holding their ground on the terrain of property, building their values into how they own. A historic unbundling and rebundling is happening again, and how it turns out will depend on how we organize ownership.

The transitions apparently underway come with a choice. Will lordship emerge as the more dominant principle, or will the commons? Clean air, free time, private data—these could each end up as luxuries for a few or as common goods. Together, we are writing the next social contracts as we go, deciding what goes in and what we ignore. Yet the questions that the cooperative movement persisted in raising for generations have too often been neglected: Who owns the engines of the economy, and how are they governed?

In early 2017, Facebook CEO (and Ibn Khaldun enthusiast) Mark Zuckerberg posted a nearly 6,000-word letter called

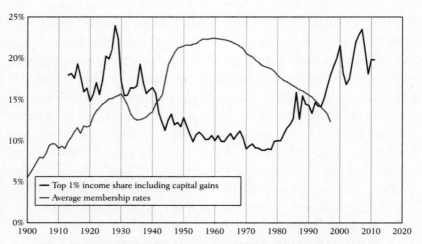

The inverse relationship between organization membership and inequality in the United States.

"Building Global Community." The name *Trump* doesn't appear in it, but it's hard not to read as a postmortem on the election several months before, in whose aftermath Facebook came under scrutiny for enabling foreign interventions to spread. "Democracy is receding in many countries," Zuckerberg observed, "and there is a large opportunity across the world to encourage civic participation." The last third of the letter outlines how Facebook can "explore examples of how community governance might work at scale."[10]

His proposal amounts to a cascading series of online experiments in which users may or may not know they are taking part. Artificial intelligence would cull and interpret user inputs, fine-tuning Facebook's discursive habitats to suit various world cultures while also encouraging healthy, cross-cluster integration. By "community governance," he seems to mean a never-ending focus group.

It may well be true that online platforms are the best hope for democracy in a time of reactionary politics. There are more Facebook users in the world than citizens of any country, or even adherents of any religion. But meaningful democracy begins with meaningful control. In a corporation like Facebook, even while users wishfully treat it as a commons, control begins with ownership.

A century ago in the North Atlantic countries, as heavy industry matured from disruption to normalcy, the social contract was up for grabs in this same way. We're still living the consequences of how that struggle played out. The modern corporation was born, streamlined for competition in capital markets. Even so, in certain sectors, more democratic structures took hold. What if US farmers had been left to rely on big-city firms to decide where electricity would come and when? What if northern Italy's food industry were the purview of conglomerates rather than artisanal producers linked by co-ops? What if credit unions weren't able to lend in areas where big banks fear to tread?

Maybe Enric Duran's FairCoop really will become a credit union on the scale of a transnational bank, powering local co-ops. New sorts of passports or medical insurance might span borders with agreements among co-ops, undermining the walls that states erect as they try to shore up their power. Networks of unMonasteries might become the next capillaries of innovation, sharing their inventions under licenses that favor fellow co-ops. Neighbors might replace the old electric grid with small solar panels, windmills, and batteries that they control, like the members of Delta-Montrose Electric Association; next, they could drop the monopoly internet-service providers and set up their own broadband service as well. And so on, in every part of life—with local nodes federating every turn, reaching upward to economies of scale with accountability to the roots.

If the social contracts to come are to be democratic ones, democratic experiments need to take hold in how we produce, trade, and consume. We need the lessons of the cooperative tradition in generations past—as well as the learnings of its latest equitable pioneers. Without them, less-democratic urges will offer to lead us through the maelstrom of change instead. These are times when what seems like far-off sci-fi turns into reality before we know it.

———————

Singularity University inhabits a small cluster of buildings in the NASA Research Park between downtown Mountain View and the San Francisco Bay. Around it are the crumbling remains of government-backed adventurism—the steel skeleton of a gigantic hangar designed to house airships, the rusting fuselages of airplanes, the dull barracks. They're reminders of the public investment that long ago dug the foundations of Silicon Valley's business empires, but it's a memory easy to forget in the thrall of private venture capital. Not far away, across a string of high-voltage wires, a bike path, and a trailer park, one finds a sprawl of parking lots and office parks, all with signs for the same familiar company, spread out around their mothership, the Googleplex. Singularity University doesn't grant degrees in the normal sense; it is a kind of secular seminary devoted to the faith that technology is the harbinger of human progress, until it outwits us altogether.

Students pay for the experience with an ownership stake in the startups they create there. "Be exponential," Singularity's slogan reminds them.[11]

In June 2014, the institution's co-founder and chairman, Peter Diamandis, a space-tourism entrepreneur, convened a gathering of fellow tech luminaries to discuss the conundrum of automation-caused unemployment. "Tell me something that you think robots cannot do, and I will tell you a time frame in which they can actually do it," claims Federico Pistono, a young Italian who spoke there. Among other accomplishments, Pistono had written a book called *Robots Will Steal Your Job, but That's OK*. At the Singularity meeting, he was the chief proponent of universal basic income, an idea that at the time still seemed novel. He cited recent basic-income experiments in India that showed promise for combating poverty among people the tech economy has left behind. Diamandis later reported having been "amazed" by the potential.[12]

That year, also, celebrity investor Marc Andreessen told *New York* magazine that he considered basic income "a very interesting idea," and Sam Altman of the elite startup accelerator Y Combinator called its implementation an "obvious conclusion."[13] Those were just the early salvos.

What people generally mean by universal basic income is the idea of giving everyone enough money to provide for the necessities of life. Imagine, say, a $20,000 check every year for every US citizen. The idea appeals to hopeful longings for a humane, egalitarian sort of commonwealth—a recognition that people, including those who are currently poor, will know better than any top-down welfare program what to spend the money on. It also appeals to Silicon Valley's preference for simple, elegant algorithms that can solve big problems once and for all. Supporters list the possible outcomes: It could end poverty and reduce inequality with hardly any bureaucracy. Recipients with more time and resources at hand would dream up startups and attend to their families. Some, as critics complain, would surf.[14] But perhaps most attractively for the executive class, the payouts would ensure that even an underemployed population could maintain the consumer demand that the robot companies would need to function.

As if Silicon Valley hasn't given us enough already, it may have to start giving us all money. Less clear, however, are the answers to those old cooperative questions: Who owns what, and who governs?

Karl Widerquist, a professor of political philosophy at Georgetown University's School of Foreign Service in Qatar, has been preaching basic income since he was in high school in the early 1980s. He says that we are now in the third wave of US basic-income activism. The first was during the economic crises between the world wars. The second was in the 1960s and 1970s, when libertarian heroes such as Milton Friedman were advocating a negative income tax, when ensuring a minimum income for the poor was just about the only thing Martin Luther King Jr., and President Richard Nixon could agree on. (Nixon's Family Assistance Plan, which bore some resemblance to basic income, passed the House but died in the Senate.) The present wave seems to have picked up in late 2013, as the news went viral about a mounting campaign in Switzerland to put basic income to a vote. Widerquist is glad to see the renewed interest, but he's cautious about what the techies have in mind.

One of the attendees at the Singularity University meeting was Marshall Brain, the founder of HowStuffWorks.com, who outlined his vision for basic income in a novella published on his website. It's called *Manna*. The book tells the story of a man who loses his fast-food job to robots, only to find salvation in a basic-income colony carved out of the Australian Outback by a visionary entrepreneur named Eric. (The fate of whatever Aboriginal peoples might live there already is unclear.) The colony is a kind of cooperative, held by its citizens on a one-person, one-share basis. They pass the time by innovating. They become a venture capitalist's ideal subjects, a vast supply of flexible entrepreneurs with the time and privilege to pursue worthy projects. Yet the colony's guiding principles declare, "Nothing is owned"—and, "Obey the rules," which are Eric's to make.[15] It's innovation on his terms, like the paternalism of Robert Owen's textile factory. Eric's commonwealth in the Outback conspicuously lacks the human friction of politics.

Chris Hawkins, an investor in his thirties who made his money building software that automates office work, credits *Manna* as an influence. To him, the appeal of basic income lies in its bureaucracy-killing potential. "Shut down government programs as you fund redistribution," he told me—mothball public housing, food assistance, Medicaid, and the rest—and replace them with a single check. Do away, also, with debates and decisions about common priorities; let the market of cash-equipped consumers vote among competing corporations with their purchases.

This kind of reasoning soon started to find a constituency in Washington. The Cato Institute, Charles Koch's libertarian think tank, published a series of essays in 2014 debating the pros and cons of basic income. That same week, an article appeared in the *Atlantic* making a "conservative case for a guaranteed basic income" on the basis of devolving federal powers.[16] This is one of those rare notions that is sneaking into plausibility from both the political left and right, more quickly than many proponents expected.

The idea gets less utopian by the moment. Barack Obama mentioned basic income approvingly in the waning days of his presidency. Governments from Finland to Hawaii are exploring policy options, and Y Combinator's nonprofit arm is funding a private experiment of its own in Oakland. For years, the journalist and entrepreneur Peter Barnes has been calling for a universal dividend funded through the use of common goods, particularly a tax on carbon emissions; now, governments in places from California and Oregon to the District of Columbia have considered plans to implement such a system. One of Barnes's champions is digital organizer Natalie Foster, who teamed up with Facebook co-founder Chris Hughes to mobilize executives, unions, and thought leaders of many stripes to unite behind payouts for all.[17]

Some basic income schemes bypass regular money altogether. Cryptocurrencies derived from Bitcoin or Ethereum have been designed to come into being as basic income, and to gain value through their universality. These attempt to form an entire monetary system in which basic income is the starting point.[18] Under the present regime, new money appears when banks lend it out.

What if money began its life, instead, as an apparition in equal quantities to everyone?

With a guaranteed income to count on, in whatever form, the liberations could pile on top of each other. Feminist scholar Kathi Weeks envisions a world of expanding time, where women wouldn't be so caught between housework and job work. Some labor organizers hope that workers, not forced to take whatever job they can get, would regain leverage lost in the decline of unions.[19] And more—for in the liberated time a basic income might afford, that unpredictable democracy-to-come would have new ground in which to germinate. But feudalisms might find roots there, too.

There are signs of such a situation on hand already. One way to think about the economic arrangement most users have with, say, their Gmail or Facebook account is that it amounts to a small stream of income—the value of whatever price they might otherwise pay for the service. The more universal these services become, the more we depend on them, just as people of the future might depend on their basic income check. The recipients could end up with no more say in where their income comes from than Facebook users have in how the company monetizes their data. We could wind up with a basic income generated by churning the data of our online habits or by polluting the air we breathe, without levers of ownership or governance to stop it. As algorithms take charge of important decisions, the lines of accountability would become harder to draw. We'd be bought in and bought off.

Giving people free money could surely help vanquish poverty, lessen inequality, and liberate time. But under what terms would the lords of the platforms deliver it? Those left out of economies past have learned that shared prosperity only really comes with shared power.

Ed Whitfield doesn't get the same starry-eyed look at the thought of basic income proposals as the techies do. He co-directs the Fund for Democratic Communities and its offshoot, the Southern Reparations Loan Fund. A big man with round, dark glasses who likes to play exotic musical instruments, Whitfield talks about the future with stories about the past. Once, in a conversation with Kali Akuno and Jessica Gordon Nembhard, I heard him point out that when their ancestors shed off slavery and demanded forty acres and a mule, they wanted the means of *production*, not the means of *consumption*.[20] They wanted a hand in shaping the economy, not just a portion of its output. To keep their freedom from getting snatched away again, they knew they had to be owners.

———

The evidence, anyway, doesn't fully agree that the wonders of automation are doing away with jobs on their own. Productivity growth has been sluggish by historical standards in the United States, and a decade after the 2008 crash, job numbers are back up. The trouble is, those jobs are less secure or reliable than before, and the owners are taking more of the spoils. More than machines replacing humans, the new jobs seem to expect humans to act like machines.[21] Perhaps the real visionaries of the future of work are not the app makers but those organizing co-ops in the fast-growing care sectors, ensuring that the most difficult work remains accountable to flesh and blood and heart. If the cooperative legacy did not exist, their task might seem insurmountable. But it's really no worse than hard.

As the stories I've told in this book declare, cooperation is no drop-in solution-for-everything. It's a process that happens a million ways at once, a diversified democracy. The troubles are as endemic as the promise. It starts with the capacities we already have, recombined to solve common problems. The commonwealth doesn't defer its business until after the world passes through some revolutionary event. It doesn't wait for things to get worse so they can get better. It doesn't appear from nowhere and disrupt everything. Instead, it grows through what Grace Lee Boggs called "critical connections"—bridging generations, forging bonds too strong for profiteers to break. It requires people who know their own strengths.

A lot of those who have been drawn into the co-op movement in recent years hope it can be something like universal basic income—a drastic, radical fix that changes everything. They try

to create co-ops for the hardest of problems, using the most untested of means, building their dreams out of policy proposals and
foundation grants and panels at conferences. I watch the news
of these developments closely. But some of the most remarkable
things are happening more quietly, making use of latent resources
already in our midst.

When I first took a phone call from Felipe Witchger, the
young executive director of the Community Purchasing Alliance
in Washington DC, I'd never heard of him or his organization. I'd
never come across it on the newsletters and feeds I follow. And
when I attended CPA's 2017 annual meeting, I realized what a
lapse this was.

Seated around me were representatives of the 160 DC-area
organizations—mainly churches and charter schools, largely people of color—that used CPA for purchasing such unglamorous
things as electricity, security, sanitation, and landscaping. After
three years in existence, CPA had saved them and the people they
serve nearly $3 million. (A woman seated next to me, a part-time
church staffer, said she'd cut out $17,000 on copier contracts
alone.) The co-op had helped many of them switch to renewable
energy, and their purchase of 580 solar panels, so far, had already
brought down the price of solar for everyone in the region.[22] On
one end of the room were employees of a black-owned security
company whose size more than doubled because of CPA contracts. Witchger was talking with some of CPA's contractors about
converting their businesses to worker co-ops.

This kind of stepwise, ground-up cooperation has enjoyed less
fanfare since the Great Recession than the pursuit of theoretical
tropes that seem fresh and radical. Some, for instance, regard the
precise locus of production as so important that they would reserve
governance rights in a worker-owned co-op solely to "producer"
workers, who physically make a given widget, over the "enablers,"
who answer phones, sweep floors, craft contracts, and the like.[23]
This kind of doctrinal fixation doesn't do much to anticipate automated or offshore production, rising demand for service work,
and the disguised labor of online platforms. It also inclines us to
neglect how pockets of commonwealth might emerge from zones

of economic life other than factory floors—from schools, from churches, from taking out the trash. Hints from the cooperative past, and latent opportunities in the present, might be better suited to survive among profiteers with a multibillion-dollar head start.

Rusty old farmer co-ops could show urban contract workers how to organize joint bargaining and insurance. A buttoned-up mutual fund like Vanguard might be the model for a basic income grounded in genuine shared ownership.

Whether or not the Silicon Valley prognosticators are right to expect an economy less dependent on human labor, cooperators need to build on a diverse foundation, one that recognizes the diverse ways people interact with their economies—not only as certain kinds of workers but as consumers, users, contributors, small-business owners, and crowdfunders. We can learn to revive the democratic spirits dormant in so many credit unions, electric co-ops, insurance mutuals, and employee stock-ownership plans. There is no single, gleaming, out-of-the-box model. Commonwealths spread through variety.

The largest worker co-op in my town is Namasté Solar, a solar-panel installation company with more than one hundred member-owners. Since converting to a co-op in 2011, it has been a thriving business—and a certified B Corp whose members get six paid weeks off every year. It has no trouble finding investors willing to finance growth without demanding control. But its greatest systemic effect has happened outside the worker-ownership structure. First, Namasté spawned a spin-off, Amicus Solar, a purchasing cooperative that helps small solar companies across North America stay competitive against large corporations. That, in turn, spun off another co-op that pools maintenance services. Now the Namasté team is helping to create the Clean Energy Federal Credit Union, designed to provide loans for homeowners nationwide switching to renewables. One thing led to another, and out came a sizable chunk of commonwealth. Our newly legalized housing co-ops did much the same thing; cooperative grocery stores have never done well in Boulder, as the market for good food is already crowded, but when the co-op houses put their purchasing power together, they created a business that sells local and organic food for a fraction of the retail price. They realized their latent power and put it to use.

When we know the diversity and dexterity of past models, we'll be better at finding the combinations we need for the present. The trouble is, longings for a perfect order can tempt us more than the unfinished commonwealths of the past, whose salvation remains incomplete and locked in procedural dullness. Unlike capitalism's penchant for perpetual disruption, cooperation works best when it can work with what is already at hand.

––––––

The eminent scholars of the Italian co-op sector are Vera and Stefano Zamagni—historian and economist, wife and husband. Vera once served as the equivalent of lieutenant governor for the Emilia-Romagna region; Stefano was an architect of Pope Benedict XVI's economic statements, which baffled Cold War–minded readers with critiques of capitalism and socialism alike. Both teach at the University of Bologna, Europe's oldest university; it began in 1088 as a kind of cooperative among students who hired professors to teach them. When the Zamagnis talk about

Vera Zamagni lecturing in front of notes written earlier by Stefano Zamagni.

the origins of what modern Italian cooperation has accomplished, they start not with Rochdale or Italy's 1948 constitution, or with the earliest Italian co-ops a century before. They go back to the Middle Ages.

Since then, says Vera Zamagni, "Italy has tried to substitute economies of scale with economies of network." The northern Italian districts where cooperation now flourishes tended to be republican city-states, even in the age of emperors and princes and monasteries. From these came some basic features of the modern market economy—double-entry accounting, insurance, municipal regulation, professional guilds. The Zamagnis distinguish this region's "civil economy" from the capitalism that would emerge elsewhere in Europe to fund colonial expansion and exploitation.

Like Prime Produce and the unMonks, they see utility in old patterns. The system of interlinked, human-scaled co-ops in northern Italy, the Zamagnis believe, is a remnant of habits learned long ago; the comparative lack of co-ops in the southern part of the country reflects the monarchic rule that long prevailed there. When political scientist Robert Putnam studied variations among Italian regional governments starting in the 1970s, he also noticed this correlation. "Mirroring almost precisely that area where the communal republics had longest endured five centuries earlier," he wrote, "the medieval traditions of collaboration persisted, even among poor peasants."[24]

According to the International Cooperative Alliance, "Cooperatives are businesses owned and run by and for their members." This is part of the basic definition, recognized around the world, including in Italy. But in Italy one hears executives and boards also insisting that their co-ops are *not* for their members—they're for future generations. They're for the community. One hears this from both the big-time manufacturing executives and back-to-the-land farmers. The members are stewards, like a family with an apartment in what was once a regal palazzo, like the people who sweep the tourists' trash at a Roman ruin. This sense of history has helped make Italy's co-ops among the world's strongest. But history also tolerates their contradictions, their tendencies to drift into oligarchic control or capitalist conformity.

I want to take members from small, radical, and allegedly pure grocery co-ops in the United States on a field trip to visit an Ipercoop in Italy. They will find a dilemma. Ipercoop is the largest kind of store in the Coop Italia system, the country's largest grocery chain, resulting from decades of mergers among local consumer cooperatives throughout the country. It is not pure. Picture, on one end of a sprawling strip mall, a gigantic superstore with globalization's full variety of cheap, imported household goods beneath fluorescent suns overhead. Employees, many of them part-time, aren't especially well-paid or empowered in their workplace. Only twenty thousand of nearly nine million consumer-members take part in meetings. But the in-house brands have no genetically modified organisms or palm oil, and suppliers—many of which are themselves Italian co-ops—must conform to certain codes of ethics in their labor practices. Things could be worse. But this is unapologetic consumerism, for a competitive price.

Would the visiting cooperators want this for their co-ops? Most of them probably wouldn't. If it's our company, we might like it to be pure. But purity means accepting the fact that in addition to shopping at our co-op, we are probably also stopping by Target or Walmart for bulk necessities, or condescending toward our neighbors who do so. Ipercoop stands for the impure claim that if people are going to do gross consumerism anyway, they can at least not funnel the profits to investor-owners somewhere; they can add the leftovers to their savings. They can manage their own compromises.

Florescent superstores are only the start of the contradictions in Italy's cooperative commonwealth. At the headquarters of SACMI, an international manufacturing conglomerate near Bologna, one finds a prosperous machinery factory behind a pristine office building with a museum on the ground floor. SACMI is a worker co-op in which only about one-third of the more than one thousand eligible Italian workers are actually members; among the company's dozens of international subsidiaries, the Italian worker-owners don't bother promulgating cooperative values or possibilities in any way. ("We do not intend to do it," confirms one executive.) And this is one of the real co-ops—a dues-paying, upstanding Legacoop member. There are also tens of thousands of "false" co-ops in the country, firms that permit no oversight from the big associations and whose sole purpose may be to enable erstwhile employers to bypass workers' collective-bargaining rights. Even the storied social co-ops can play this kind of role; as critics feared, their rise has coincided with a long process of privatizing public services, enabling local governments to deliver services without paying government-level wages.

"Cooperatives have transformed into institutional loopholes," contends Lisa Dorigatti, a young researcher at the University of Milan who has studied co-op labor markets. Even Pope Francis, a frequent co-op advocate, has noticed the problem. "Counter the false cooperatives," he told a 2015 Confcooperative meeting, "because cooperatives must promote an economy of honesty."[25]

Today, the pioneering types of people who built Italy's cooperative movement a century ago are not necessarily flooding into co-ops. They're not attending Coop Italia's annual meetings or holding out hope of becoming a SACMI member. If they're organizing co-ops, they're often treating the required board structures as a legal formality and governing themselves more like an open-source software project—whether they're writing code or growing vegetables. They're forgoing co-op language altogether, speaking instead about "political consumerism" and "solidarity purchasing." Yet according to University of Bergamo sociologist Francesca Forno, "I think we are going back to the roots of cooperativism."[26] They want something more cooperative than Ipercoop.

Insiders and outsiders alike frequently mistake cooperative enterprise for a utopian project. But it never has been, or it never remains one for long. Constructing a commonwealth means insisting on principles while tolerating compromise.

"I rebuke them every day," Stefano Zamagni says of the big co-ops. But he's patient. With time, even partial manifestations of the commonwealth help the ideals spread.

The canon of international co-op values and principles that I began this book with can be deceptive; it seems to claim that there's a formula. Shared principles really just string together the cooperative habits that diverse peoples have carried with them, and that they bring to the common challenges of twenty-first-century survival. Economy is a form of culture. This is why a Kenyan woman I know who works at Vancity credit union in Canada could start a lending circle with fellow Kenyans, though the idea baffles her native-born Canadian friends—even ones at the credit union where she works. They didn't grow up watching their mothers going to lending-circle meetings.

Cooperators today neglect the local, diverse, compromised legacies at their peril—the aging cooperative grain elevators across the rural United States, or the gleaming aisles of an Italian Ipercoop. These are achievements that can lend the commonwealth of the future a leg up, and that can help it cross lines of political party and social class. Small, pioneering experiments help new generations hone their ambitions. But we also need to build on what we already have, where we already are.

If advocates for a cooperative commonwealth in the United States were to encourage not just worker co-ops but agricultural, utility, purchasing and credit co-ops as well, they might see their political support become drastically wider—not just Bernie Sanders, a longtime champion of worker ownership in Vermont, but Mike Pence, whose base has included electric co-ops and credit unions. That kind of bridge-crossing can seem unpleasant in hyperpartisan times, but it's possible. If Italy's Catholics and communists could unite around the practical work of building a commonwealth, perhaps Democrats and Republicans can, too.

Now, co-ops in Italy have to reach across an even wider gulf than political divisions. Migrants from Africa and the Middle East have upended the demographics of the country in less than a generation, and social co-ops have made a point of employing and integrating the newcomers. These people can't claim the same medieval inheritances that the native-born Catholics and communists had in common. Yet migrants are creating co-ops of their own now in Italy, bringing their cultures and cooperative habits with them. Just as for my own family's immigrant story, this kind of business opens doors that would otherwise be shut. People seeking an inclusive, responsive economy must continually relearn the lessons of commonwealths past—to work with what they have, to seek out the fullness of what they might share with one another.

———

There is a trap built into that International Cooperative Alliance formula about how co-ops are "businesses owned and run by and for their members." When all a business does is serve its existing members, and those members' perceptions of their worlds, it can fall stagnant, and stagnation in a changing world is no help to members. Investor-owned businesses attract investor-owners on the premise that they'll forever exceed expectations; it is both a virtue and a peril that co-ops tend to find their members under the humbler premise of meeting known, day-to-day needs.

A generation gap divides the cooperative movement today. The wealth and know-how and power is in older co-ops, which first arose to serve a sedentary economy no longer with us. Their directors are used to being maintainers; they're rarely equipped to mentor founders. Meanwhile, the new cooperators, confronting more nomadic forces, act as if they have to build the commonwealth they need all on their own, starting from zero. They can't find financing to support their startups, even if there's a massive cooperative bank just down the road (as there is from me); if they study business in school and they're taught to furnish investor profits, even though businesses all around them quietly practice cooperation. Today's equitable pioneers have invented new cooperative forms and pushed the commonwealth into untried territories, often because they didn't know any better and didn't have a choice.

A commonwealth must evolve—its technology, of course, but also its cultures and its structures. Somehow, despite the co-ops' laudable risk aversion, they need to find means of taking the risks necessary to support new ventures. Democracy has always been a risk; the inheritors of a co-op deserve the chance to take risks just as the founders did.

The future need not be a province reserved for profiteers. More or less democratic institutions have put people on the moon. They sponsored much of the technology that Silicon Valley investors now act as if they invented. And cooperatives have been taking care of people in ways that the reigning economy found otherwise impossible. The future may yet be, more than the present, a commonwealth.

———

I was still little when my Colorado grandfather died, but I remember the silver belt buckle he'd wear as if he were here right now. There was a brand name on it: *TRUSTWORTHY*, with the *T*s in *TRUST* reaching down into *WORTHY* below. Long before I knew that word's significance to him, I could tell it signified something important. He seemed to wear that buckle like he meant it.

I think I know a bit more now about why. Trustworthy was a brand that his company, Liberty Distributors, offered the stores it served. They could use it if they wanted to, or they could stick with their own. The brand was a claim to authenticity and reality against an ever-more big-box hardware industry, a claim that Liberty

Two of my grandfather's buttons.

Distributors backed up with its cooperative ownership design and its bulk purchasing for local stores. It was a claim my grandfather wore on his belt even after he retired from the business.

The equitable pioneers I meet lately don't much resemble my grandfather. They turn to cooperation for different reasons and in different ways. The achievements of commonwealths past have receded to an unremembered memory, a door on which they don't know how to knock. But it doesn't have to be that way. When the pioneers start to find each other, they also start piecing together what patches of commonwealth they've individually found. They become less alone. What they'd thought was pioneering becomes more like continuing, like pressing on.

While writing this book, I helped put together a group we call the Colorado Co-ops Study Circle. First it was just me and a friend in Denver who was struggling to start up her own co-op development consultancy. We tried to make it easy on ourselves— simple gatherings, announced online, on topics we were interested in, with a few snacks.

It wasn't long before twenty or thirty or forty people were coming to meetings. They were grilling a co-op lawyer we'd invited with questions, or learning esoteric secrets from a real-live Grange member, or tussling with divides of race and class. The people who came were working with partial knowledge, and partial experience, and eagerness to do more—to be, together, the makings of a new Colorado commonwealth. As we started, it could seem like we were starting from nothing. We weren't. On our simple website, I spent some late nights assembling a directory of co-ops in Colorado, thinking it would be an easy exercise, until night after night the list worked its way up to nearly four hundred entries.[27] We were surrounded. We had shoulders on which to stand. We would soon begin an effort to try linking that commonwealth together through joint marketing and purchasing, in partnership with one of the country's biggest co-ops, and we formed an investment club of diverse, largely first-time investors to put our own money into the cooperatives to come.

When the Association of Cooperative Educators met in Denver during the Study Circle's first year, we decided it was time for a party. We'd been talking about a party for months, but finally we did it. The residents of Queen City Cooperative welcomed us to their house for supper with a full spread of home-cooked dishes. One Queen City member held court behind the bar out back, with a tap from a friendly brewery and a mojito punchbowl. An elder neighbor wanted to teach us a levitation trick. Most of us who had been at the conference found our way there late, but we came—co-op business consultants, a researcher studying how co-ops document themselves, a recent college graduate who'd just joined Denver's Community Language Cooperative as an interpreter. The farmers, young and old, mostly stayed home that night. I sat on the porch for a while with one of the political operatives from Boulder's housing co-ops; he updated me about the new house he was trying to fill and his new worker co-op, which was making software to analyze incriminating data about fossil-fuel power plants. He had the co-op symbol of the twin pines tattooed on one arm. But the champions of the evening were the Puerto Rican cooperators, their ages spanning four decades or more, who had already blown the mainlanders away with a presentation about their youth programs. They had swimming lessons and art contests and Olympic athletes as spokespeople. That night, as promised, they blew us away on the dance floor.

I'd been to Queen City on a few occasions before, but this was the first time I noticed the sign just inside the front door, to the left—one of those enclosed boxes with movable white plastic letters on black felt. It had come from a chiropractor's office; near the bottom it still said, "Ask us about our gift certificates." Above that were the first names of the members and "est. 2015." But the central item was a quotation, duly attributed to "MLK." It was the one that goes, "We may have come here on different ships, but we're in the same boat now."

Acknowledgments

Throughout the preceding, I remix material—sometimes verbatim, often not—from previously published articles of mine, listed below. I am grateful for the collaboration of the editors, fact-checkers, copy-editors, transcribers, patrons, and readers who helped me hone the reporting that serves as the backbone of this book.

Chapter 1

"Commies for Christ," *New Inquiry* (December 13, 2013).

"'Truly, Much Can Be Done!': Cooperative Economics from the Book of Acts to Pope Francis," in *Laudato Si': Ethical, Legal, and Political Implications*, ed. Frank Pasquale (Cambridge University Press, forthcoming).

"Can Monasteries Be a Model for Reclaiming Tech Culture for Good?" *Nation* (November 27, 2014).

Chapter 2

"10 Lessons from Kenya's Remarkable Cooperatives," *Shareable* (May 4, 2015).

"Interviewed: The Leaders of Kenya's College for Cooperatives," *Shareable* (April 24, 2015).

"'Truly, Much Can Be Done!': Cooperative Economics from the Book of Acts to Pope Francis," in *Laudato Si': Ethical, Legal, and Political Implications*, ed. Frank Pasquale (Cambridge University Press, forthcoming).

"How Communists and Catholics Built a Commonwealth," *America* (September 7, 2017).

"A New Way to Work," *America* (August 15–22, 2016).

"Curricular Cop-Out on Co-ops," *Chronicle of Higher Education* (October 9, 2016).

Chapter 3

"Detroit at Work," *America* (October 24, 2014).

"Denver Taxi Drivers Are Turning Uber's Disruption on Its Head," *Nation* (September 7, 2016).

"Sharing Isn't Always Caring," *Al Jazeera America* (May 18, 2014).

"Owning Is the New Sharing," *Shareable* (December 21, 2014).

"Figuring Out the Freelance Economy," *Vice* (September 2016).

"Living, Breathing Platforms," *Enspiral Tales* (June 23, 2016).

"Why One City Is Backing a Different Kind of Family Values: Housing Co-ops," *America* (January 4, 2017).

Chapter 4

"For These Borrowers and Lenders, Debt Is a Relationship Based on Love," *YES! Magazine* (September 21, 2015).

"After the Bitcoin Gold Rush," *New Republic* (February 24, 2015).

"Code Your Own Utopia," *Al Jazeera America* (April 7, 2014).

"Are You Ready to Trust a Decentralized Autonomous Organization?" *Shareable* (July 14, 2014).

"A Techy Management Fad Gives Workers More Power—Up to a Point," *YES! Magazine* (September 30, 2015).

"Be the Bank You Want to See in the World," *Vice* (April 2015).

Chapter 5

"The Joy of Slow Computing," *New Republic* (May 29, 2015).

"A Techy Management Fad Gives Workers More Power—Up to a Point," *YES! Magazine* (September 30, 2015).

"Can Monasteries Be a Model for Reclaiming Tech Culture for Good?" *Nation* (November 27, 2014).

"An Internet of Ownership: Democratic Design for the Online Economy," *Sociological Review* 66, no. 2 (March 2018).

"How the Digital Economy Is Making Us Gleaners Again," *America* (October 17, 2015).

"Intellectual Piecework," *Chronicle of Higher Education* (February 16, 2015).

"Users Should Be Able to Own the Businesses They Love Instead of Investors," *Quartz* (March 27, 2017).

"Our Generation of Hackers," *Vice* (November 11, 2014).

"The Rise of a Cooperatively Owned Internet," *Nation* (October 13, 2016).

"The Associated Press Is a Joint Media Venture. Maybe Twitter Should Be Too," *America* (April 21, 2017).

Chapter 6

"Economic Democracy and the Billion-Dollar Co-op," *Nation* (May 8, 2017).

"How Colorado Voters Could Usher in the Future of Healthcare in America," *Vice* (December 14, 2015).

"Colorado's Universal Health Care Proposal Is Also a Seismic Expansion of Democracy," *America* (June 30, 2016).

"How Communists and Catholics Built a Commonwealth," *America* (September 7, 2017).

"Free the Land," *Vice* (April 2016).

Chapter 7

"Why We Hack," in *Wisdom Hackers* (The Pigeonhole, 2014).

"Why the Tech Elite Is Getting Behind Universal Basic Income," *Vice* (January 2015).

"Dear Mark Zuckerberg: Democracy Is Not a Facebook Focus Group," *America* (February 21, 2017).

"How Communists and Catholics Built a Commonwealth," *America* (September 7, 2017).

I also stand in debt to the teams at Nation Books, Hachette, and Stuart Krichevsky Literary Agency for their aid in reassembling and reimagining that reporting here, particularly my agent David Patterson and my editor Katy O'Donnell. Barbara Croissant and Doug O'Brien provided generous feedback on drafts. My colleagues at the University of Colorado Boulder, especially through the leadership of Nabil Echchaibi, have shown me the solidarity of an ancient guild. And I've learned constantly from the cooperativism of my wife, Claire Kelley, in the business of our growing family and beyond.

This book would not be possible, finally, without those who allowed me to experience their stories and share them, the new equitable pioneers. In addition to people profiled herein, these guides include (but are not limited to) Nicole Alix, Martijn Arets, Ahmed Attia, Devin Balkind, Kaeleigh Barker Van Valkenburgh, Harriet Barlow, Paul Bindel, Joseph Blasi, David Bollier, Becks Boone, Jennifer Briggs, Greg Brodsky, Howard Brodsky, Alexa Clay, Nithin Coca, Matt Cropp, Brendan Denovan, Avery Edenfield, Hanan El Youssef, Laura Flanders, Natalie Foster, Karen Gargamelli, Shamika Goddard, Marina Gorbis, Jonathan Gordon-Farleigh, Jessica Gordon Nembhard, Neal Gorenflo, Stephanie Guico, Yessica Holguin, Jen Horonjeff, Sara Horowitz, Brent Hueth, Alanna Irving, Camille Kerr, Ben Knight, Corey Kohn, Marcia Lee, Rhys Lindmark, Pia Mancini, Annie McShiras, Micky Metts, Melina Morrison, Doug O'Brien, Janelle Orsi, Linda Phillips, Ludovica Rogers, Douglas Rushkoff, Caroline Savery, Trebor Scholz, Adam Schwartz, Zane Selvans, Palak Shah, Nuno Silva, Danny Spitzberg, Armin Steuernagel, Bill Stevenson, Michelle Sturm, Keith Taylor, Stacco Troncoso, Sandeep Vaheesan, Margaret Vincent, Halisi Vinson, Tom Webb, Jason Wiener, Elandria Williams, Felipe Witchger, and Erik Olin Wright. May what I've gleaned from you be of use.

Notes

Introduction: Equitable Pioneers

1. LeRoy Croissant, *Ancestors and Descendants of Fred Henry Croissant (1791–2001)*, private family history (2001); the cassette tapes were made as part of Croissant's research for the book, recorded January 14 and 15, 1989.
2. Liberty Distributors, *Policies and Procedures* (December 1978). The manual, found by my aunt Janet Finley in her basement, includes documents with various dates. The financial data comes from 1980, when the company's estimated sales volume was $660 million. I also spoke about the company with Chuck Short of Amarillo Hardware, one of Liberty's member-owners. Liberty dates back to 1935, and according to Short, it was not legally a cooperative but operated as one. In 1991, through a merger, what had been Liberty Distributors became part of another co-op, Distribution America.
3. Croissant, *Ancestors and Descendants*; according to Western Sugar Cooperative, "History," westernsugar.com/who-we-are/history, the company became a co-op in 2002.
4. Repeated throughout Peter Maurin, *Easy Essays* (Wipf and Stock, 2010).

5. John Curl, *For All the People: Uncovering the Hidden History of Co-operation, Cooperative Movements, and Communalism in America*, 2nd ed. (PM Press, 2012), 190–191; for analysis of earlier repression of US co-ops, see Marc Schneiberg, "Movements as Political Conditions for Diffusion: Anti-Corporate Movements and the Spread of Cooperative Forms in American Capitalism," *Organization Studies* 34, no. 5–6 (2013).

6. The term *cooperative commonwealth* first took hold with Laurence Gronlund, *The Co-operative Commonwealth in Its Outlines: An Exposition of Modern Socialism* (Lee and Shepard, 1884), which translated Karl Marx into a more gradualist, explicitly Darwinist evolution into cooperative arrangements, while retaining Marx's all-encompassing state; Norman Thomas, *The Choice Before Us: Mankind at the Crossroads* (AMS Press, 1934); on Du Bois and the commonwealth, see Olabode Ibironke, "W.E.B. Du Bois and the Ideology or Anthropological Discourse of Modernity: The African Union Reconsidered," *Social Identities* 18, no. 1 (2012), and Jessica Gordon Nembhard, *Building a Cooperative Solidarity Commonwealth* (The Next System Project, 2016); see also Edward K. Spann, *Brotherly Tomorrows: Movements for a Cooperative Society in America, 1820–1920* (Columbia University Press, 1989), and Alex Gourevitch, *From Slavery to the Cooperative Commonwealth: Labor and Republican Liberty in the Nineteenth Century* (Cambridge University Press, 2014).

7. Although the 1912 speech is frequently used as its source text, the phrase predated that occasion, as it had already inspired a poem by James Oppenheim in 1911. Minerva K. Brooks, "Votes for Women: Rose Schneiderman in Ohio," *Life and Labor* (September 1912), 288; Margaret Dreier Robins, "Self-Government in the Workshop," *Life and Labor* (April 1912), 108–110; for an account of US struggles over working hours, see Benjamin Kline Hunnicutt, *Free Time: The Forgotten American Dream* (Temple University Press, 2013).

8. The laws in question are the Joint Stock Companies Act of 1856 and the Industrial and Provident Societies Partnership Act of 1852; Henry Hansmann, "All Firms Are Cooperatives—and So Are Governments," *Journal of Entrepreneurial and Organizational Diversity* 2, no. 2 (2013).

9. *State of the Global Workplace* (Gallup, 2017); Francesca Gino, "How to Make Employees Feel Like They Own Their Work," *Harvard Business Review* (December 7, 2015); Jocko Willink and Leif Babin, *Extreme Ownership: How U.S. Navy SEALs Lead and Win* (St. Martin's

Press, 2015); see also widespread examples such as Micah Solomon, "The Secret of a Successful Company Culture: Spread a Sense of Ownership," *Forbes* (July 7, 2014), and Joel Basgall, "Build a Culture of Ownership at Your Company," *Entrepreneur* (October 1, 2014); on diverse forms of employee ownership, see Joseph R. Blasi, Richard B. Freeman, and Douglas L. Kruse, *The Citizen's Share: Reducing Inequality in the 21st Century* (Yale University Press, 2012).

10. "ESOPs by the Numbers," National Center for Employee Ownership, nceo.org/articles/esops-by-the-numbers; however, only about two million workers experience an ESOP with significant scale or governance rights, according to Thomas Dudley, "How Big Is America's Employee-Owned Economy?" *Fifty by Fifty,* on Medium (June 22, 2017).

11. The alliance uses *"Co-operative"* in its name, but I omit the hyphen (which is standard British usage) for consistency, as with other deviations from US usage; I will continue to use "cooperative" in the main text but retain hyphens in these notes for bibliographic correctness. Dave Grace and Associates, *Measuring the Size and Scope of the Cooperative Economy: Results of the 2014 Global Census on Co-operatives* (United Nations Secretariat Department of Economic and Social Affairs Division for Social Policy and Development, 2014); Hyungsik Eum, *Cooperatives and Employment: Second Global Report* (CICOPA, 2017); International Cooperative Alliance, "Facts and Figures," ica.coop/en/facts-and-figures.

12. Liminality, "Cooperative Awareness Survey" (April 2017), commissioned by Cooperatives for a Better World.

13. Brent Hueth, "Missing Markets and the Cooperative Firm," Toulouse School of Economics, Conference on Producer Organizations (September 5–6, 2014).

14. Roberto Stefan Foa and Yascha Mounk, "The Danger of Deconsolidation: The Democratic Disconnect," *Journal of Democracy* 27, no. 3 (July 2016).

15. President George W. Bush sought to promote both democratic politics abroad and an "ownership society" at home; this ownership society, however, was based on schemes that would replace shared, public ownership of health-care and education with individual purchasing of private-sector services. His British counterpart, Tony Blair, envisioned an ownership society with somewhat more cooperative components.

16. On Apple, see Lori Emerson, *Reading Writing Interfaces: From the Digital to the Bookbound* (University of Minnesota Press, 2014),

77 and 81; Naisbitt quoted in Theodore Roszak, *The Cult of Information: The Folklore of Computers and the True Art of Thinking* (Pantheon, 1986), 161.

17. International Cooperative Alliance, "Cooperative Identity, Values, and Principles," ica.coop/en/whats-co-op/co-operative-identity -values-principles; see also *Guidance Notes to the Cooperative Principles* (International Cooperative Alliance, 2015). There are other sets of principles as well. The US government has its own set, focused on agricultural co-ops, discussed in Bruce J. Reynolds, *Comparing Cooperative Principles of the US Department of Agriculture and the International Cooperative Alliance* (US Department of Agriculture, June 2014); worker co-ops in particular articulate distinct sets, largely overlapping with those of the ICA, in International Organisation of Industrial and Service Cooperatives, *World Declaration on Worker Cooperatives*, approved by the ICA General Assembly in Cartagena, Colombia (September 23, 2005); Mondragon Corporation, "Our Principles," mondragon-corporation .com/en/co-operative-experience/our-principles.

18. Jonathan Stempel, "Arconic Is Sued in US over Fatal London Tower Fire," *Reuters* (July 13, 2017); Geoffrey Supran and Naomi Oreskes, "What Exxon Mobil Didn't Say About Climate Change," *New York Times* (August 22, 2017).

19. On union-cooperative alliances, see 1worker1vote.org and cincinnatiunioncoop.org; on Pope Francis, see my article "How Pope Francis Is Reviving Radical Catholic Economics," *Nation* (September 9, 2015); on the Movement for Black Lives platform, see policy.m4bl.org/economic-justice; on the Labour Party, see Anca Voinea, "Corbyn's Digital Democracy Manifesto Promotes Co-operative Ownership of Digital Platforms," *Co-operative News* (August 30, 2016); Bernie Sanders's original campaign website included "creating worker co-ops" as the last of its twelve policy proposals, but he rarely spoke of this publicly, and the idea was soon demoted to a lesser bullet point in his platform (see web.archive .org/web/20150430045208/berniesanders.com/issues); for a general discussion on the relationship between social movements and cooperation, see Schneiberg, "Movements as Political Conditions for Diffusion."

20. George Lakey, *Viking Economics: How the Scandinavians Got It Right—and How We Can, Too* (Melville House, 2016); Jessica Gordon Nembhard, *Collective Courage: A History of African*

American Cooperative Economic Thought and Practice (University of Pennsylvania Press, 2014); M. K. Gandhi, *Constructive Programme: Its Meaning and Place*, 2nd ed. (Navajivan, 1945).

21. This is AnyShare, an online platform designed through Fair-Shares, a UK-based framework for developing multi-stakeholder co-ops; Josef Davies-Coates, "Open Co-ops—An Idea Whose Time Has Come?" Open Co-op blog (January 7, 2014); Michel Bauwens, "Open Cooperativism for the P2P Age," P2P Foundation blog (June 16, 2014); Pat Conaty and David Bollier, *Toward an Open Co-operativism: A New Social Economy Based on Open Platforms, Co-operative Models and the Commons* (Commons Strategies Group, 2014), commonsstrategies.org /towards-an-open-co-operativism.

22. A useful critical discussion, for instance, is Matthew D. Dinan, "Keeping the Old Name: Derrida and the Deconstructive Foundations of Democracy," *European Journal of Political Theory* 13, no. 1 (2014).

Chapter 1: All Things in Common

1. John Coney (dir.), *Space Is the Place* (1974), 32:00.

2. Jean Leclercq, *The Love of Learning and the Desire for God* (Fordham University Press, 1961), 175.

3. E.g., Lynn Margulis, *Symbiotic Planet: A New Look at Evolution* (Basic Books, 1998); Martin A. Nowak and Roger Highfield, *Super-Cooperators: Altruism, Evolution, and Why We Need Each Other to Succeed* (Free Press, 2012).

4. Margaret Mead, ed., *Cooperation and Competition Among Primitive Peoples* (McGraw-Hill, 1937), 16; Alexa Clay, "Neo-Tribes: The Future Is Tribal," keynote at re:publica in Berlin, Germany (May 4, 2016).

5. Adapted, not verbatim, from Elinor Ostrom, *Governing the Commons: The Evolution of Institutions for Collective Action* (Cambridge University Press, 1990), 90; for applications of Ostrom's framework to historical commons, see "Collective Action Institutions in a Long-Term Perspective," a special issue of the *International Journal of the Commons* 10, no. 2 (2016); an excellent primer on the commons is David Bollier, *Think Like a Commoner: A Short Introduction to the Life of the Commons* (New Society Publishers, 2014).

6. Ed Mayo, *A Short History of Co-operation and Mutuality* (Co-operatives UK, 2017).

7. Acts 2:43–45. This and all subsequent biblical quotations are from the New American Bible.

8. Acts 4:32 and 5:12.

9. Acts 6:1–6.

10. Augustine of Hippo, *The Rule of St. Augustine*, trans. Robert Russell (Brothers of the Order of Hermits of Saint Augustine, 1976); Benedict of Nursia, *RB 1980: The Rule of St. Benedict in English*, trans. Timothy Fry (Liturgical Press, 1981), chap. 3; the relevance of the Benedictine rule to modern cooperativism is the subject of Greg MacLeod, "The Monastic System as a Model for the Corporate Global System," Work as Key to the Social Question conference, Vatican City (September 12–15, 2001).

11. Chap. 4 of the Rule of St. Clare, in *Francis and Clare: The Complete Works*, trans. R. J. Armstrong (Paulist Press, 1988), 215–216. The words "among us" are in brackets in the original.

12. For an extended discussion of this debate, see Giorgio Agamben, *The Highest Poverty: Monastic Rules and Form-of-Life*, trans. Adam Kotsko (Stanford University Press, 2013).

13. Robert Harry Inglis Palgrave, ed., *Dictionary of Political Economy*, vol. 1 (Macmillan, 1915), 212; I've changed "all men" to "everyone," which is also the translation used in Agamben, *The Highest Poverty*, 112. *Catechism of the Catholic Church*, 2nd ed. (Liberia Editrice Vaticana, 1993), pt. 3, sec. 2, chap. 2, art. 7.I.

14. Benedict of Nursia, *RB 1980*, chap. 33.

15. Steven A. Epstein, *Wage Labor and Guilds in Medieval Europe* (University of North Carolina Press, 1995), 40–41.

16. Thomas Müntzer, *Sermon to the Princes* (Verso, 2010), 96–97.

17. A more Protestant-oriented version of the history of Christian cooperation can be found in Andrew McLeod, *Holy Cooperation! Building Graceful Economies* (Cascade Books, 2009).

18. See Peter Linebaugh, *The Magna Carta Manifesto: Liberties and Commons for All* (University of California Press, 2009); Karl Polanyi, *The Great Transformation: The Political and Economic Origins of Our Time* (Beacon Press, 2001 [1944]); Silvia Federici, *Caliban and the Witch: Women, the Body and Primitive Accumulation* (Autonomedia, 2014 [2004]).

19. "The True Levellers Standard Advanced," in Gerrard Winstanley, *A Common Treasury* (Verso, 2011), 17.

Chapter 2: The Lovely Principle

1. James Peter Warbasse, *Cooperative Democracy Through Voluntary Association of the People as Consumers*, 3rd ed. (Harper and Brothers, 1936), 61–62. Originally called the Cooperative League of America, its name first changed in 1922. The organization was partly an outgrowth of the Jewish Cooperative League, founded in 1909 on New York's Lower East Side.

2. Murray D. Lincoln, *Vice President in Charge of Revolution* (McGraw-Hill, 1960), 108.

3. Warbasse, *Cooperative Democracy*, 270.

4. Here, and for much of the early history of US cooperation, I draw from John Curl, *For All the People: Uncovering the Hidden History of Cooperation, Cooperative Movements, and Communalism in America*, 2nd ed. (PM Press, 2012); Jessica Gordon Nembhard, *Collective Courage: A History of African American Cooperative Economic Thought and Practice* (University of Pennsylvania Press, 2014); Joseph G. Knapp, *The Rise of American Cooperative Enterprise: 1620–1920* (Interstate, 1969); and Edward K. Spann, *Brotherly Tomorrows: Movements for a Cooperative Society in America, 1820–1920* (Columbia University Press, 1989). The cod-fishery story is recounted in the introduction to Joseph R. Blasi, Richard B. Freeman, and Douglas L. Kruse, *The Citizen's Share: Reducing Inequality in the 21st Century* (Yale University Press, 2012).

5. Quoted in Gordon Nembhard, *Collective Courage*, 36.

6. Abraham Lincoln, "Address Before the Wisconsin State Agricultural Society, Milwaukee, Wisconsin," in *Collected Works of Abraham Lincoln*, vol. 3 (University of Michigan Digital Library Production Services, 2001).

7. For the longer philosophical tradition, David Ellerman, "On the Renting of Persons," *Economic Thought* 4, no. 1 (2015); the account of Lowell is from Bruce Laurie, *Artisans into Workers: Labor in Nineteenth-Century America* (University of Illinois Press, 1997), 87; the lyric was a parody of a popular song, "I Won't Be a Nun."

8. George Jacob Holyoake, *The History of Cooperation*, rev. ed. (T. Fisher Unwin, 1908 [1875]), 11 and 13. Another prominent, parallel chronicle of the period is Beatrice Potter Webb, *The Co-operative Movement in Great Britain* (Allen and Unwin, 1899).

9. Holyoake, *The History of Cooperation*, 34.

10. Holyoake, 40.

11. There are suggestions that the significance of Rochdale has been overblown by the influence of Holyoake, for instance, in Brett Fairbairn, *The Meaning of Rochdale: The Rochdale Pioneers and the Co-operative Principles* (Centre for the Study of Co-operatives, University of Saskatchewan, 1994), and John F. Wilson, Anthony Webster, and Rachael Vorberg-Rugh, *Building Co-operation: A Business History of The Co-operative Group, 1863–2013* (Oxford University Press, 2013); a map of pre-Rochdale cooperatives in England can be found in Ed Mayo, *A Short History of Co-operation and Mutuality* (Co-operatives UK, 2017); but given the role of Rochdale in the establishment of Britain's dominant cooperative organizations, such revisionist histories don't fully contradict Holyoake's boosterism.

12. Holyoake, *The History of Cooperation*, 280–281; Webb, *The Co-operative Movement in Great Britain*, emphasizes the comparison in approaches to private property.

13. George Jacob Holyoake, *The History of the Rochdale Pioneers*, 10th ed. (George Allen and Unwin, 1893), 21; Holyoake, *The History of Cooperation*, 287–288.

14. The definitive source for this history is Wilson, *Building Co-operation*.

15. Missing markets: Brent Hueth, "Missing Markets and the Co-operative Firm," Toulouse School of Economics, Conference on Producer Organizations (September 5–6, 2014); Kazuhiko Mikami, *Enterprise Forms and Economic Efficiency: Capitalist, Co-operative and Government Firms* (Routledge, 2013); E. G. Nourse, "The Economic Philosophy of Co-operation," *American Economic Review* 12, no. 4 (December 1922). Startup costs: Hueth, "Missing Markets." Productivity benefits: Peter Bogetoft, "An Information Economic Rationale for Cooperatives," *European Review of Agricultural Economics* 32 (2005); Peter Molk, "The Puzzling Lack of Cooperatives," *Tulane Law Review* 88 (2014); Virginie Pérotin, *What Do We Really Know About Worker Cooperatives?* (Co-operatives UK, 2016). Protection: Henry Hansmann, *The Ownership of Enterprise* (Harvard University Press, 2000); Pérotin, *What Do We Really Know*. Information sharing: Bogetoft, "An Information Economic Rationale"; Timothy W. Guinnane, "Cooperatives as Information Machines: German Rural Credit Cooperatives, 1883–1914," *Journal of Economic History* 61, no. 2 (2001); Mikami, *Enterprise Forms*. Chance of failure: John W. Mellor, *Measuring Cooperative Success: New Challenges and Opportunities*

in Low- and Middle-Income Countries (United States Overseas Cooperative Development Council and United States Agency for International Development, 2009); Molk, "The Puzzling Lack"; Erik K. Olsen, "The Relative Survival of Worker Cooperatives and Barriers to Their Creation," in *Sharing Ownership, Profits, and Decision-Making in the 21st Century*, ed. Douglas Kruse (Emerald Group Publishing, 2013); Pérotin, *What Do We Really Know*. Resilience: Johnston Birchall, *Resilience in a Downturn: The Power of Financial Cooperatives* (International Labour Organization, 2013); Clifford Rosenthal, *Credit Unions, Community Development Finance, and the Great Recession* (Federal Reserve Bank of San Francisco, 2012); Guillermo Alves, Gabriel Burdín, and Andrés Dean, "Workplace Democracy and Job Flows," *Journal of Comparative Economics* 44, no. 2 (May 2016). Cost savings: Hansmann, *The Ownership of Enterprise*; Hueth, "Missing Markets"; Pérotin, *What Do We Really Know*.

16. Quoted from an epigraph in Holyoake, *The History of Cooperation*, 312 and 355–356; Curl, *For All the People*, pt. I, chap. 3, epub; Victor Rosewater, *History of Cooperative News-Gathering in the United States* (D. Appleton, 1930).

17. Poster for the Union Co-operative Association No. 1 of Philadelphia, quoted in Steve Leikin, *The Practical Utopians: American Workers and the Cooperative Movement in the Gilded Age* (Wayne State University Press, 2005), 1; *Iron Molders' International Journal* (May 1868), quoted in Leikin, 28.

18. David T. Beito, *From Mutual Aid to the Welfare State: Fraternal Societies and Social Services, 1890–1967* (University of North Carolina Press, 2000); Blasi, Freeman, and Kruse, *The Citizen's Share*, 141–142.

19. Curl, *For All the People*, pt. I, chaps. 5–6, epub; Lawrence Goodwyn, *The Populist Moment: A Short History of the Agrarian Revolt in America* (Oxford University Press, 1978); Knapp, *The Rise of American Cooperative Enterprise*; Leikin, *The Practical Utopians*.

20. W. E. Burghardt Du Bois, ed., *Economic Co-operation Among Negro Americans* (Atlanta University Press, 1907), 4. See also Gordon Nembhard, *Collective Courage*.

21. Gordon Nembhard, *Collective Courage*, 85.

22. Charles Caryl, *New Era: Presenting the Plans for the New Era Union* [...] (1897); Silvia Pettem, *Only in Boulder: The County's Colorful Characters* (History Press, 2010); Bradford Peck, *The World a Department Store: A Story of Life Under a Coöperative*

System (1900); Spann, *Brotherly Tomorrows*, 216–219. The works of both Caryl and Peck resemble the style of Edward Bellamy's hugely popular *Looking Backward*, published in 1888.

23. See especially Knapp, *The Rise of American Cooperative Enterprise*; on antitrust, see John Hanna, "Antitrust Immunities of Cooperative Associations," *Law and Contemporary Problems* 13 (Summer 1948), and Christine A. Varney, "The Capper-Volstead Act, Agricultural Cooperatives, and Antitrust Immunity," *Antitrust Source* (December 2012).

24. Cooperative League of the USA, *The Co-ops Are Comin'* (1941), archive.org/details/the-co-ops-are-comin-1941. In the film, "study groups" is italicized.

25. Andrea Gagliarducci, "The Man Who Put *Laudato Si* into Practice in Ecuador—Forty Years Ago," *Catholic News Agency* (July 8, 2015).

26. J. Carroll Moody and Gilbert C. Fite, *The Credit Union Movement: Origins and Development, 1850-1980* (Kendall/Hunt, 1984); Susan MacVittie, "Credit Unions: The Farmers' Bank," *Watershed Sentinel* (January 16, 2018); William Foote Whyte and Kathleen King Whyte, *Making Mondragón: The Growth and Dynamics of the Worker Cooperative Complex*, 2nd ed. (ILR Press, 1991).

27. On Judaism, see Noémi Giszpenc, "Cooperatives: The (Jewish) World's Best-Kept Secret," *Jewish Currents* (Autumn 2012); on Protestantism, see Andrew McLeod, *Holy Cooperation! Building Graceful Economies* (Cascade Books, 2009); cooperatives are widespread in many Muslim- and Buddhist-majority regions, as well as among their diasporic communities elsewhere, and cooperators reinterpret the model through the local religious vernacular.

28. Leo XIII, *Rerum Novarum*, sec. 46.

29. The ideological foundations of Catholic cooperativism make for a checkered pedigree. Pope Pius XI, who echoed Leo XIII in more explicitly cooperative form, became caught up in prewar entanglements with Benito Mussolini, and Belloc and Chesterton harbored fascist, racist sympathies alongside their distributist longings. These tendencies were less common among the actual practitioners of Catholic cooperation.

30. José María Arizmendiarrieta, *Reflections* (Otalora, 2013), sec. 213; see also Race Mathews, *Jobs of Our Own: Building a Stakeholder Society; Alternatives to the Market and the State*, 2nd ed. (Distributist Review Press, 2009), and *Of Labour and Liberty:*

Distributism in Victoria 1891–1966 (Monash University Publishing, 2017); another important account of the Mondragon system is Whyte and Whyte, *Making Mondragón*. As one Basque biographer put it in the opening lines of his book, "Arizmendiarrieta did not start—historically or systematically—from the philosophical analysis of a theory of history or production; his primary source of inspiration, rather, is in a concrete philosophical conception of the person" (Joxe Azurmendi, *El Hombre Cooperativo: Pensamiento de Arizmendiarrieta* [Lan Kide Aurrezkia, 1984], via a draft translation by Steve Herrick of the Interpreters' Cooperative of Madison).

31. "Father Albert McKnight," Cooperative Hall of Fame, heroes.coop /archive/father-albert-mcknight; Albert J. McKnight, *Whistling in the Wind: The Autobiography of The Rev. Albert J. McKnight, C. S. Sp.* (Southern Development Foundation, 2011), epub; Mary Anne Rivera, "Jubilee: A Magazine of the Church and Her People: Toward a Vatican II Ecclesiology," *Logos: A Journal of Catholic Thought and Culture* 10, no. 4 (Fall 2007); see Catholic Relief Services, "Agency Strategy," crs.org/about/agency-strategy; "Interfaith Partners," Equal Exchange, equalexchange.coop/our -partners/interfaith-partners; for more on Catholic tradition, Pope Francis, and cooperation, see my chapter "'Truly, Much Can Be Done!': Cooperative Economics from the Book of Acts to Pope Francis," in *Laudato Si': Ethical, Legal, and Political Implications*, ed. Frank Pasquale (Cambridge University Press, forthcoming).

32. L. Cannari and G. D'Alessio, "La Distribuzione del Reddito e della Ricchezza nelle Regioni Italiane," Banca d'Italia, *Temi di Discussione del Servizio Studi* no. 482 (June 2003); Flavio Delbono, "The Sources of GDP in [the] Emilia Romagna Region and the Role of Co-operation," Emilia Romagna Cooperative Study Tour lecture at the University of Bologna (June 8, 2017); Delbono, a prominent economist and former mayor of Bologna, argued both in that lecture and in subsequent correspondence for a causal relationship that the co-ops have on the region's economic indicators. I draw here considerably from the experience of the study tour, co-organized by the Co-operative Management Education program at Saint Mary's University and the Department of Economics at the University of Bologna.

33. Spelled "Co-operative Bank," following British usage.

34. For overviews of the Kenyan cooperative economy and its history, see Ndwakhulu Tshishonga and Andrew Emmanuel Okem, "A

Review of the Kenyan Cooperative Movement," in *Theoretical and Empirical Studies on Cooperatives*, ed. Andrew Emmanuel Okem (Springer, 2016); Fredrick O. Wanyama, "The Qualitative and Quantitative Growth of the Cooperative Movement in Kenya," in *Cooperating Out of Poverty: The Renaissance of the African Cooperative Movement*, ed. Patrick Develtere, Ignace Pollet, and Fredrick Wanyama (International Labour Organization, 2008).

35. E. N. Gicheru, "Engaging Co-operatives in Addressing Local and Global Challenges: The Role of Co-operatives in Generating Sustainable Livelihood," presented at a United Nations meeting on cooperatives in Addis Ababa, Ethiopia (September 4–6, 2012); CoopAfrica, "Kenya," International Labour Organization, ilo.org /public/english/employment/ent/coop/africa/countries/eastafrica /kenya.htm.

36. Roderick Hill, "The Case of the Missing Organizations: Co-operatives and the Textbooks," *Journal of Economic Education* (Summer 2000); see also Panu Kalmi, "The Disappearance of Cooperatives from Economics Textbooks," *Cambridge Journal of Economics* 31, no. 4 (2007).

37. Quoted in Lee Altenberg, "An End to Capitalism: Leland Stanford's Forgotten Vision," *Sandstone and Tile* 14, no. 1 (Winter 1990).

38. Joss Winn, "Democratically Controlled, Co-operative Higher Education." *openDemocracy* (April 23, 2015); The Schools Co-operative Society, co-operativeschools.coop.

39. Altenberg, "An End to Capitalism."

Chapter 3: The Clock of the World

1. See the final summary of her thinking, Grace Lee Boggs with Scott Kurashige, *The Next American Revolution: Sustainable Activism for the Twenty-First Century*, 2nd ed. (University of California Press, 2012).

2. See Kathi Weeks, *The Problem with Work: Feminism, Marxism, Antiwork Politics, and Postwork Imaginaries* (Duke University Press, 2011).

3. Jared Bernstein coined the term based on 2011 Bureau of Labor Statistics data comparing productivity to private-sector employment: Bernstein, "The Challenge of Long Term Job Growth: Two Big Hints," *On the Economy* (blog) (June 5, 2011), jaredbernsteinblog .com/the-challenge-of-long-term-job-growth-two-big-hints; Andrew

McAfee, "Productivity and Employment (and Technology): In the Jaws of the Snake" (March 22, 2012), andrewmcafee.org/2012/03/mcafee-bernstein-productivity-employment-technology-jaws-snake. See also Lawrence Mishel, "The Wedges Between Productivity and Median Compensation Growth," Economic Policy Institute, Issue Brief no. 330 (April 26, 2012).

4. Jim Tankersley, "Meet the 26-Year-Old Who's Taking on Thomas Piketty's Ominous Warnings About Inequality," *Washington Post* (March 19, 2015).

5. Joseph L. Bower and Clayton M. Christensen, "Disruptive Technologies: Catching the Wave," *Harvard Business Review* (January–February 1995); Clayton M. Christensen, *The Innovator's Solution: Creating and Sustaining Successful Growth* (Harvard Business Press, 2003). Between the former and the latter, he adjusted the term from "disruptive technology" to "disruptive innovation."

6. James Manyika et al., *Jobs Lost, Jobs Gained: Workforce Transitions in a Time of Automation* (McKinsey Global Institute, 2017).

7. See Thomas I. Palley, *Financialization: The Economics of Finance Capital Domination* (Palgrave Macmillan, 2013).

8. Johnston Birchall, *Resilience in a Downturn: The Power of Financial Cooperatives* (International Labour Organization, 2013); Clifford Rosenthal, *Credit Unions, Community Development Finance, and the Great Recession* (Federal Reserve Bank of San Francisco, 2012).

9. For seminal accounts of these and other major examples from the recent cooperative movement, see John Restakis, *Humanizing the Economy: Co-operatives in the Age of Capital* (New Society Publishers, 2010), J. Tom Webb, *From Corporate Globalization to Global Co-operation: We Owe It to Our Grandchildren* (Fernwood Publishing, 2016); Jonathan Michie, Joseph R. Blasi, and Carlo Borzaga, eds., *The Oxford Handbook of Mutual, Co-operative, and Co-owned Business* (Oxford University Press, 2017). For more examples of worker co-governance, which doesn't necessarily involve cooperative ownership, see Immanuel Ness and Dario Azzellini, eds., *Ours to Master and to Own: Workers' Control from the Commune to the Present* (Haymarket, 2011); Catherine P. Mulder, *Transcending Capitalism Through Cooperative Practices* (Palgrave Macmillan, 2015); Daniel Zwerdling, *Workplace Democracy: A Guide to Workplace Ownership, Participation and Self-Management Experiments in the United States and Europe* (Harper Colophon, 1980). On ESOPs, "ESOPs by the Numbers," National Center for

Employee Ownership, nceo.org/articles/esops-by-the-numbers; the initiative Fifty by Fifty (fiftybyfifty.org) seeks to reach fifty million employee owners by 2050. Visa has since demutualized; Dee Hock described this fate to me in an email as "organizationally inevitable, economically greedy, socially unjust, creatively barren, philosophically foolish, and a disappointment to its founder." I also can't mention the Park Slope Food Co-op without confessing to having broken its rules by not becoming a member myself while sharing a household with my wife, a member and a far better co-operator than I am.

10. Oscar Perry Abello, "NYC Set to Triple Number of Worker Co-operatives," *Next City* (January 11, 2016); Marielle Mondon, "Co-Op Success in Cleveland Is Catching On," *Next City*, (March 17, 2015); for more on the "Cleveland model," see community -wealth.org, produced by the Democracy Collaborative, and a critique at Atlee McFellin, "The Untold Story of the Evergreen Cooperatives," *Grassroots Economic Organizing* (November 7, 2016); Ajowa Nzinga Ifateyo, "$5 Million for Co-op Development in Madison," *Grassroots Economic Organizing* (January 26, 2015); Malcolm Burnley, "Oakland Is Claiming Its Worker Cooperative Capital Title," *Next City* (September 22, 2015); "Legislative Package Introduced to Encourage Employee-Owned Companies," Senator Bernie Sanders press release (May 11, 2017); Mary Hoyer, "Labor Unions and Worker Co-ops: The Power of Collaboration," *Grassroots Economic Organizing* (July 9, 2015).

11. Kari Lydersen, *Revolt on Goose Island: The Chicago Factory Take-over and What It Says About the Economic Crisis* (Melville House, 2009); Astra Taylor, "Hope and Ka-ching," *The Baffler* 25 (2014); the Working World's loans to New Era appear at theworkingworld .org/us/loans/loans/1344.

12. For more on Airbnb's special relationship with Paris, see Jeff Sharlet, "Cult of Hospitality," *Travel + Leisure* (April 21, 2016).

13. Trebor Scholz, notably, challenged Botsman's enthusiasm for on-line labor markets: "This is a total affront to what the labor movement has struggled for for centuries"; find his argument, in book form, in *Uberworked and Underpaid: How Workers Are Disrupting the Digital Economy* (Polity, 2017). For a broader account of debates over the sharing economy, see Juliet Schor, "Debating the Sharing Economy," Great Transition Initiative (October 2014).

14. For an overview of similar responses to precarious work, see Pat Conaty, Alex Bird, and Cilla Ross, *Working Together: Trade Union*

and Co-operative Innovations for Precarious Workers (Co-operatives UK, 2018).

15. The organization's internal documentation is public at handbook .enspiral.com.

16. Alex Burness, "At Long Last, Boulder Approves New Co-op Housing Ordinance," *Daily Camera* (January 4, 2017).

17. James Howard Kunstler, "The Ghastly Tragedy of the Suburbs," TED talk (May 2007).

Chapter 4: Gold Rush

1. See John T. Noonan Jr., *The Scholastic Analysis of Usury* (Harvard University Press, 1957); Jacques Le Goff, *Your Money or Your Life: Economy and Religion in the Middle Ages* (Zone Books, 1988).

2. See Nathan Schneider, "How a Worker-Owned Tech Startup Found Investors—and Kept Its Values," *YES! Magazine* (April 26, 2016).

3. Credit Union National Association, "Credit Union Data and Statistics," cuna.org/Research-And-Strategy/Credit-Union-Data-And -Statistics; CoBank, "About CoBank," cobank.com/About-CoBank .aspx.

4. Satoshi Nakamoto, "Bitcoin Open Source Implementation of P2P Currency," P2P Foundation Ning forum (February 11, 2009), p2pfoundation.ning.com/forum/topics/bitcoin-open-source; see also the original Bitcoin white paper at bitcoin.org/bitcoin.pdf; for a fuller account of the rise of Bitcoin, see Nathaniel Popper, *Digital Gold: Bitcoin and the Inside Story of the Misfits and Millionaires Trying to Reinvent Money* (Harper, 2015).

5. Daniela Hernandez, "Homeless, Unemployed, and Surviving on Bitcoins," *Wired* (September 13, 2013); Kim Lachance Shandrow, "Bill Gates: Bitcoin Is 'Better Than Currency,'" *Entrepreneur* (October 3, 2014); for an eloquent critique of bitcoin, see Brett Scott's "Visions of a Techno-Leviathan: The Politics of the Bitcoin Blockchain," *E-International Relations* (June 1, 2014) and "How Can Cryptocurrency and Blockchain Technology Play a Role in Building Social and Solidarity Finance?" working paper for the United Nations Research Institute for Social Development (February 2016).

6. Because many people who were writing about Bitcoin early on were also holders of bitcoins, reliable analysts were few and far between; Swanson's work was a welcome exception. See his books at ofnum bers.com. Although Bitcoin's open ledger is a statistician's dream,

it's not easy to associate accounts to actual human beings. For demographic data, see Lui Smyth, "Bitcoin Community Survey 2014" (February 1, 2014), http://simulacrum.cc/2014/02/01/bitcoin -community-survey-2014; Neil Sardesai, "Who Owns All the Bitcoins—An Infographic of Wealth Distribution," *CryptoCoins-News* (March 31, 2014); CoinDesk, *Who Really Uses Bitcoin?* (June 10, 2015), coindesk.com/research/who-really-uses-bitcoin; Olga Kharif, "The Bitcoin Whales: 1,000 People Who Own 40 Percent of the Market," *Bloomberg Businessweek* (December 8, 2017); Coin Dance, "Bitcoin Community Engagement by Gender Summary," coin.dance/stats/gender (94.73 percent male in March 2018).

7. Buterin's original white paper can be found at github.com /ethereum/wiki/wiki/White-Paper.

8. Perhaps the first scholarly presentation to take Ethereum seriously was Primavera De Filippi, "Ethereum: Freenet or Skynet?" luncheon at Berkman Klein Center for Internet and Society at Harvard University (April 15, 2014), cyber.harvard.edu/events /luncheon/2014/04/difilippi; see also the widely circulated video "Vitalik Buterin Reveals Ethereum at Bitcoin Miami 2014," youtube.com/watch?v=l9dpjN3Mwps; a compelling early analysis of Buterin's worldview is Sam Frank, "Come With Us If You Want to Live," *Harper's Magazine* (January 2015); for a technical perspective, see Ethereum Foundation, "How to Build a Democracy on the Blockchain," ethereum.org/dao.

9. Vitalik Buterin, comment on Reddit thread (April 6, 2014), reddit .com/r/ethereum/comments/22av9m/code_your_own_utopia.

10. Follow the ongoing contest of currencies at coinmarketcap.com; for CU Ledger, see culedger.com.

11. Joon Ian Wong and Ian Kar, "Everything You Need to Know About the Ethereum 'Hard Fork,'" *Quartz* (July 18, 2016).

12. Duran served as a significant informant, referred to as "Pau," in Jeffrey S. Juris, *Networking Futures: The Movements Against Corporate Globalization* (Duke University Press, 2008).

13. Enric Duran, *Abolim la Banca* (Ara Llibres, 2009).

14. For a more recent overview of the CIC, as well as more details on its organizational structure, see George Dafermos, *The Catalan Integral Cooperative: An Organizational Study of a Post-Capitalist Cooperative* (P2P Foundation and Robin Hood Coop, 2017).

15. The mysterious first chapter of FairCoin's life remains archived in a popular cryptocurrency forum: bitcointalk.org/index .php?topic=487212.0.

Chapter 5: Slow Computing

1. Christopher M. Kelty, *Two Bits: The Cultural Significance of Free Software* (Duke University Press, 2008).
2. Jodi Dean, "The Communist Horizon," lecture at No-Space in Brooklyn, New York (July 28, 2011), vimeo.com/27327373.
3. W3Techs, "Usage of Operating Systems for Websites," w3techs.com /technologies/overview/operating_system/all.
4. E. Gabriella Coleman, *Coding Freedom: The Ethics and Aesthetics of Hacking* (Princeton University Press, 2012); Christopher M. Kelty, *Two Bits*; David Bollier, "Inventing the Creative Commons," in *Viral Spiral: How the Commoners Built a Digital Republic of Their Own* (New Press, 2008).
5. Theodore Roszak, *The Cult of Information: The Folklore of Computers and the True Art of Thinking* (Pantheon, 1986), 138–141; see also Fred Turner, *From Counterculture to Cyberculture: Stewart Brand, the Whole Earth Network, and the Rise of Digital Utopianism* (University of Chicago Press, 2006), and Judy Malloy, ed., *Social Media Archeology and Poetics* (MIT Press, 2016).
6. Coleman, *Coding Freedom*; Brian J. Robertson, *Holacracy: The New Management System for a Rapidly Changing World* (Henry Holt, 2015); Frederic Laloux, *Reinventing Organizations: A Guide to Creating Organizations Inspired by the Next Stage of Human Consciousness* (Nelson Parker, 2014). Perhaps it's worth noting that I used Git to manage version-control for this book.
7. Jennifer Reingold, "How a Radical Shift Left Zappos Reeling," *Fortune* (March 4, 2016).
8. Evgeny Morozov, "The Meme Hustler," *Baffler* 22 (2013).
9. GitHub, "Open Source Survey," opensourcesurvey.org/2017; Coraline Ada Ehmke, "The Dehumanizing Myth of the Meritocracy," *Model View Culture* 21 (May 19, 2015); Ashe Dryden, "The Ethics of Unpaid Labor and the OSS Community," (November 13, 2013), ashedryden.com/blog/the-ethics-of-unpaid-labor -and-the-oss-community.
10. Roszak, *The Cult of Information*, 175.
11. Aaron Smith, "Gig Work, Online Selling and Home Sharing," Pew Research Center (November 17, 2016); on the platform economy in general, see Martin Kenney and John Zysman, "The Rise of the Platform Economy," *Issues in Science and Technology* 32, no. 3 (Spring 2016), and Geoffrey G. Parker, Marshall W. Van Alstyne, and Sangeet Paul Choudary, *Platform Revolution: How Networked*

Markets Are Transforming the Economy and How to Make Them Work for You (W. W. Norton, 2016); for a critique of the "platform" concept, see Tarleton Gillespie, "The Platform Metaphor, Revisited," Social Media Collective research blog (August 24, 2017); valuation statistics based on *Forbes* magazine data via statista.com /statistics/263264.

12. Julia Cartwright, *Jean François Millet: His Life and Letters* (Swan Sonnenschein, 1902), 177; for an exploration of the economic significance of gleaning in Jewish tradition, see Joseph William Singer, *The Edges of the Field: Lessons on the Obligations of Ownership* (Beacon Press, 2000).

13. See Anna Bernasek and D. T. Mongan, *All You Can Pay: How Companies Use Our Data to Empty Our Wallets* (Nation Books, 2015); Nick Couldry, "The Price of Connection: 'Surveillance Capitalism,'" *Conversation* (September 22, 2016); Virginia Eubanks, *Automating Inequality: How High-Tech Tools Profile, Police, and Punish the Poor* (St. Martin's Press, 2018); Frank Pasquale, *The Black Box Society: The Secret Algorithms That Control Money and Information* (Harvard University Press, 2015); Astra Taylor, *The People's Platform: Taking Back Power and Culture in the Digital Age* (Metropolitan Books, 2014); Joseph Turow et al., *The Tradeoff Fallacy: How Marketers Are Misrepresenting American Consumers and Opening Them Up to Exploitation*, report from the Annenberg School for Communication at the University of Pennsylvania (June 2015); James Joyce quoted from *Finnegans Wake* in Marshall McLuhan, *The Gutenberg Galaxy: The Making of Typographic Man* (University of Toronto Press, 1962), 278.

14. Greetje F. Corporaal and Vili Lehdonvirta, *Platform Sourcing: How Fortune 500 Firms Are Adopting Online Freelancing Platforms* (Oxford Internet Institute, 2017); Lawrence F. Katz and Alan B. Krueger, "The Rise and Nature of Alternative Work Arrangements in the United States, 1995–2015," National Bureau of Economic Research working paper no. 22667 (September 2016).

15. David de Ugarte, "Tipologías de las Cooperativas de Trabajo," *El Jardín Indiano* (September 18, 2011); Sebastiano Maffettone et al., "Manifesto" (2012), www.cooperativecommons.coop/index .php/en/manifesto; Janelle Orsi, "The Next Sharing Economy" (October 17, 2014), youtube.com/watch?v=xpg4PjGtbu0; her call was echoed in Brian Van Slyke and David Morgan, "The 'Sharing Economy' Is the Problem," *Grassroots Economic Organizing* (July 3, 2015); see a directory of North American tech worker co-ops at

techworker.coop and coops.tech for the UK; for accounts of the rationale for tech co-ops, see Brian Van Slyke, "The Argument for Worker-Owned Tech Collectives," *Fast Company* (November 20, 2013), and Gabrielle Anctil, "Can Coops Revolutionize the Tech Industry?" *Model View Culture* 34 (March 16, 2016).

16. Nathan Schneider, "Owning Is the New Sharing," *Shareable* (December 21, 2014); Trebor Scholz, "Platform Cooperativism vs. the Sharing Economy" (December 5, 2014), medium.com/@trebors /platform-cooperativism-vs-the-sharing-economy-2ea737f1b5ad. See also Scholz's subsequent, fuller account of the concept in his pamphlet *Platform Cooperativism: Challenging the Corporate Sharing Economy* (Rosa Luxemburg Stiftung, 2016), as well as the collective manifesto he and I coedited, *Ours to Hack and to Own: The Rise of Platform Cooperativism, a New Vision for the Future of Work and a Fairer Internet* (OR Books, 2016). Scholz also writes at length about platform cooperativism in *Uberworked and Underpaid: How Workers Are Disrupting the Digital Economy* (Polity, 2017). Douglas Rushkoff, the concluding speaker at the 2015 Platform Cooperativism conference, advocates the model in *Throwing Rocks at the Google Bus: How Growth Became the Enemy of Prosperity* (Portfolio, 2016).

17. Highly recommended: Marjorie Kelly, *Owning Our Future: The Emerging Ownership Revolution* (Berrett-Koehler Publishers, 2012); Managed by Q, "Managed by Q Stock Option Program Press Conference," (March 18, 2016), vimeo.com/159580593.

18. See platform.coop for the conferences and the consortium, and ioo.coop for the directory. For my use of "ecosystem," apologies to Adam Curtis (dir.), *All Watched Over by Machines of Loving Grace*, BBC (2011).

19. E.g., selfhosted.libhunt.com and ioo.coop/clouds.

20. Anand Sriraman, Jonathan Bragg, and Anand Kulkarni, "Worker-Owned Cooperative Models for Training Artificial Intelligence," *CSCW '17 Companion* (February 25–March 1, 2017).

21. José María Arizmendiarrieta, *Reflections* (Otalora, 2013), sec. 486.

22. John Geraci, "Interviewed: Venture Capitalist Brad Burnham on Skinny Platforms," *Shareable* (June 22, 2015).

23. On November 17, 2017, the ICA General Assembly in Malaysia unanimously passed a resolution in support of platform co-ops, sponsored by Co-operatives UK and the US National Cooperative Business Association; Brewster Kahle, "Difficult Times at Our Credit Union," *Internet Archive Blogs* (November 24, 2015).

24. Dmytri Kleiner, *The Telekommunist Manifesto* (Institute of Network Cultures, 2010); Stacco Troncoso, "Think Global, Print Local and Licensing for the Commons," P2P Foundation blog (May 10, 2016).

25. Devin Balkind, founder of coopData.org and a collaborator of mine in building the Internet of Ownership, offers a critique of data practices in the co-op sector in "When Platform Coops Are Seen, What Goes Unseen?" The Internet of Ownership blog (February 10, 2017).

26. See platform.coop/2015/participants/maria-del-carmen-arroyo; on Austin and the aftermath, Jeff Kirk, "The Austin Ride-Hail Chronicles: Game Over for RideAustin?" *Austin Startups* (June 15, 2017); Anca Voinea, "Corbyn's Digital Democracy Manifesto Promotes Co-operative Ownership of Digital Platforms," *Co-operative News* (August 30, 2016).

27. Lina Khan, "Amazon's Antitrust Paradox," *Yale Law Journal* 126, no. 3 (January 2017); Jonathan Taplin, "Is It Time to Break Up Google?" *New York Times* (April 22, 2017); Ryan Grim, "Steve Bannon Wants Facebook and Google Regulated Like Utilities," *Intercept* (July 27, 2017).

28. David Talbot, Kira Hessekiel, and Danielle Kehl, *Community-Owned Fiber Networks: Value Leaders in America* (Berkman Klein Center for Internet and Society, 2018); for resources on co-op and municipal broadband programs, see muninetworks.org, a project of the Institute for Local Self-Reliance.

29. Victor Rosewater, *History of Cooperative News-Gathering in the United States* (D. Appleton, 1930), 351; William Bryk, "A False Armistice," *New York Sun* (November 10, 2004).

30. Walter R. Mears, "A Brief History of AP," in Reporters of the Associated Press, *Breaking News: How the Associated Press Has Covered War, Peace, and Everything Else* (Princeton University Press, 2007); Rosewater, *History of Cooperative News-Gathering*; Jonathan Silberstein-Loeb, *The International Distribution of News: The Associated Press, Press Association, and Reuters, 1848–1947* (Cambridge University Press, 2014).

31. Liana B. Baker, "Twitter CEO Calls Company 'People's News Network,'" *Reuters* (October 10, 2016).

32. Nathan Schneider, "Here's My Plan to Save Twitter: Let's Buy It," *Guardian* (September 29, 2016).

33. Twitter, Inc., *Proxy Statement: Notice of 2017 Annual Meeting of Stockholders* (April 7, 2017); the SEC ruling can be

found at sec.gov/divisions/corpfin/cf-noaction/14a-8/2017
/mcritchiesauerteig031017-14a8.pdf; for a comprehensive account, see also Danny Spitzberg, "#GoCoop: How the #BuyTwit-
ter Campaign Could Signal a New Co-op Economy," *Cooperative
Business Journal* (Summer 2017); a relevant precedent to the
Twitter proposal is the "consumer stock ownership plan" model
proposed by Louis Kelso (who also first proposed the widespread employee stock ownership plan), see Louis O. Kelso
and Patricia Hetter Kelso, *Democracy and Economic Power: Extending the ESOP Revolution Through Binary Economics* (Ball-
inger, 1986).

34. Fred Wilson, "The Golden Age of Open Protocols," *AVC* (July 31,
2016). There is a typo in the original, which reads "more disruptive that."

Chapter 6: Free the Land

1. "Full Speech: Donald Trump Event in Gaffney, SC (2-18-16),"
Right Side Broadcasting Network (February 18, 2016), youtube
.com/watch?v=pq4wA_jQ8-k.

2. Data from various National Rural Electric Cooperative Association publications; see maps at cooperative.com/public/maps.

3. For the political history of electric co-ops, see Jack Doyle, *Lines
Across the Land: Rural Electric Cooperatives: The Changing Politics
of Energy in Rural America* (Environmental Policy Institute, 1979),
and Ted Case, *Power Plays: The U.S. Presidency, Electric Cooperatives, and the Transformation of Rural America* (self-published,
2013); contribution data from the Center for Responsive Politics,
opensecrets.org; Steven Johnson, "Mike Pence Familiar to Indiana
Co-ops," National Rural Electric Cooperative Association press release (July 25, 2016); Abby Spinak, "Infrastructure and Agency: Rural Electric Cooperatives and the Fight for Economic Democracy in
the United States" (PhD diss., Massachusetts Institute of Technology, 2014).

4. Cathy Cash, "'Co-ops Vote' Called a Success," National Rural
Electric Cooperative Association press release (November 14,
2016).

5. "NRECA Statement on Budget Proposal," National Rural Electric Cooperative Association press release (March 16, 2017); Re-
becca Harvey, "Trump's Budget Blueprint Sees Cuts for Co-ops
and Credit Unions," *Co-operative News* (March 17, 2017); Cathy

Cash, "Trump Orders Clean Power Plan Review," National Rural Electric Cooperative Association press release (March 28, 2017).

6. G&T numbers courtesy of the National Rural Electric Cooperative Association; "What Is U.S. Electricity Generation by Energy Source?" US Energy Information Administration (April 1, 2016), eia.gov/tools/faqs/faq.php?id=427&t=3.

7. "Cooperative Solar Skyrockets," National Rural Electric Cooperative Association press release (March 9, 2017).

8. Doyle, *Lines Across the Land*, 141 and 300. I'm grateful for the guidance of longtime electric co-op consultant and expert Adam Schwartz.

9. Rural Electrification Administration, *A Guide for Members of REA Cooperatives* (US Department of Agriculture, 1939); for examples of government films, see Rural Electrification Administration, *Power and the Land* (1951 [1940]), and United States Information Service, *The Rural Co-op* (c. 1950).

10. For explanations of this and other financial abuses among electric co-ops, see Jim Cooper, "Electric Co-operatives: From New Deal to Bad Deal?" *Harvard Journal on Legislation* 45, no. 2 (Summer 2008).

11. For an account of the Co-op Democracy Project, see a special issue on the subject, *Southern Changes* 18, no. 3–4 (1996).

12. "Subpoenaed Witnesses Evade House Oversight Committee," Congressman Jim Cooper press release (June 26, 2008).

13. John Farrell, *Re-Member-ing the Electric Cooperative* (Institute for Local Self-Reliance, 2016).

14. Murray D. Lincoln, *Vice President in Charge of Revolution* (McGraw-Hill, 1960), 133.

15. Cooper, "Electric Co-operatives," 346.

16. For an extended comparison of the USDA and ICA principles, see Bruce J. Reynolds, *Comparing Cooperative Principles of the US Department of Agriculture and the International Cooperative Alliance* (US Department of Agriculture, June 2014).

17. James Peter Warbasse, *Cooperative Democracy Through Voluntary Association of the People as Consumers*, 3rd ed. (Harper and Brothers, 1936), 25, 266, and 7.

18. Corey Hutchins, "Bernie Sanders: Colorado Could 'Lead the Nation' with Its Universal Healthcare Ballot Measure," *Colorado Independent* (October 26, 2015).

19. Michael A. Shadid, *A Doctor for the People: The Autobiography of the Founder of America's First Co-operative Hospital* (Vanguard

Press, 1939); Paul Starr, *The Social Transformation of American Medicine: The Rise of a Sovereign Profession and the Making of a Vast Industry* (Basic Books, 1984), 302–306; Sabrina Corlette, Kevin Lucia, Justin Giovannelli, and Sean Miskell, "The Affordable Care Act CO-OP Program: Facing Both Barriers and Opportunities for More Competitive Health Insurance Markets," *To the Point*, published by the Commonwealth Fund (March 12, 2015).

20. Financing: Camile Kerr, *Local Government Support for Cooperatives* (Democracy at Work Institute, 2015); Peter Molk, "The Puzzling Lack of Cooperatives," *Tulane Law Review* 88 (2014); Laura Hanson Schlachter, "MCDC Milestone Reflections: City of Madison Grant Writing Process" (University of Wisconsin–Madison Center for Cooperatives, August 2016); USDA Rural Development, *Income Tax Treatment of Cooperatives* (US Department of Agriculture, June 2013). Development: Oscar Perry Abello, "NYC Set to Triple Number of Worker Cooperatives," *Next City* (January 11, 2016); Kerr, *Local Government Support for Cooperatives*; Lauren McCauley, "'An Idea Whose Time Has Come': Lawmakers Roll Out Plan to Expand Worker Ownership," *Common Dreams* (May 11, 2017); Schlachter, "MCDC Milestone Reflections." Mandates: Kerr, *Local Government Support for Cooperatives*; Molk, "The Puzzling Lack of Cooperatives." Enablers: Antonio Fici, "Cooperation Among Cooperatives in Italian and Comparative Law," *Journal of Entrepreneurial and Organizational Diversity* 4, no. 2 (2015); Sustainable Economies Law Center, "Worker Coop City Policies," theselc.org/worker_coop_city_policies.

21. Antonio Fici, "Italy," in *International Handbook of Cooperative Law*, ed. Dante Cracogna et al. (Springer-Verlag, 2013); Tito Menzani and Vera Zamagni, "Co-operative Networks in the Italian Economy," *Enterprise and Society* (2009).

22. Laura Flanders, "Remembering Chokwe Lumumba," *YES! Magazine* (February 26, 2014); see also Flanders's excellent profile of Lumumba, "After Death of Radical Mayor, Mississippi's Capital Wrestles with His Economic Vision," *YES! Magazine* (April 1, 2014).

23. See the results of a 2014–2016 Freedom of Information Act request, archived on muckrock.com at perma.cc/H6T3-GPYM; Donna Ladd, "Jackson Tragedy: The RNA, Revisited," *Jackson Free Press* (March 5, 2014).

24. National Conference of Black Lawyers, "Chokwe Lumumba: A Legal Biography" (March 3, 2014); R. L. Nave, "A 'New Justice Frontier,'" *Jackson Free Press* (April 3, 2014).

25. The slogan comes from an event in 1971, when hundreds of revelers broke a vigilante and law-enforcement blockade that attempted to prevent them from celebrating the purchase of land in Mississippi by the Provisional Government of the Republic of New Afrika; the story is retold in Rukia Lumumba, "All Roads Lead to Jackson," in *Jackson Rising: The Struggle for Economic Democracy, Socialism and Black Self-Determination in Jackson, Mississippi*, ed. Kali Akuno and Ajamu Nangwaya (Daraja Press, 2017).

26. See Kali Akuno, *Casting Shadows: Chokwe Lumumba and the Struggle for Racial Justice and Economic Democracy in Jackson, Mississippi* (Rosa Luxemburg Siftung, 2015); for extensive reporting on the Lumumba candidacy and mayoral administration, see the archives of the *Jackson Free Press*, a local paper, which also posted the campaign-finance documents on its website.

27. Details can be found in Ajamu Nangwaya, "Seek Ye First the Worker Self-management Kingdom: Toward the Solidarity Economy in Jackson, MS," in *Jackson Rising*.

28. Allen was convicted of embezzlement in 2017 but continues to hold his post at the downtown development corporation.

29. Overviews of this history appear in Jessica Gordon Nembhard, *Collective Courage: A History of African American Cooperative Economic Thought and Practice* (University of Pennsylvania Press, 2014), and Michael Miles, "Black Cooperatives," *New Republic* (September 21, 1968); Matt Cropp, "Martin Luther King, Jr., Credit Unionist," *Credit Union History* (blog) (January 20, 2014); the role of Student Nonviolent Coordinating Committee comes to me from the testimony of SNCC organizer Mary Elizabeth King.

30. R. L. Nave, "Candidate Profile: Tony Yarber," *Jackson Free Press* (April 2, 2014); see also *Jackson Jambalaya* archives at kingfish1935 .blogspot.com.

31. Donna Ladd, "Making of a Landslide: Chokwe A. Lumumba and a Changing Jackson," *Jackson Free Press* (May 10, 2017); D. D. Guttenplan, "Is This the Most Radical Mayor in America?" *Nation* (December 4–11, 2017).

32. Prieto is mentioned in Andy Greenberg's profile of Taaki, "How an Anarchist Bitcoin Coder Found Himself Fighting ISIS in Syria," *Wired* (March 29, 2017).

33. "The Social Economy," in Michael Knapp, Anja Flach, and Ercan Ayboga, *Revolution in Rojava: Democratic Autonomy and Women's Liberation in the Syrian Kurdistan*, trans. Janet Biehl (Pluto Press, 2016); Strangers in a Tangled Wilderness, eds., *A Small Key Can*

Open a Large Door: The Rojava Revolution (AK Press, 2015). The Institute for Solidarity Economics and Corporate Watch maintain a useful blog on "Co-operative Economy in Rojava and Bakur" at cooperativeeconomy.info.

34. Fabrice Balanche, "The Kurdish Path to Socialism in Syria," The Washington Institute (May 16, 2017).

Chapter 7: Phase Transition

1. An archive of the original website is at web.archive.org/web /20131210152950/http://floksociety.org:80/cuando-va-a-suceder.

2. The wiki is now at p2pfoundation.net/Main_Page; more accessible presentations of the foundation's work, built on the basis of the FLOK research, are available at commonstransition.org.

3. For more on such open accounting, see Michel Bauwens and Vasilis Niaros, *Value in the Commons Economy: Developments in Open and Contributory Value Accounting* (Heinrich-Böll-Foundation and P2P Foundation, 2017); this is tied, also, with the vision of "open cooperativism": Michel Bauwens, "Open Cooperativism for the P2P Age," P2P Foundation blog (June 16, 2014).

4. See Vasilis Kostakis and Michel Bauwens, *Network Society and Future Scenarios for a Collaborative Economy* (Palgrave Macmillan, 2014); Michel Bauwens, "Blueprint for P2P Society: The Partner State and Ethical Economy," *Shareable* (April 7, 2012); John Restakis, *Cooperative Commonwealth and the Partner State* (The Next System Project, 2017).

5. Ibn Khaldun, *The Muqaddimah: An Introduction to History*, trans. Franz Rosenthal (Princeton University Press, 2015).

6. An early statement of the trend is Derek Thompson and Jordan Weissmann, "The Cheapest Generation," *Atlantic* (September 2012); for a statistical critique of the "myth of the 'don't own' economy," see *The Millennial Study* (Accel and Qualtrics, 2017); for a critique of this "investment" see Malcolm Harris, *Kids These Days: Human Capital and the Making of Millennials* (Little, Brown, 2017).

7. On housing, see Laura Gottesdiener, "The Empire Strikes Back," *TomDispatch* (November 26, 2013); on employment, see Guy Standing, *The Precariat: The New Dangerous Class* (Bloomsbury Academic, 2011); on citizenship, see Atossa Araxia Abrahamian, *The Cosmopolites: The Coming of the Global Citizen* (Columbia Global Reports, 2015); on clouds, see John Durham Peters, *The*

Marvelous Clouds: Toward a Philosophy of Elemental Media (University of Chicago Press, 2015).

8. Richard Florida, *Who's Your City? How the Creative Economy Is Making Where to Live the Most Important Decision of Your Life* (Basic Books, 2008), argued for a tripartite distinction among the "mobile," the "stuck," and the "rooted"; for a more recent policy analysis, see David Schleicher, "Stuck! The Law and Economics of Residential Stability," *Yale Law Journal* 127 (2017).

9. Jeff Abbott, "Indigenous Weavers Organize for Collective Intellectual Property Rights," *Waging Nonviolence* (July 17, 2017).

10. Richard Feloni, "Why Mark Zuckerberg Wants Everyone to Read the Fourteenth-Century Islamic Book *The Muqaddimah*," *Business Insider* (June 2, 2015); Mark Zuckerberg, "Building Global Community" (February 16, 2017), facebook.com/notes/mark -zuckerberg/building-global-community/10154544292806634.

11. I have been a guest speaker at Singularity University's Global Solutions Program.

12. Peter Diamandis, "I Am Peter Diamandis, from XPRIZE, Singularity University, Planetary Resources, Human Longevity Inc., and More. Ask Me Anything," Reddit AMA discussion (July 11, 2014), reddit.com/r/Futurology/comments/2afiw5/i_am_peter_diamandis _from_xprize_singularity/ciulffv.

13. Kevin Roose, "In Conversation: Marc Andreessen," *New York* (October 19, 2014); Sam Altman, "Technology and Wealth Inequality" (January 28, 2014), blog.samaltman .com/technology-and-wealth-inequality.

14. Recent overviews of universal basic income include Philippe Van Parijs and Yannick Vanderborght, *Basic Income: A Radical Proposal for a Free Society and a Sane Economy* (Harvard University Press, 2017), and Rutger Bregman, *Utopia for Realists: How We Can Build the Ideal World* (Little, Brown, 2017).

15. Marshall Brain, *Manna: Two Views of Humanity's Future* (2012), marshallbrain.com/manna1.htm; for another perspective on parallels between basic income and venture capital, see Steve Randy Waldman, "VC for the People" (April 16, 2014), interfluidity.com /v2/5066.html.

16. Matt Zwolinski, Michael Huemer, Jim Manzi, and Robert H. Frank, "Basic Income and the Welfare State," *Cato Unbound* (August 2014); Noah Gordon, "The Conservative Case for a Guaranteed Basic Income," *Atlantic* (August 6, 2014).

17. In Scott Dadich, "Barack Obama, Neural Nets, Self-Driving Cars, and the Future of the World," *Wired* (November 2016), Obama said, "Whether a universal income is the right model—is it gonna be accepted by a broad base of people?—that's a debate that we'll be having over the next ten or twenty years." On universal dividends funded through common goods, see, for example, Peter Barnes, *With Liberty and Dividends for All: How to Save Our Middle Class When Jobs Don't Pay Enough* (Berrett-Koehler Publishers, 2014); for the Oregon case, see Nathan Schneider, "Soon, Oregon Polluters May Have to Pay Residents for Changing the Climate," *YES! Magazine* (December 9, 2015); Foster's and Hughes's organization is called the Economic Security Project, and more about its approach can be found in Chris Hughes, *Fair Shot: Rethinking Inequality and How We Earn* (St. Martin's Press, 2018).

18. Cryptocurrency basic-income projects go by such names as Circles, Grantcoin, Group Currency, and Resilience; they interact at reddit.com/r/CryptoUBI.

19. Kathi Weeks, *The Problem with Work: Feminism, Marxism, Antiwork Politics, and Postwork Imaginaries* (Duke University Press, 2011); Andy Stern and Lee Kravitz, *Raising the Floor: How a Universal Basic Income Can Renew Our Economy and Rebuild the American Dream* (PublicAffairs, 2016).

20. "Black Cooperatives and the Fight for Economic Democracy," session at the Left Forum at the John Jay College of Criminal Justice (May 31, 2015); see also Marina Gorbis's calls for "universal basic assets" rather than merely income.

21. On technological unemployment, see a summary in James Surowiecki, "Robopocalypse Not," *Wired* (September 2017); on employment and inequality, see (among many other studies) Michael Förster and Horacio Levy, *United States: Tackling High Inequalities, Creating Opportunities for All* (OECD, 2014); on workplace surveillance, see Esther Kaplan, "The Spy Who Fired Me," *Harper's* (March 2015); on human computerization, see Brett M. Frischmann, "Human-Focused Turing Tests: A Framework for Judging Nudging and Techno-Social Engineering of Human Beings," Cardozo Legal Studies Research Paper no. 441 (2014).

22. Community Purchasing Alliance, *2016 Annual Report* (February 2017). I delivered the keynote address at that meeting and was compensated for doing so.

23. E.g., Richard D. Wolff, *Democracy at Work: A Cure for Capitalism* (Haymarket, 2012); for an application of Wolff's framework, see Catherine P. Mulder, *Transcending Capitalism Through Cooperative Practices* (Palgrave Macmillan, 2015).

24. Robert D. Putnam, *Making Democracy Work: Civic Traditions in Modern Italy* (Princeton University Press, 1993), 142; appendix F of the same volume identifies statistical correlations between the presence of cooperatives and other forms of civic involvement. Among the Zamagnis' many writings, see especially Stefano Zamagni and Vera Zamagni, *Cooperative Enterprise: Facing the Challenge of Globalization* (Edward Elgar, 2010).

25. Lisa Dorigatti, "Workers' Cooperatives and the Transformation of Value Chains: Exploiting Institutional Loopholes and Reducing Labour Costs," presentation at Cooperative Pathways Meeting, University of Padua (June 8, 2017); see more about the overall project, Erik Olin Wright's Pathways to a Cooperative Market Economy, at ssc.wisc.edu/~wright/Cooperative-pathways.htm; "Pope Francis Encourages Cooperatives to Build Solidarity," *Vatican Radio* (May 5, 2015); for more on Francis, see my chapter "'Truly, Much Can Be Done!': Cooperative Economics from the Book of Acts to Pope Francis," in *Laudato Si': Ethical, Legal, and Political Implications*, ed. Frank Pasquale (Cambridge University Press, forthcoming).

26. Comment during Francesca Forno and Paolo Graziano, "Reconnecting the Social: How Political Consumerism Enacts Collective Action," presentation at Cooperative Pathways Meeting, University of Padua (June 9, 2017).

27. The directory is at coloradocoops.info/directory; I received decisive help from the Rocky Mountain Farmers Union, which had developed a list based on state incorporation data.

Illustration Credits

All photographs were taken by me in the course of reporting. For charts, maps, and other graphics, I draw from the following sources, with permission from relevant organizations.

3   Liberty Distributors, *Policies and Procedures* (December 1978).

42   James Peter Warbasse, *Cooperative Democracy Through Voluntary Association of the People as Consumers*, 3rd ed. (Harper and Brothers, 1936).

57   University of Wisconsin Center for Cooperatives.

74   Southeastern Michigan Council of Governments and Courtney Flynn, Wayne State University Center for Urban Studies.

77   Lawrence Mishel, "The Wedges Between Productivity and Median Compensation Growth," Economic Policy Institute, Issue Brief no. 330 (April 26, 2012).

108   Blockchain Luxembourg SA, api.blockchain.info/charts/preview /market-price.png?timespan=all&lang=en.

145   Richard Florida and Karen M. King, "Spiky Venture Capital: The Geography of Venture Capital Investment by Metro and Zip Code," Martin Prosperity Institute (February 22, 2016).

176 Rural Electrification Administration, *A Guide for Members of REA Cooperatives* (US Department of Agriculture, 1939), 20–21.

218 Concept from Peter Turchin, "The Strange Disappearance of Cooperation in America," *Cliodynamica* (blog) (June 21, 2013), peterturchin.com/cliodynamica/strange-disappearance. Data from Robert D. Putnam, *Bowling Alone: The Collapse and Revival of American Community* (Simon & Schuster, 2000), 54, and Facundo Alvaredo, Anthony B. Atkinson, Thomas Piketty, and Emmanuel Saez, "The Top 1 Percent in International and Historical Perspective," *Journal of Economic Perspectives* 27, no. 3 (Summer 2013): 3–20.

Index

PHOTO BY EMILY HANSEN

Nathan Schneider is a professor of media studies at the University of Colorado Boulder. He is the author, most recently, of *Thank You, Anarchy: Notes from the Occupy Apocalypse* and coeditor of *Ours to Hack and to Own: The Rise of Platform Cooperativism, a New Vision for the Future of Work and a Fairer Internet.*